THE SUPREME COURT AND JUVENILE JUSTICE

The Supreme Court and Juvenile Justice

Christopher P. Manfredi

 University Press of Kansas

© 1998 by the University Press of Kansas

Published by the University Press of Kansas (Lawrence, Kansas 66049),
which was organized by the Kansas Board of Regents and is operated and
funded by Emporia State University, Fort Hays State University, Kansas
State University, Pittsburg State University, the University of Kansas, and
Wichita State University

Library of Congress Cataloging-in-Publication Data

Manfredi, Christopher P.
    The Supreme Court and juvenile justice / Christopher P. Manfredi.
        p.   cm.
    Includes bibliographical references and index.
    ISBN 0-7006-0851-6 (alk. paper)
    1. Juvenile justice, Administration of—United States.   2. Law
reform—United States.   3. Unites States. Supreme Court.
    I. Title.
    KF9779.M36   1997
    345.73'08—dc21   97-18993

British Library Cataloguing in Publication Data is available.

Printed in the United States of America

10 9 8 7 6 5 4 3 2 1

The paper used in this publication meets the minimum requirements of the
American National Standard for Permanence of Paper for Printed Library
Materials Z39.48-1984.

To Paula and Sophie

Contents

Preface

On March 21, 1966, the U.S. Supreme Court announced its discovery in *Kent v. United States* that juvenile defendants were living in the "worst of both worlds," receiving neither "the protections accorded to adults" nor the "solicitous care and regenerative treatment postulated for children" by the nineteenth-century juvenile court movement. In a majority opinion by Justice Abe Fortas, the Court made clear that it would no longer tolerate "procedural arbitrariness" in juvenile courts. In particular, the majority held that juveniles in the District of Columbia were entitled to representation by counsel at a judicial hearing before the juvenile court could waive jurisdiction and transfer their cases for trial in ordinary criminal courts. Although the Court decided *Kent* on statutory grounds and applied it in principle to a single jurisdiction, the majority opinion signaled for the first time that the Court had serious doubts about the constitutional status of juvenile proceedings, which had remained relatively undisturbed in most states since the turn of the century.[1]

The Court transformed these doubts into new constitutional law fourteen months later in *In re Gault*.[2] In another majority opinion by Justice Fortas, the Court declared that "neither the Fourteenth Amendment nor the Bill of Rights is for adults alone."[3] Under Fortas's direction, a majority of the Court held that the Sixth Amendment's notice, confrontation, and right to counsel clauses, as well as the Fifth Amendment's self-incrimination clause, apply to the adjudication phase of state delinquency proceedings through the Fourteenth Amendment's due process clause. Although the Court continued its self-styled "constitutional domestication" of juvenile courts three years later in *In re Winship* (1970)[4] and rendered other important juvenile justice decisions throughout the 1970s and 1980s, *Gault* stands out because it was both the first and the most extensive decision imposing constitutionally derived standards of due process on juvenile courts. Nevertheless, except to acknowledge its obvious impact on the legal framework of juvenile justice, scholars have paid relatively little attention to *Gault* in the literature concerning constitutional litigation and social reform.[5]

This lack of interest stems partly from the fact that the case was, on one level, a straightforward due process claim in which an individual sought release from state custody because of alleged constitutional deficiencies in the process that led to that loss of liberty. In its origins and outcome, *Gault* lacked the drama, political visibility, and apparent sweep of the racial discrimination and other institutional reform decisions that have usually captured the attention of political scientists. Indeed, to the casual observer, the Court's decision in *Gault* would undoubtedly appear to have been a natural and unremarkable extension of the Warren Court's application of the federal Bill of Rights to state judicial proceedings. Although this interpretation of *Gault* is to some degree accurate, it nonetheless understates the case's importance as an example of institutional reform through constitutional litigation. Indeed, by demonstrating the Court's willingness to extend constitutional rights to minors, *Gault* opened the door to other children's rights litigation.[6] In more precise terms, the objective of *Gault* was to alter the operational rules of juvenile courts, which are the core institution within a complex of policy instruments designed to solve the problem of juvenile criminality. In this book I attempt to describe how juvenile court reform became part of the constitutional agenda of the 1960s, why *Gault* became the principal vehicle for carrying out that reform, and how the Court's constitutional domestication of juvenile courts affected the further development of juvenile justice policy.

In order to achieve this objective, I pursue three parallel tasks. First, I provide a detailed examination of the historical, political, and legal events that led to the constitutional domestication of juvenile justice. Historically, *Gault* and the other cases were the product of a general loss of faith in the rehabilitative ideal underlying traditional juvenile court procedures. Politically, they reached the Supreme Court during a period when that body was deeply engaged in the supervision of state criminal procedure. Legally, the Court had to accept and legitimize the novel proposition that children possess liberty interests similar to those of adults in order to bring juvenile court procedures within the ambit of the Bill of Rights.

My second task is to examine how each of these factors influenced the outcome and impact of the cases, including the implementation of the Court's *Gault* decision by local juvenile court judges and officials, the evaluation and refinement of that decision by the Court itself in subsequent cases, and legislative reactions to the new principles of juvenile justice underlying the decision. The aspect that makes *Gault* particularly intriguing is that developments in juvenile justice policy after 1967 were precisely the opposite of the results that the Court predicted would be the immediate and long-term impact of its decision. The majority asserted that juveniles would reap immediate procedural benefits from the increased use of criminal due process in juvenile proceedings and that there would be little or no long-term negative impact on the unique character of juvenile justice. Nevertheless, the anticipated short-term procedural improvements were short-circuited by local officials who failed to implement the decision as expected. The legal success of the movement represented by *Gault* was not matched by success at the level of policy. To call the movement a failure, however, is not to say that juvenile justice policy has remained unchanged in the three decades since *Gault*. Indeed, a period of legislative activity followed the decision during which juvenile justice moved substantially closer to conventional criminal justice. One of my aims in this book is to provide a systematic, theoretically grounded discussion of the reasons for the initial combination of legal success and policy failure, of the consequences of the policy failure, and of the degree to which those consequences can be attributed to a tension between the legal revolution announced by the Court in *Gault* and the failure to translate that revolution directly into policy.

The third general task is to situate the detailed case study of *Gault* within the general theoretical and empirical literature on institutional reform litigation. Placing the case in this context carries both risks and opportunities. On the one hand, there is the risk that any analysis of the case may be prejudiced simply because very few studies have reached positive conclusions concerning the ability of courts to reform complex institutions.[7] Critics have argued that judicial efforts in this area are hampered by problems of both constitutional legitimacy and institutional capacity. On the other hand, conventional wisdom suggests that, since judges are "experts on process," and therefore competent to formulate policy in procedural areas, courts themselves may be the one institution that judges can effectively reform. Thus, the *Gault* case provides an opportunity to explore judicial reform of an institution that should be more amenable to court-ordered change than other types of institutions.[8]

By undertaking these three tasks, I attempt to combine two related research traditions in my analysis of constitutional domestication and its impact. One of these traditions is the detailed historical and political study of constitutional cases.[9] Although the case study approach is open to the criticism of narrowness, it compensates for this limitation through analytical depth. This counterbalance is particularly true here because I examine the development of institutional reform litigation in a single policy area over a series of cases. The second tradition is concerned with the legal and extralegal factors that influence the process by which judicial decisions are generated and the impact of those decisions.[10] These two traditions are thus combined in the process of analysis. First, drawing on both classical works and more recent scholarship, I begin by setting out a theory of institutional reform litigation. In chapter 1 I provide a definition of institutional reform litigation; focus on the origins of such litigation, how it is conducted, and its impact; and place the case study of constitutional domestication within the general context of the due process revolution of the 1960s and 1970s. I also examine the political and social environment in which *Gault* and its associated cases arose, including the internal dynamics of the Supreme Court and its decisional trends. Next, to illustrate the context of the cases, especially for readers unfamiliar with the history and principles of juvenile justice, I turn in chapter 2 to a discussion of the founding principles of juvenile courts, the decline of the rehabilitative ideal underlying juvenile justice, and the emergence of a juvenile court reform movement after World War II. In chapter 3 I examine the juvenile justice case that preceded *Gault* in the Supreme Court: *Kent v. United States* (1966). Although not launched as a juvenile court case, *Kent* had the effect of announcing the Court's willingness to entertain constitutional challenges to traditional juvenile proceedings. In chapter 4 I deal with the legal path that led the Gault family to the Supreme Court by examining the law and policy context of juvenile justice in Arizona, the character and history of Gerald Gault's involvement with juvenile court authorities, the juvenile court proceedings to which he was subjected, appellate proceedings in the state, and preparations for taking *Gault* to the Supreme Court (including the role of the American Civil Liberties Union in the case). In chapter 5 I examine the development of briefs on all aspects of the case before closely analyzing the various opinions issued in *Gault*. Attention then shifts in chapter 6 to juvenile procedure cases decided by the Court after 1967, with a special emphasis on *In re Winship* (1970).[11] In chapter 7 I assess the Supreme Court's impact on juvenile justice policy by focusing on the short-term implementation of procedural reform and on the legislative reforms that followed its decisions. An important element here is a comparison of the contemporary vision of juvenile justice with the vision articulated by the Court during the 1966 to 1970 period. In the concluding chapter I reflect on the general lessons concerning the impact of constitutional decisions on policy that might be drawn from this episode of institutional reform.

The juvenile court movement of the nineteenth century represented more than a legal innovation; it also represented a crucial development in social policy toward children whose circumstances and behavior fell outside the expected norms of the period. Similarly, the constitutional domestication of juvenile courts in the late 1960s concerned more than procedure; it struck at the core assumptions of the paradigm that had guided juvenile justice policy for more than sixty years. In so doing, the Court prepared the ground for the fundamental changes in juvenile justice policy that characterized the late 1970s and 1980s. What follows in this book is an attempt to describe and understand the external and internal dynamics of the litigation process that produced this particular instance of institutional reform.

Acknowledgments

This project could not have been completed without the assistance of several individuals and organizations. Ralph A. Rossum of Claremont McKenna College first encouraged me to think about the role of courts as policy-making institutions and about the impact of that role in the area of juvenile justice policy. Without the help of several of the participants in *Kent, Gault,* and *Winship,* who answered my queries about the cases and provided me with key documents, I would have been unable to reconstruct the stories behind those cases. In particular, I owe a debt of gratitude to the library staff at Princeton University, who provided documents from the ACLU archives. The reviewers for the University Press of Kansas, Donald Jackson, Lee Epstein, and Sanford Fox, provided invaluable comments that made this a much better book. Financial assistance at various stages of the project came from the Social Sciences and Humanities Research Council of Canada, the Rose Institute of State and Local Government at Claremont McKenna College, and McGill University. Finally, Michael Briggs of the University Press of Kansas never wavered in his support for the project, and for that I am grateful. My acknowledgment of the assistance of these individuals and organizations does not, of course, impute any responsibility to them for the final product.

1. Litigation and the Dynamics of Social Reform

Until the 1950s the Supreme Court's exercise of judicial review did not raise many expectations that constitutional litigation could be an important engine of social reform. The Court's second invalidation of a federal statute, for example, occurred in *Dred Scott v. Sandford* (1857), in which it declared that "persons of the Negro [*sic*] race" could not be U.S. citizens, thus preventing Congress from prohibiting the expansion of slavery into federal territory.[1] Similarly, in other decisions involving civil rights[2] and economic regulation[3] the Court established judicial review as an impediment to social progress in the eyes of many observers. The Court shed this image in dramatic fashion, however, in *Brown v. Board of Education* (1954).[4] The moral soundness of the Court's rejection of racial segregation in public education in *Brown* granted new legitimacy to judicial review in American political life and transformed it from an obstacle to social progress to one of the principal means of achieving progress.[5] Since *Brown,* the Supreme Court and the lower federal courts have actively responded to litigants' claims to reform public policy involving, among other issues, zoning and land-use planning, housing, welfare, transportation, education, and the operating conditions of prisons and mental health institutions.[6] The constitutional domestication of juvenile courts was clearly a part of this post-*Brown* link between constitutional litigation and social reform.

The dramatic increase in judicial activism after the *Brown* decision made constitutional litigation fertile ground not only for social reformers but also for scholars.[7] This interest has generated an important body of theoretical and empirical literature on the use of litigation to pursue policy change in areas outside the usual scope of judicial expertise. Analysts have focused on such matters as why litigation is selected by certain groups to pursue their reform efforts, how these groups construct and execute their litigation campaigns, the factors determining the success or failure of those campaigns, and the practical impact of judicially generated policy reform. I shall extract a set of concepts from this literature that can assist in understanding the legal campaign to bring juvenile court practices within constitutionally defined procedural boundaries, offering first a general discussion of institutional reform litigation and then an examination of three factors that affect such litigation.

The Nature of Institutional Reform Litigation

The principal concern of institutional reform litigation is to modify the framework of procedural and substantive rules according to which social and political institutions operate.[8] Although institutional reform litigation can be grounded in statutory rules, the objectives of litigation based on statutes tend to be limited to correcting marginal flaws in the implementation of an institution's original design. In its most comprehensive and powerful form, institutional reform litigation seeks to use constitutional rules, particularly those concerned with the rights of individuals, to alter the fundamental nature of the institution in question. In this sense, constitutional rights possess two important characteristics. On the one hand, they represent the highest, legally enforceable claim to justice available in liberal-democratic political regimes, providing protection against the potential oppression of certain groups and individuals that may occur through the normal operation of majoritarian decisionmaking bodies. On the other hand, constitutional rights also represent powerful political resources that state-based actors (generally courts) distribute and that society-based actors can acquire and mobilize to serve broader policy objectives, including institutional reform.

Not only do constitutional rights possess these related legal and political characteristics, but they also exist at two distinct levels. The most visible level is in the constitutional text itself, which I call primary rights. The Bill of Rights and the Fourteenth Amendment's due process and equal protection clauses are obvious examples of primary constitutional rights. The practice of judicial review, however, means that these primary rights are subject to judicial interpretation and construction, the product of which can be described as secondary rights. The Supreme Court's decision in *Brown* that segregation in public education violates the equal protection clause is one example of a secondary right. In addition, secondary rights may encompass the policy directives issued by courts to remedy violations of constitutional rights, such as the judicial requirement that states take positive measures (e.g., busing) to remedy educational segregation. In essence, institutional reform activists, engaged in specific programs of legal change through constitutional modification, are seeking to limit and redefine the policy choices available to legislators and other government officials.[9] Although this goal can be accomplished by modifying primary rights through formal amendment, that approach faces two important constraints. First, the rules are designed to make formal amendment difficult. Second, the necessity of judicial interpretation makes the future meaning of the new right uncertain, which undermines its value as an instrument of institutional reform. Consequently, the preferred route is constitutional rulemaking and institutional design through litigation.

Institutional reform litigation can thus be conceptualized as the manipulation of primary rights to acquire and mobilize secondary rights that can be used to alter the structure or operating rules or both of public organizations such as educational systems, prisons, hospitals, and mental health institutions. It is, as Susan Lawrence argues, "a planned effort to influence the course of judicial policy development to achieve a particular policy goal."[10] The principal objective of institutional reform litigation is to acquire a remedial decree, which contains a set of policy directives from courts to institutions that are derived from both primary and secondary rights. Remedial decrees can take many forms, ranging from simple declarations of rights to injunctions that mandate dispute-resolution processes, performance standards that institutions should meet, or specific actions that officials must take to remedy constitutional violations.[11] The nature of remedial decree litigation has been described best by Philip J. Cooper, who argues that institutional reform cases can be analyzed as a process consisting of trigger, liability, remedy, and postdecree phases.[12] The trigger phase consists of both the general historical practices and specific triggering events that lead to the initiation of a case. According to Cooper, the importance of these factors suggests that remedial decree litigation is as much reactive as it is the product of carefully planned reform strategies. Moreover, since litigants must meet threshold requirements connected with the rules of standing and amicus curiae status, a significant degree of judicial choice is involved at the earliest stages of institutional reform litigation. Indeed, at the highest levels of the judicial process, courts have virtually complete control over their dockets, which provides them with the discretion to select the most appropriate cases for resolving complex policy issues. These two aspects of this phase of remedial decree litigation were evident in *Gault*. The specific event that triggered the case, for example, was the use of traditional juvenile court procedures to restrain an individual's liberty for a period out of proportion to the seriousness of the offense. The case would not have reached the Supreme Court, however, had it not arisen in the context of a general loss of faith in the rehabilitative ideal underlying juvenile court procedures, which made the Court more open to reviewing those procedures.

The liability and remedy phases, in which rights violations are determined and remedies formulated to correct the violations, constitute the central components of institutional reform litigation. These phases may occur simultaneously or be the subject of separate proceedings. Moreover, they may encompass certain elements of the trigger phase, such as determining whether litigants have met threshold requirements like standing. Several aspects of the liability phase affect the ultimate success of litigation, including the development of an accurate record to support any liability findings and subsequent remedial orders. If the record is weak and the court's liability findings equivocal, the subsequent remedy will be vulnerable to attack on appeal. Although remedies may be the product of judicially supervised and approved negotiations between parties, they may also be imposed by courts following adversarial remedial hearings. In *Gault*, the liability and remedy phases revolved around two critical questions: first, whether juveniles possessed constitutional rights that could be violated in juvenile proceedings, and second, the level of due process that would be necessary to protect those rights.

The final step in institutional reform litigation is the postdecree phase, during which remedies are implemented, evaluated, and refined. This phase is characterized by interaction between litigants and judges, with the degree of interaction determined by the nature of the initial remedy. Three variables shape the degree of judicial supervision necessary to ensure proper implementation of any institutional reform remedy: the extent of the constitutional violation, the organizational capacity of the institution to change, and the surrounding political culture. If the constitutional violations are narrow, organizational capacity is high, and the political culture supportive, usually it will be possible to formulate a process-oriented consent decree that requires relatively little judicial supervision. By contrast, if the constitutional violations are extensive, organizational capacity low, and the political culture hostile, it may be necessary to place the institution into court-supervised receivership.[13] Closely connected to these variables and the remedies they generate is the question of when courts should disengage from the project of institutional reform they were asked to undertake, with disengagement occurring more quickly in cases involving process-oriented consent decrees.[14] In formulating its remedy in *Gault*, the Supreme Court assumed that its new due process requirements were relatively narrow, that juvenile courts were amenable to change, and that the surrounding culture supported constitutional domestication. Consequently, the Court imposed a process-oriented remedy that contained few provisions for judicial supervision by higher courts. These assumptions had an important impact on local implementation of the Supreme Court's remedy, state legislative initiatives, and refinement by the Court itself.

As Cooper's remedial decree litigation model suggests, several phenomena, including individual or group demands, local political forces, and conditions in the broader political system, influence both the process and outcome of institutional reform litigation. These phenomena have been summarized by Lee Epstein and Joseph Kobylka, who identify three general factors that affect the outcome of constitutional litigation in the Supreme Court in instances where the aim is to produce legal change that has direct and immediate policy consequences.[15] One factor is the composition of the Court itself, since the behavioral attributes of individual justices affect their receptiveness to various constitutional claims. To this factor might be added institutional attributes, such as the capacity of a legal institution to gather and process the information necessary to make important policy decisions.[16] A second factor is the efforts of organized interest groups, who are most often responsible for litigation involving significant legal reform and policy change. Finally, Epstein and Kobylka point to the political environment in which the litigation takes place, with the success of constitutional claims directly dependent on the level of support for those claims in that environment. Each of these factors must be examined in more detail in order to build an analytical framework for the analysis of *Gault* and the legal/policy reforms for which it was responsible.

Judicial Behavior and Institutional Capacity

In the early 1960s, under the influence of legal realism, studies of judicial decisionmaking shifted significantly from an emphasis on legal and doctrinal analysis to an emphasis on individual judicial voting behavior. Guided by Oliver Wendell Holmes's aphorism that the "life of the law has not been logic, but experience,"[17] proponents of legal realism rejected the idea that law is a set of fixed concepts and replaced it with a functionalist approach that viewed law as an evolving element of a dynamic social process.[18] Law, according to the realists, was both a product of that process and a potential tool for taking the process in new directions. Legal realism thus had both descriptive and prescriptive pretensions. On the one hand, it purported to describe the "real" process by which judges decide cases; on the other hand, it attempted to prescribe how judges could use the law—particularly administrative and constitutional law—to engineer a better society.

Rooted in legal realism's assertion that judicial decisionmaking is the product of relatively stable individual value orientations rather than of logical deductions from legal first principles, the political science literature on judicial decisionmaking has developed in roughly three phases. In the first phase, scholars such as C. Herman Pritchett and Glendon Schubert sought empirical verification for the theoretical assertions of legal realism by examining the voting behavior of individual Supreme Court justices. Focusing on the obvious fact that Supreme Court justices often disagree about important questions of constitutional law, Pritchett's pioneering work on the Roosevelt Court verified that these disagreements were not random but represented discernible decisionmaking patterns linked to individual value systems.[19] Schubert's innovation was to apply the quantitative techniques of behavioralism to the same questions posed by Pritchett in order to construct a theoretical model that might have predictive value.[20] Building on the work of social psychologists, Schubert emphasized the link between ideology and decisionmaking. Applying his analysis to the Vinson and Warren Court eras, Schubert identified three distinct ideological blocs that consistently voted together.

The Pritchett/Schubert approach led naturally to the second phase in the development of this literature, which focused on deeper questions of explanation and prediction by analyzing individual judicial behavior through models based on social background characteristics, individual political attitudes, and role theory.[21] According to one analysis, for example, age at appointment, federal administrative experience, and religious affiliation are three characteristics that explain and predict judicial decisionmaking in certain types of cases. In other analyses, scholars have asserted that individual background characteristics are filtered through the orientation that judges have toward their proper role in the political system.[22] In essence, these role orientations affect the degree to which judges believe that it is appropriate to use their own attitudes and personal belief systems as a guide to decisionmaking. Nevertheless, whatever the source of judicial attitudes, for the second phase scholars, as for Pritchett and Schubert, the principal explanation for changes in constitutional doctrine became changes in the composition of the Court.

The changing fate of juvenile rights before the Supreme Court certainly appears to support the basic assertions of these first two phases of research

Table 1.1. Supreme Court Juvenile Justice Decisions, 1966–1984

	Originating Jurisdiction	*Year*	*Issue Decided*	*Accept/Reject (M/C/D)*[a]
Kent v. United States	District of Columbia	1966	Waiver hearing	Accept (5/0/4)
In re Gault	Arizona	1967	Notice, counsel, cross-examination, self-incrimination	Accept (5/3/1)
In re Winship	New York	1970	Burden of proof	Accept (4/1/3)
McKeiver v. Pennsylvania	Pennsylvania	1971	Jury trial	Reject (4/2/3)
Breed v. Jones	California	1975	Double jeopardy	Accept (9/0/0)
Fare v. Michael C.	California	1979	*Miranda*	Reject (5/0/4)
Schall v. Martin	New York	1984	Pretrial detention	Reject (6/0/3)

[a](Majority/Concurring/Dissenting)

on judicial behavior, since the composition of the Court and the individual voting behavior of its justices unquestionably affected the development of juvenile jurisprudence. Between 1966 and 1984, the Court decided seven important juvenile justice cases (see Table 1.1).[23] After deciding in favor of the rights claimant in the first three of these cases, the Court then rejected the claim in three of the next four cases. Although the changing nature of the claims made in these cases was certainly important, so too were changes in the Court's composition. For example, by 1971 Chief Justice Earl Warren and Justices Tom Clark and Abe Fortas, who had each supported all the juvenile rights claims presented in *Kent* and *Gault,* had been replaced by Thurgood Marshall, Warren Burger, and Harry Blackmun, of whom only one (Marshall) would be consistently sympathetic to such claims.

The loss of Fortas was particularly important. Born in Memphis in 1910 to an Orthodox Jewish family who had emigrated to Tennessee from England, Fortas's judicial philosophy had been forged in the legal realism of Yale University, nurtured by his mentor William O. Douglas, and honed in the bureaucratic battles of the early New Deal. When Fortas entered Yale Law School in 1930 at the age of twenty, it had begun to surpass Columbia University as the intellectual center of legal realism. In 1928, under the leadership of Robert Maynard Hutchins, Yale acquired two prestigious members of Columbia's law faculty, Underhill Moore and twenty-eight-year-old William O. Douglas.[24] Douglas was about to embark on his quest to develop a functional approach to business law that would eventually lead him to the chairmanship of the Securities and Exchange Commission and finally to a seat on the Supreme Court in 1939.

Fortas's relationship with Douglas began in 1932, when Douglas selected Fortas to undertake a study with him on consumer credit in Chicago.[25] The relationship continued after Fortas's graduation from Yale, with Douglas acting as Fortas's patron and guide through the complex world of the New Deal bureaucracy. Fortas left government service in 1946 to enter private practice, where he acquired Lyndon Johnson as a client and acted as the court-appointed attorney in the landmark right to counsel case, *Gideon v. Wainwright* (1963).[26] In 1965, Fortas's former client, by then the president, rewarded him with a seat on the Supreme Court. In matters of criminal procedure, Fortas was generally considered a staunch advocate of defendants' rights over state interests. This orientation was clear in his support of Chief Justice Warren's decision in *Miranda v. Arizona* (1966)[27] and in his opinions for the Court majority in the first two juvenile justice cases.

Despite the important insights into the Supreme Court's actions generated by the first two phases in the development of the judicial decision-making literature, its behavioral emphasis left it vulnerable to critics who accused its proponents of ignoring legal variables and the dynamics surrounding the collective decisions of courts as institutions. These criticisms led to a third phase of development, characterized by a revival of interest in the role of legal doctrine and the influence of institutional variables. For example, Jeffrey Segal has applied the quantitative techniques of behavioral analysis to study how legal doctrine influences case outcomes.[28] According to Segal, Supreme Court justices, faced with an overwhelming number of complex cases to decide each term, use existing legal doctrine to extract informational cues from those cases to guide their decisions. Similarly, Lee Epstein, Thomas Walker, and William Dixon have conceptualized the U.S. Supreme Court as a political institution and examined how institutional variables such as the political composition of the Court, attitude stability, policymaking priorities, and the external political environment affect the Court's policy outputs.[29] These approaches both recognize that individual judicial decisions are made in a particular institutional and political context that brackets decisionmaking within certain parameters.

One means of understanding these institutional parameters is to consider Donald Horowitz's argument that the structure or "attributes" of adjudication impose constraints on the policymaking capacity of courts, even in fields that they presumably know and understand well.[30] This approach is based on the notion that courts do not constitute an exception to the rule that different political institutions approach and resolve policy questions in distinctive ways.[31] More specifically, the traditional structure of adjudication—in which lawsuits are bipolar and self-contained, litigation is retrospective, rights and remedies are interdependent, and the process is party-initiated and party-controlled—limits the capacity of courts to shift comfortably from strictly legal issues to policy analysis.[32] As Colin Diver argues, judicial policy analysis forces judges to act as political powerbrokers, a role to which traditional adjudication is not well-suited.[33] Unlike politics, which is a bargaining process that relies on exchange to accommodate conflicting interests and which is characterized by flexibility, dynamism, and power, adjudication resolves conflicts through the authoritative articulation of norms.[34] This difference means, Horowitz argues, that adjudication has "its own devices for choosing problems, its own habits of analysis, its own criteria of the relevance of phenomena to issues, [and] its own repertoire of solutions."[35]

The first, and most obvious, attribute of adjudication is that courts speak the language of rights. Unlike legislatures, which are concerned with weighing the costs and benefits of different courses of action, the emphasis on rights and remedies in adjudication limits the range of policymaking alternatives available to courts and precludes explicit cost-benefit analyses; courts are supposed to provide remedies to vindicate rights violations regardless of the cost. This emphasis on rights and remedies leads to a second attribute of adjudication: It is designed to ascertain historical or adjudicative facts about discrete events that transpired during the past rather than social or legislative facts about causal relationships and the future impact of decisions. Although one might expect the policymaking capacity of courts to be enhanced by a third attribute of adjudication—incremental decisionmaking—this is not necessarily the case, since courts tend to react slowly to new information. Moreover, when they do react, that reaction tends to be in the form of grafting qualifications onto prior decisions rather than through a fresh consideration of the issues. The weaknesses of judicial incrementalism are further exacerbated by a fourth attribute: Courts are passive institutions that must wait for others to bring cases and issues before them. Although this passivity can be mitigated through judicial control of court dockets, there remains the danger that the pool of available cases may not accurately represent the general impact of the policies under review. Judicial passivity also contributes to the final attribute of adjudication: It contains inadequate provision for policy review. Courts, Horowitz argues, tend to neglect consequentialist facts about the "impact of a decision on behavior."[36]

Most of the attributes identified by Horowitz—that adjudication is singularly focused on rights and remedies, that it produces change in small increments, and that the process is dominated by historical (or adjudicative) facts—characterize the liability and remedy phases of institutional reform litigation. The trigger phase of institutional reform litigation, however, is shaped by the fact that adjudication is passive and must be triggered by litigants rather than by courts themselves. Finally, the postdecree phase suffers from the absence of an effective mechanism for initiating policy review. Taken as a whole, these attributes of adjudication give courts limited vision, make litigation a poor means of gathering and processing policy-relevant information, and lead to numerous implementation difficulties. In this respect, Horowitz's approach epitomizes the perspective that Gerald Rosenberg calls the "constrained court view," which asserts that courts will seldom be effective generators of social reform.[37] According to Rosenberg, the constraints that courts face as social reformers can be overcome only when one or more key conditions are met: incentives exist for the institution under review to change, costs are imposed for not changing, the possibility exists for the emergence of parallel institutions that are willing to implement the change, and key actors have the ability to use court orders as a rationale for action or as leverage in extracting additional resources.[38] However, the limited nature of constitutional rights, the lack of judicial independence, and the judiciary's inability to develop and implement appropriate policies make institutional reform litigation an exceptionally unreliable path to social change.[39]

Interest Groups and Litigation

Though the early extralegal models of judicial voting behavior focused primarily on internal factors, more recent versions have also emphasized external factors such as the nature, skill, and experience of litigants.[40] To a large extent this development can be attributed to Clement Vose, whose study of the restrictive covenant cases and others raised scholars' awareness of organized interest groups and the degree to which they employ litigation systematically to advance their policy agendas.[41] The research tradition resulting from this awareness has subsequently focused on two broad theoretical concerns. One area is the conditions under which interest groups choose litigation, rather than another form of political activity, to pursue their policy objectives. The second is with the factors that influence how interest groups select their specific litigation strategies and tactics.

The object of this research—public interest litigation—can trace its roots to the early twentieth century, when the National Consumers' League used litigation to advance the interests of working women and children.[42] Litigation campaigns blossomed during the 1960s as a response to perceived weaknesses in the political process. In contrast to legislatures, courts were considered relatively open institutions with numerous points of entry that could be accessed with relative ease.[43] Law journals provided one access point, with interest groups able to sensitize judges to their concerns through information contained in scholarly articles. Amicus curiae briefs provided a second, and more direct, form of access. Finally, test cases and class action suits sponsored by interest groups provided the greatest potential for achieving fundamental social reform through litigation. The importance of such litigation stems from the fact that it puts to the test "not only the legal rules but the limits of the legal system itself."[44]

Credit for the systematic development of public interest litigation techniques goes to two groups: the National Association for the Advancement of Colored People (NAACP) and the American Civil Liberties Union (ACLU). The NAACP adopted litigation as a tool for implementing broad social reform and developed "a strategic plan for cumulative litigation efforts aimed at achieving specified social objectives."[45] The ACLU, however, approached litigation in a rather piecemeal fashion, adjusting its litigation activities to current events. Thus, although law reform projects concerning specific issues have always been at the core of the ACLU's activities, it has avoided incremental, case-by-case development of constitutional doctrine, choosing instead to be highly selective and to expend its resources only in cases that raise major constitutional issues.[46] The different approaches taken by the NAACP and the ACLU have been described as programmatic and as reactive.[47]

Until recently, conventional wisdom held that programmatic interest group litigation is the ultimate weapon of political outsiders and occurs when other avenues of political change are closed. Termed the "political disadvantage" theory, this explanation is closely associated with the experiences of the NAACP. Until the 1960s restrictive election laws and voting requirements in a significant portion of the United States ensured that African Americans remained a "discrete and insular minority"[48] unable to defend or advance their interests through normal democratic political participation. Thus, in 1915 the NAACP entered the judicial arena to defend the legal rights of African Americans, and in 1939 it established an independent Legal Defense and Education Fund (LDF) to undertake a systematic program of social reform through constitutional litigation.[49] These legal struggles achieved important constitutional victories in the areas of restrictive covenants on property ownership, segregated education, and voting rights.[50] To be sure, each of these victories required further legal and political action to become effective, but the LDF's experience provided both a theoretical and a practical model of interest group litigation in the United States.

In the 1970s, however, this experience began to appear increasingly anomalous. First, scholars noted that not every interest group litigant suffered from the same political disadvantages experienced by the NAACP. Second, politically advantaged interest group litigants were often more successful in court than their disadvantaged counterparts. Some groups, in other words, appeared to seek constitutional change even where policy change through ordinary politics was possible. In an important 1974 article, Marc Galanter attempted to explain these departures from the model of interest group litigation based on the NAACP experience.[51] According to Galanter, participants in the legal process can be divided into one-shot (OS) and repeat-player (RP) litigants. The OS litigants are intensely interested in the outcome of specific disputes, but the RP litigants are concerned with long-term interests, and they expend resources on litigation only when there is a high probability of affecting the development of fundamental legal and political rules.[52] Moreover, RP litigants enjoy an advantage in the judicial process because their accumulated expertise and more extensive legal resources permit them to manipulate existing rules effectively and to promote the creation of even more favorable rules. As systematic, repeat-player litigants, interest groups will initiate constitutional litigation whenever fundamental rules affecting their long-term interests are at stake. Moreover, these groups stress law reform and interest representation rather than client service and representation as their organizational mandate.[53]

Modifications have also been made to the political disadvantage theory by Susan Olson.[54] What Olson found particularly inadequate about the theory is its assumption that interest group litigants would prefer to pursue their objectives through the majoritarian political process but are forced into the legal arena because of their status as political outsiders. Olson argued instead that litigation and other forms of interest advocacy are complementary political activities that interest groups pursue simultaneously. The choice between these two alternatives in specific instances, according to Olson, is a function of the mix of legal and political resources controlled by interest groups and their adversaries.[55] In her view, constitutional, statutory, and common law rights are the most important legal resources that groups possess. The value of these resources varies, however, according to their scope and stability. By contrast, political resources are those characteristics of a group or organization that give it access to and influence over legislators, executive officials, and bureaucrats. These resources include money and number of supporters, both of which allow groups to compete effectively for the attention of political decisionmakers. Olson's point is that a group without political resources is also unlikely to possess legal resources. Indeed, even the NAACP had political resources in the form of financial support from philanthropic organizations and influential (or merely dedicated and hard-working) individuals with ties to the majority political community.[56] According to Olson, groups will initiate litigation when their ratio of political to legal resources is smaller than their opponents' ratio of these two sets of resources. Thus, since the absolute level of political resources is not the key variable, Olson's theory explains why politically strong groups would choose litigation.

The dual contribution of legal and political resources to interest group litigation is particularly evident in a model of interest group litigation developed by Kim Scheppele and Jack Walker on the basis of their survey of a wide spectrum of literature on the litigation strategies of interest groups.[57] The organizational resources commanded by an interest group constitute one key element of this model. According to Scheppele and Walker, the most relevant organizational resources for litigation purposes are financial support (preferably from diffuse sources), access to legal expertise, and longevity (since litigation is a time-consuming strategy). At least two of these organizational resources—money and longevity—are also valuable for political activity outside the judicial arena. A second element of the model is the structure of the policy conflicts in which interest groups are engaged. Since litigation is defined by adversarial confrontation, there is an incentive to develop alternative mechanisms for resolving disputes with potential partners in future policy alliances. Consequently, litigation will become a more common strategy in instances where groups are engaged in intense conflict with regular opponents. A third element of the model is the political sensitivity of group demands. Since litigation is aimed at constitutionalizing policy change, it is a particularly valuable strategy for groups whose political fortunes, and hence policy success, are particularly sensitive to electoral shifts.

Finally, consistent with the political disadvantage theory, Scheppele and Walker include within their model the political status of groups, with political outsiders having a special incentive to litigate. Following Olson, however, Scheppele and Walker recognize that political insiders can acquire legal rights that make subsequent litigation more attractive.[58]

Whatever an interest group's motivation for shifting its energies toward the judicial arena, the success or failure of interest group litigation depends on a number of strategic and tactical choices.[59] The basic strategic choice that interest groups must make is between direct sponsorship of test cases designed to alter legal rules and participation as amicus curiae in cases brought by others. Direct sponsorship of test cases maximizes interest group control of litigation but is very expensive; amicus curiae participation is less costly but affords far less control over the development of legal rules. In general, a complete litigation strategy will encompass both types of activities. Choosing to litigate test cases imposes additional strategic constraints, however. First, since social change through litigation is the quintessential example of incremental policymaking,[60] it is important that cases be brought in the proper sequence. Second, cases must be brought in favorable venues in order to increase the probability of success. Further, a systematic reform litigation strategy requires centralized control in order to ensure that other strategic constraints are met and that counterproductive litigation does not occur in the target policy field.

These strategic choices are to a large degree interdependent. For example, the NAACP preferred to litigate in U.S. federal courts rather than in state courts not only because federal judges were considered more sympathetic to the NAACP's cause but also because this decision meant that LDF lawyers had to master only a single set of procedural rules that applied throughout the United States. Litigating in state courts would have forced LDF lawyers to learn multiple sets of rules and to rely more extensively on local counsel, which would have increased the costs of litigation and reduced the level of central control exercised in specific cases.[61] Consequently, venue selection was a function of three factors: estimates of the probability of success in each venue, costs of litigation, and the need for central control.

The strategic choices that interest groups make are closely related to the principal tactical choice they face: selecting specific cases and determining the arguments to make in those cases. The incremental character of judicial policymaking means that the ultimate constitutional objectives of a litigation campaign can be achieved only through the gradual development of discrete rules that eventually form the basis for a new, overarching, constitutional doctrine. Thus in practical terms, cases raising the easiest constitutional questions must be identified and litigated first, before moving on to cases raising more problematic constitutional issues. The NAACP's experience is again instructive on this point. Its ultimate objective was to establish the constitutional doctrine that segregation in public education violates the equal protection clause of the Fourteenth Amendment. In order to establish this doctrine, the NAACP attacked three cornerstones of educational segregation: differential teaching salaries based on race, segregation of public graduate and professional schools, and inequalities in the physical facilities of African American and white elementary and secondary schools.[62] Both the nature and sequencing of these attacks were important, because at each step the NAACP broadened the legal concept of educational equality and applied it to progressively more difficult cases. These cases made the final step to the constitutional doctrine—that separate public education facilities are inherently unequal—less drastic than it might otherwise have been.

Interest groups, particularly the American Civil Liberties Union, were active in *Gault* and *Winship* (see Table 1.2).[63] Moreover, various interest groups, including the National Council of Juvenile Court Judges, the National Council on Crime and Delinquency, the Public Defender Service of the District of Columbia, the California Public Defenders Association, and Americans for Effective Law Enforcement, participated in the cases that followed *Winship*. Among the more interesting groups involved in the constitutional domestication of juvenile justice was the Legal Services Program (LSP), which had been established by the Office of Economic Opportunity (OEO) in 1965. Emphasizing the legal problems of the poor, LSP represented an effort to combine the two traditional functions of interest group litigants by pursuing law reform in the context of providing strong client service. Because a large proportion of juvenile defendants suffered from economic disadvantage, it was inevitable that LSP would become involved in these cases. Indeed, LSP participated in *Gault* and *Winship* as amicus curiae, and in *McKeiver* and *Breed v. Jones* as the actual sponsors of the litigation. Overall, LSP enjoyed an unusually high success rate in the cases it brought before the Supreme Court, and the juvenile justice cases were no exception. In three of the four cases in which LSP participated, the Court extended the due process rights of juveniles. Perhaps because of this success, Congress amended the Equal Opportunity Act to restrict LSP's criminal representation services, which also affected its work in juvenile justice.[64]

These groups showed overwhelming support for juvenile court reform in *Gault* and *Winship* (see Table 1.2). Indeed, nongovernmental interest group

Table 1.2. Interest Group Participants, 1966–1970

	Group	Mode of Participation	Position
Gault	American Civil Liberties Union	Litigant	For
	National Legal Aid and Defender Association	Amicus	For
	New York Legal Aid Society	Amicus	For
	Children's Committee for the City of New York	Amicus	For
	American Parents' Committee	Amicus	For
	Ohio Association of Juvenile Court Judges	Amicus	Against
Winship	New York Legal Aid Society	Litigant	For
	Neighborhood Legal Services Program (District of Columbia)	Amicus	For
	Legal Aid Association (District of Columbia)	Amicus	For

participants in the seven cases considered in this book supported additional procedural safeguards for juveniles by approximately a three-to-one margin. Existing studies of interest group litigation suggest that the analysis of this aspect of the constitutional domestication of juvenile courts begin by assessing the impact of this alignment of legal and political resources on each side of the controversy over juvenile justice policy during the 1960s. The next step is to determine whether choices concerning modes of participation, sequencing of cases, and venue selection were consistent with an effective strategy of systematic reform litigation or whether they even reflected a strategic approach to the problem.

Political Environment

Although it may not be entirely true, as Finley Peter Dunne's Mr. Dooley suggested, that "th' supreme coort follows th' iliction returns,"[65] there can be little doubt that external political forces shape judicial decisionmaking. In particular, political developments change patterns of participation in and access to the Court, which in turn affect its agenda setting and decisionmaking.[66] Two such developments facilitated the constitutional attack on juvenile courts. One development was a broad conceptual revolution in the judicial understanding of due process and its components and the spread of that revolution to the states through the Fourteenth Amendment. This due process revolution radically altered the law with respect not only to the rights of juvenile defendants but also in the areas of search and seizure, the rights of criminal defendants (including the right to counsel and the right against self-incrimination), and the rights of prison inmates.[67] The second, more narrow, development was the simultaneous rise in juvenile arrest rates and the decline of faith in discretionary justice and the rehabilitative ideal, which combined to make juvenile proceedings vulnerable to the implications of the broader development.

The best place to begin any examination of the revolution in criminal procedure that occurred throughout the 1960s is with Herbert Packer's distinction between the crime control and due process models of that procedure. Although they represent different approaches, the models share a number of common assumptions by virtue of their existence within an adversarial system of justice. Among these assumptions are the prohibition against ex post facto laws (i.e., conduct must be defined as criminal prior to its being punished as such), the limited power of governments to investigate and apprehend persons suspected of committing crimes, and the idea that alleged criminals are independent subjects who can force the state to demonstrate their guilt to an independent authority. Nevertheless, even if both models are constrained within the parameters set by the minimal procedural requirements of the adversarial/accusatorial system of justice characteristic of common law jurisdictions, they emphasize different values and have different practical implications.

According to Packer, the crime control model views "the repression of criminal conduct [as] the most important function to be performed by the criminal process." From this perspective, the criminal process is seen as a positive guarantor of social and individual liberty. To achieve its purpose, the crime control model focuses attention on "the efficiency with which the criminal process operates to screen suspects, determine guilt, and secure appropriate dispositions of persons convicted of crime." In order to justify itself, this approach to criminal procedure must produce a high rate of apprehension and conviction in a context where criminal activity is high and resources are limited. This model requires that a premium be placed on speed, which depends on informality and uniformity, and on finality, which depends on minimizing opportunities to challenge the process's decisional outputs. Consequently, the crime control model tends to deemphasize the formal adversarial components of the criminal process in favor of the preadjudicative, investigative phase of the process.[68] In this model, police, prosecutors, defense lawyers, and judges work together to ensure the efficient administration of criminal justice and the rapid processing of criminal cases. This is not to imply, however, that the objective of efficiency completely eclipses the desire for accurate decisionmaking. Indeed, according to the crime control model, inaccuracy reduces efficiency by undermining the credibility of the process, which interferes with the goal of repressing crime.

In contrast to this approach, the due process model is principally concerned with the factual integrity and accuracy of the criminal process. As such, it is willing to trade efficiency for reliability in order to eliminate the possibility of erroneous fact-finding. This approach leads the due process model to reject "informal fact-finding processes as definitive of factual guilt and to an insistence on formal, adjudicative, adversary fact-finding processes in which the factual case against the accused is publicly heard by an impartial tribunal."[69] The due process model is skeptical of the motivations and fact-determining skills of law enforcement officers and prosecutors; rigorous procedures are considered to be the best instrument for guaranteeing correct outcomes. Moreover, the due process model also emphasizes the prevention of official oppression of the individual by maintaining a strict distinction between factual and legal guilt. Rigorous due process requires that the state prove both, and the purpose of the adversarial system is to make determinations of legal guilt difficult. Taken to its extreme, the due process model exhibits a deep skepticism about both the morality and utility of the criminal sanction.

Although every system of criminal procedure will encompass elements of both models, it is possible to determine where, at a particular moment, any system falls on the spectrum between the two ideal models as well as the direction of any changes in the principles and practices of a system. There can be little dispute that the core assumptions underlying the due process model provided the basis for the Supreme Court's review of criminal procedure during the postwar period, particularly under the leadership of Chief Justice Earl Warren during the 1960s. Indeed, consistent with the precepts of the due process model, the Court's concern with maintaining the factual integrity of the criminal process led it gradually to expand the protections of the Bill of Rights to the earliest stages of criminal investigation, as was particularly evident in search and seizure and self-incrimination cases. In both areas, the Court abandoned the common law admissibility standards of relevance and reliability in order to focus on the manner in which evidence is gathered. For example, to ensure that the fact-finding process would not be tainted by evidence gathered illegally, the Court eventually applied the federal exclusionary rule to state criminal proceedings as a way of deterring law enforcement officers from violating the Fourth Amendment's prohibition against unreasonable searches and seizures. Although this rule first emerged in *Weeks v. United States* (1914), the Court explicitly refused to impose it on the states in *Wolf v. Colorado* (1949).[70] The Court's rationale in *Wolf* was that the exclusionary rule was simply a practical remedy, without constitutional status, developed as part of the Court's general supervisory power of the federal judiciary.[71] The Warren Court began to abandon this rationale in *Elkins v. United States* (1960), when it rejected the so-called "silver platter doctrine," according to which federal officials had been permitted to use evidence seized illegally by state officials.[72] Finally, in *Mapp v. Ohio* (1961) the Warren Court applied the exclusionary rule to state proceedings in order to ensure that no defendant would be convicted by evidence obtained through constitutionally prohibited means.[73]

This attempt to "constitutionalize" the preadjudicative phase of the criminal process reached its apex in the Court's consideration of confessions in *Miranda v. Arizona* (1966).[74] Referring to several police interrogation manuals, Chief Justice Warren argued that modern interrogation practices are "psychologically rather than physically oriented." Custodial interrogation (i.e., "incommunicado interrogation of individuals in a police-dominated atmosphere"), Warren continued, "exacts a heavy toll on individual liberty and trades on the weakness of individuals." This practice results in "inherently compelling pressures which work to undermine the individual's will to resist and to compel him to speak where he would not otherwise do so freely." Warren found these procedures inconsistent with the privilege against self-incrimination, whose "constitutional foundation . . . is the respect a government must accord to the dignity and integrity of its citizens."[75] In order to protect individual dignity and integrity in the coercive atmosphere of custodial interrogation, the *Miranda* Court developed the constitutional rule that law enforcement officers must fully inform arrested suspects of their Fifth and Sixth Amendment rights.

As Warren's comments in *Miranda* might suggest, the decision to extend the exclusionary rule to the states and to control the use of confessions derived chiefly from a view of due process that was largely unrelated to its instrumental contribution to the factual integrity of the criminal process. During the Warren Court era, commentators began to argue that the strict procedural requirements of the due process model possess an intrinsic value since they equalize the relationship between individuals and the state and provide individuals with an opportunity to express "their dignity as persons."[76] According to this "dignity enhancement" aspect of the due process model, the interpretation and application of procedural rights should maximize the capacity of individuals to make decisions free from state coercion.[77] In seeking to control the investigative techniques of law enforcement officers, the Court actively attacked practices that it perceived as "strip[ping] individuals of their self-respect" on the grounds that "forcing an individual to be the instrument of his own undoing degrades the dignity of man."[78]

Traditional juvenile procedures were obviously inconsistent with these jurisprudential developments. To begin with, juvenile proceedings did not share the adversarial assumptions common to both models of criminal procedure. More important, and somewhat ironically, the procedures that juvenile courts did employ were firmly rooted in crime-control values. Traditional juvenile procedures assumed that any young person brought within a juvenile court's jurisdiction needed some form of correction, and the objective was to determine the content of that correction rather than the factual basis of the petition against the youth. It is not surprising, therefore, that juvenile procedures would appear increasingly anomalous to a Court that was rapidly shifting criminal procedure toward the due process end of the spectrum. Moreover, as *Mapp* had clearly demonstrated, it was a Court increasingly willing to impose its vision of due process on state criminal proceedings.

Until the Fourteenth Amendment's ratification in 1868, there was little controversy that the Bill of Rights applied only to the national government, leaving the states free to develop criminal procedure as they saw fit. Indeed, even after the Fourteenth Amendment's due process clause raised the possibility of a broader application of the Bill of Rights, the Supreme Court largely refused to incorporate its provisions into the amendment until 1925.[79] Moreover, even after 1925, the Court's incorporation activity focused on the First Amendment, with criminal procedure receiving the Court's attention on only three occasions between 1925 and 1961. The Warren Court can be credited for most of the nationalization of criminal procedure (see Table 1.3).

Although the Warren Court as a whole generally accepted the concept of incorporating the Bill of Rights into the Fourteenth Amendment's due process clause, the justices differed in their understanding of precisely how incorporation should be accomplished and what it should mean for state proceedings.[80] The earliest approach, which first emerged in 1884, argued for the total incorporation of all guarantees in the Bill of Rights, but nothing more, into the Fourteenth Amendment's due process clause. Although this approach continued to attract supporters such as Justices Hugo Black and William Douglas as late as 1947, it never enjoyed majority support on the

Table 1.3. Incorporation and Criminal Procedure

	Amendment	Year	Case
Fair trial and counsel in capital cases	6	1932	*Powell v. Alabama*
Public trial	6	1948	*In re Oliver*
Unreasonable searches and seizures	4	1949	*Wolf v. Colorado*
Exclusionary rule	4	1961	*Mapp v. Ohio*
Cruel and unusual punishments	8	1962	*Robinson v. California*
Counsel in all felony cases	6	1963	*Gideon v. Wainwright*
Self-incrimination	5	1964	*Malloy v. Hogan*
Confrontation	6	1965	*Pointer v. Texas*
Impartial jury	6	1966	*Parker v. Gladden*
Speedy trial	6	1967	*Klopfer v. North Carolina*
Compulsory process for obtaining witnesses	6	1967	*Washington v. Texas*
Jury trial in nonpetty cases	6	1968	*Duncan v. Louisiana*
Double jeopardy	5	1969	*Benton v. Maryland*
Counsel in all criminal cases involving jail terms	6	1972	*Argersinger v. Hamlin*

Source: David M. O'Brien, *Constitutional Law and Politics,* vol. 2, *Civil Rights and Civil Liberties* (New York: W. W. Norton, 1991), 280–81.

Court. The second approach, which eventually became the majority test on the Warren Court, was selective incorporation, which looked to the substantive and procedural rights that form "the essence of a scheme of ordered liberty."[81] This standard allowed the Court to incorporate those Bill of Rights' provisions it deemed fundamental as well as important federal procedural requirements not expressly enumerated in the Bill of Rights. Finally, adherents of the fundamental fairness approach viewed the Fourteenth Amendment's due process clause as a requirement that states grant defendants the "fundamental fairness essential to the very concept of justice."[82] Fundamental fairness is a context-sensitive approach in which the procedural guarantees required in any specific case vary according to the proceedings under review and the nature of the rights at stake in those proceedings. As a context-driven standard, the fundamental fairness approach is not keyed to particular procedural safeguards but to the overall climate and context of the setting. Thus, although the specific provisions of the Bill of Rights provide a guide to the meaning of fundamental fairness, it is neither determinative nor exhaustive of the procedural safeguards that are required.

Each of these theories of incorporation carried different implications for the level of due process required in juvenile proceedings. In particular, the choice between selective incorporation and the context-oriented fundamental fairness approach would prove crucial both in the application of the Bill of Rights to juvenile court hearings and in the retreat that occurred after 1970. To the justices deciding *Gault* and *Winship,* juvenile court proceedings appeared to be so similar to adult criminal courts that the constitutionally protected concept of "ordered liberty" made selective incorporation of crucial components of due process into juvenile proceedings necessary. By contrast, to the majority of justices on the post-*Winship* Court, the overall nature of juvenile court proceedings appeared sufficiently fair to permit the doctrine of fundamental fairness to forgive particular procedural shortcomings in those proceedings, such as the absence of jury trials. The transition from selective incorporation to fundamental fairness thus constitutes an important part of the story of the Court's approach to juvenile justice policy.

Within this framework of theoretical and analytical concepts that guide the detailed examination of the constitutional domestication of juvenile courts, the key component is institutional reform litigation: the use of litigation to establish and implement legal changes that affect the structure and operations of public institutions. Its success depends on interest group activity, judicial attitudes, and the level of political acceptability surrounding the claims in question.[83] However, as Epstein and Kobylka point out, "It is *the law and legal arguments as framed by legal actors* that most clearly influence the content and direction of legal change."[84] The framework developed here suggests that neither traditional legal analysis nor microlevel behavioral analysis is completely adequate for understanding the development, resolution, and impact of institutional reform litigation. The principal shortcomings of these two approaches are that traditional legal analysis ignores, or at least downplays, the political environment of judicial decisionmaking and that the behavioralist's focus on voting and judicial attitudes does not capture the complexity involved in developing the legal arguments necessary to mobilize constitutional rights in a favorable direction. Consequently, my approach combines traditional analysis (since legal argumentation and doctrine are important in understanding the policy significance of institutional reform cases) with certain aspects of extralegal analysis (since deciding these cases is a profoundly political exercise). Therefore I have emphasized legal arguments in the following chapters.

The success or failure of institutional reform litigation depends heavily on the skill with which judges and litigants use the tools available to them in the litigation process and on their ability to adjust to the structural constraints of adjudication. By examining how these skills were applied over a short period of time by the litigants and Supreme Court justices in a series of cases concerning the same policy issue (the centerpiece of which is *Gault*), I seek to answer several questions. How did juvenile justice policy reach the Supreme Court's agenda, and why was *Gault* the case in which the Court resolved the various issues surrounding that policy? How did the Court develop its approach to the incorporation of the Bill of Rights into state juvenile court proceedings? What were the assumptions about the relationship between rehabilitation and due process that produced the Court's predictions about the impact of its decisions? How did the structure and underlying principles of the decisions contribute to the unintended consequences evident in state legislative reforms? Finally, how did the Court react to these consequences? By analyzing in some detail the effect of individual judicial attitudes, changing Court composition, and the general development of due process, I have provided some preliminary answers to these questions. By examining the legal arguments advanced by the various actors in these cases, I hope to provide more detailed answers in order to discern the nature and legacy of a critical phase in the development of American juvenile justice policy in a way that contributes to our general understanding of institutional reform litigation.

2. Discretionary Justice and the Decline of the Rehabilitative Ideal

The second half of the nineteenth century constituted one of the most important periods of social transformation in American history. It was a time of fundamental technological, economic, and institutional change, tracing its origins and subsequent evolution to the same source: rapid urbanization.[1] The number of American cities with populations greater than 100,000 increased from nine in 1860 to twenty-eight in 1890 and from thirty-eight in 1900 to fifty in 1910. Moreover, between 1880 and 1900, the U.S. urban population increased at a rate six times faster than the rural population. With urbanization came associated problems such as population congestion, housing shortages, poverty, inadequate public hygiene, and rising crime rates. Nowhere was urbanization and its epiphenomena more evident than in Illinois and its largest city, Chicago. In 1860 Illinois had a population density of thirty-one persons per square mile; by 1900 this figure had risen to eighty-six per square mile. Much of this increase was attributable to the astounding growth experienced by Chicago, which saw its population increase from 109,620 in 1860 to 2,185,283 in 1910. Necessity, opportunity, and intellectual resources combined to make Chicago an important laboratory for social experimentation. It comes as no surprise, then, that the first juvenile court in the United States opened its doors in that city in 1899.[2]

The establishment of this novel institution and its surrounding apparatuses represented a major accomplishment for nineteenth-century social reformers. According to most conventional historical interpretations, these reformers had been searching for a means of addressing the underlying causes of criminal behavior among children while protecting them from the stigma and harm caused by criminal prosecution. Their accomplishment can be placed in a broader legal and political context through an examination of the history of juvenile justice policy from the 1820s until the early 1960s. The founding principles and legislative operationalization of the juvenile court ideal at the turn of the century and early criticisms of that ideal will be explored. Then post–World War II criticisms of juvenile justice (including historical re-interpretation) and the legislative reforms those criticisms generated will be examined, followed by a discussion of an important turning point in the legal history of juvenile courts: a speech by Supreme Court Chief Justice Earl Warren critical of traditional juvenile court procedures. Like many ambitious social reforms, the nineteenth-century juvenile court could not carry the full burden of its founders' expectations. By failing in its promise to protect both children and society, the juvenile court left itself vulnerable to the changes ushered in by the Supreme Court.

Founding Principles

Until the nineteenth century little difference existed between the public response to crimes committed by children and to those by adults. In both cases the key issue was the individual's capacity to form criminal intent, and the only advantage that children enjoyed was the common law's presumption that this capacity did not fully crystallize until the age of fourteen. As the United States became more urbanized, however, social activists increasingly emphasized the relationship between criminal behavior and the social environment. Early reformers attributed crime among children to urban economic and social systems that produced citizens "who were physically and morally unfit for social life."[3] Early nineteenth-century American reformers, David Rothman argues, were "convinced that crime was the fault of the environment, not a permanent or inevitable phenomenon." Being "eager to demonstrate the social blessings of republican political arrangements to the world," they "set out to protect the safety of society and to achieve unprecedented success in eradicating deviancy."[4]

The first manifestation of these efforts was the House of Refuge movement, which sought to remove children from the negative influences of the chaotic urban society surrounding them. Social activists argued that these institutions would eradicate the causes of crime by providing children with the "daily routine of strict and steady discipline" necessary to cope with the "open, free-wheeling and disordered community" that constituted urban America in the nineteenth century.[5] Established in the 1820s by philanthropists concerned with poverty among urban children in cities such as New York, Philadelphia, and Boston, the Houses of Refuge imposed strict discipline on their residents and trained them in useful skills. Unhappy with the corruptive influences of urban life, the Houses also sent many of their residents away to work on rural farms. Although these institutions continued to exist well into the twentieth century, by 1870 they were no longer considered panaceas for the ills that produced criminal behavior among children. Indeed, concerns about abusive practices in some Houses of Refuge, as well as scientific advances in the study of crime, combined to encourage the search for new responses to childhood crime.[6]

The juvenile court movement that emerged from this search drew its theoretical and practical inspiration largely from the maturing science of positivist criminology. Relying on a deterministic model of human behavior, positivist criminology shifted attention away from criminal acts as products of free moral choice to the personality disorders from which criminal offenders suffered.[7] The positivist understanding of criminal behavior led its adherents to advocate a system of "individualized justice" in which the background and personality traits of each offender could be considered and in which punishment and deterrence would have little relevance.[8] The concept of an individualized system of justice, designed to respond to behavioral problems rather than to acts that were the product of free moral choice, captured the imagination of reformers who were disillusioned with the House of Refuge movement yet still concerned with the problems facing urban youth.

The juvenile court movement relied for direction, energy, and support on a national network of charitable organizations and local civic improvement groups. In Chicago, the spiritual and intellectual center of the movement was a dilapidated former mansion at the corner of Halstead and Polk streets.[9] The building was the home of Hull House, which had been established in 1889 by twenty-nine-year-old Jane Addams as a place where young, college-educated men and women interested in helping the urban poor could live and work. Addams had been inspired by the example of London's Toynebee Hall, where she had observed young men serving the poor without the paternalism characteristic of more institutionalized charitable organizations. In addition to helping the poor, Addams saw Hull House as an outlet for the talent and energy of her contemporaries and particularly for the abilities of young women. In return, the residents of Hull House received experience and education in the difficulties of life among the urban underclass.[10]

Addams's observations of the children living in Hull House's surrounding neighborhood, as well as her reflections on various nineteenth-century studies of childhood and youth, convinced her that society's existing response to crime was virtually irrelevant to the vast majority of offenders, who were young.[11] She was particularly concerned about the existing practice of mixing adults and children in the same courts and jails, fearing that this system would breed even more crime. Along with Julia Lathrop, who had moved to Hull House in 1890, Addams led the movement to establish a separate justice system for children as part of Hull House's general concern with the welfare of Chicago's children and youth.[12] As Lathrop would later explain, the juvenile court movement aimed at remedying a situation in which some boys arrested as criminals received no sanction while others served up to nine months in the city prison. The residents of Hull House found the lack of intervention as disturbing as prison confinement, since it meant that boys thus released would not benefit from constructive work on their behalf.[13] The central role that Hull House played in the juvenile court movement continued after the court's establishment: Julia Lathrop became the first chairperson of the Juvenile Court Committee, and another resident of Hull House—Alzina Stevens—was the court's first probation officer. The court itself was located across the street from Hull House, and an informal arrangement existed whereby the city sought the settlement's approval before appointing the court's judge.[14]

The Hull House reformers who energized the juvenile court movement were concerned with a wide range of misbehavior that went far beyond actions that could be included within any traditional definition of criminal activity. Indeed, the ameliorative efforts of these reformers were not aimed so much at specific acts of misbehavior as they were at a behavioral condition, to which they attached the novel term "juvenile delinquency."[15] They perceived juvenile court laws as a means of bringing children before judges who, with the help of behavioral experts, could diagnose the conditions causing delinquency and prescribe treatment to meet the child's individual needs. As Judge Julian Mack of Chicago explained in 1909, the important question for juvenile courts was not "has this boy or girl committed a specific wrong, but what is he, how has he become what he is, and what had best be done in his interest and in the interest of the state to save him from a downward career?"[16] Mack urged juvenile court judges to be "willing and patient enough to search out the underlying causes of the trouble and to formulate the plan by which . . . the cure may be effected." Above all, Mack urged juvenile court judges not to treat children as criminal offenders.[17]

The reformers did not design the juvenile court to serve as a conventional legal institution but as a forum where specialists could meet to examine a child's character, lifestyle, psychology, and home environment.[18] The court's mission was to remove young offenders from the criminal process and to provide them with the care and supervision found in stable middle- and upper-middle-class families. Central to the court's activities was its assumption that the state, delinquent children, and their parents shared identical interests in the treatment of delinquency. The court thus abandoned the adversarial atmosphere of criminal courts and adopted the equity doctrine of *parens patriae* as a substitute for the cold, inflexible standards of criminal procedure. Established as a civil court of equity, the juvenile court developed a specialized vocabulary: petitions of delinquency replaced criminal charges; hearings replaced trials; adjudications of delinquency replaced findings of guilt; and dispositions replaced sentences. Finally, juvenile court statutes excluded the public from court proceedings in order to ensure that children would be protected from the stigma of criminal prosecution. The juvenile court's ultimate aim was to combine flexible decisionmaking and individualized intervention to treat and rehabilitate children rather than to punish offenses. These objectives were clearly evident in the purpose, jurisdiction, procedures, and dispositional practices of the Illinois Juvenile Court Act and its early progeny.

The purpose clause of the 1899 Illinois act articulated several objectives, most of which stressed the desirability of providing delinquent children with the "care and guidance" necessary for their rehabilitation without removing them from their homes. Where removal was necessary, the act stipulated that the state had an obligation to provide the child with "care, custody and discipline as shall approximate as nearly as possible that which should be given them by their parents." The Illinois purpose clause would serve as the model for purpose clauses in other states' legislation. In essence, it established three interests that juvenile courts were expected to pursue: the protection and proper development of children, the protection of society, and the establishment of respect for, and protection of, the family.[19] Early juvenile court laws stressed the first of these interests, and a 1910 survey of these statutes concluded that the best among them provided significant discretion for juvenile court officials to act to protect children from criminal prosecution and the conditions underlying delinquent behavior.[20]

Model juvenile court laws written early in the twentieth century reflected the widespread acceptance of the purposes embodied in the Illinois legislation. The 1914 model statute of the National Probation Association (NPA) stipulated that it "shall be construed liberally and as remedial in character; and the powers hereby conferred are intended to be general to effect the beneficial purpose herein set forth." Section 11 of the model law provided that "the court shall proceed upon the theory that said child is the ward of the State, and is subject to the discipline and entitled to the protection which the court should give such child under the conditions disclosed in the case." Moreover, to guarantee the achievement of the remedial and protective purposes of the act, it provided that no child adjudicated delinquent by the juvenile court would be considered a criminal, nor would such adjudication constitute a criminal conviction.[21]

Each of these objectives reappeared in the 1925 version of this model legislation. The purpose of the NPA's proposed standard juvenile court law of 1925 was "to secure for each child under [the court's] jurisdiction such care, guidance, and control . . . as will conduce to the child's welfare and the best interests of the state." The model's basic principle was that "children under the jurisdiction of the court are wards of the state, subject to the discipline and entitled to the protection of the state, which may intervene to safeguard them from neglect or injury and to enforce the legal obligations due to them and from them." Like the 1914 version, the 1925 model law stipulated that delinquency adjudications would not constitute criminal convictions or impose criminal status on children brought within the court's jurisdiction.[22]

The Illinois example continued to influence the development of model juvenile court laws well into the 1960s, as evidenced by the Uniform Juvenile Court Act drafted in 1968 by the National Conference of Commissioners on Uniform State Laws.[23] The commissioners' purpose in drafting the Uniform Act was to meet the new challenges of the 1960s while simultaneously preserving and promoting "the basic objectives of the juvenile court system." Consequently, the act provided for "judicial intervention when necessary for the care of deprived children and for the treatment and rehabilitation of delinquent and unruly children, but under defined rules of law and through fair and constitutional procedure." The act's purpose clause revealed the commissioners' traditional understanding of the objectives of juvenile courts. Among the act's objectives were providing "for the care, protection, and wholesome moral, mental, and physical development of children" and removing "from children committing delinquent acts the taint of criminality and the consequences of criminal behavior and [substituting] therefore a program of treatment, training, and rehabilitation."

Another principal feature of early juvenile court laws was the broad scope of juvenile court jurisdiction. The juvenile court of the early twentieth century possessed exclusive and original jurisdiction in three broad areas: delinquency, dependency, and neglect. The consensus among early juvenile court experts was that the best statutes gave jurisdiction over these matters to a special branch of an established court while specifically prohibiting police courts and justices of the peace from exercising that jurisdiction.[24] In addition, the statutes relied on an extremely broad definition of delinquency in order to ensure "that the court will not be unable, because of any technical lack of jurisdiction, to place a child under the care of the court and its officers, if that seems to be for the best interest of the child."[25] Thus, delinquency included violations of state laws and local ordinances as well as incorrigibility and a long list of noncriminal misbehavior. The list covered such actions as knowingly associating with "thieves, vicious or immoral persons"; running away; "growing up in idleness or crime"; visiting houses of ill-repute and gambling houses; wandering "about the street at night or about railroad yards or tracks"; using "vile, obscene or indecent language"; and generally acting immorally or indecently. Some later model acts defined this behavior as evidence of neglect.

The NPA's model juvenile court laws exemplified this broad view of jurisdiction. The 1914 model applied to children under eighteen who violated local penal laws or municipal ordinances, who committed offenses that could be considered crimes, or who engaged in any conduct that might endanger their morals, health, or general welfare.[26] Similarly, the 1925 model statute defined a "delinquent child" as one who violated any state law or local regulation, who was beyond parental control, who was habitually truant, or who habitually acted in a manner dangerous to the health or morals of the child or others.[27] The founders of the juvenile court believed that the court required this wide jurisdiction in order to accomplish its protective objectives. The court's advocates feared that a narrower jurisdiction would allow children who might benefit from the court's intervention to fall through the cracks of the system.

In addition to its broad jurisdiction, another cornerstone of the original juvenile court ideal was its rejection of adversary proceedings and its reliance on informal procedures. By 1910 thirteen states expressly provided that juvenile cases be heard in a "summary manner" in order to establish "an intimate, friendly relationship . . . between the judge and the child."[28] Only three states, by contrast, required that juvenile courts follow regular criminal procedure. Eight states and the District of Columbia permitted appeals, and separate juvenile records were necessary in twenty-two states.[29] Curiously, fifteen jurisdictions, including eight where juvenile courts followed summary procedures, provided for jury trials at the juvenile's request or on the judge's own motion.[30] Although only six states expressly prohibited public trials, most judges excluded persons without a direct interest in the case from the juvenile courtroom.[31]

The NPA's model acts followed the informality of these early statutes. The 1914 version provided that the juvenile court could "conduct the examination of the witnesses without the assistance of counsel" and could conduct the proceedings in chambers or exclude the public from the hearing room.[32] Similarly, the 1925 model stipulated that the court could "conduct the hearing in an informal manner, and without observing the usual requirements of criminal or civil procedure."[33] By the end of the 1950s, statutes and case law had firmly established procedural informality and the immunity of juvenile proceedings from the constitutional requirements of criminal due process as crucial elements of juvenile justice.[34]

The procedural cornerstone of traditional juvenile courts was the informality of nonadversarial proceedings; the dispositional cornerstone was the indeterminate sanction. Since dispositional practices were premised on the idea that dispositions constituted corrective responses to patterns of behavior rather than punishments for specific offenses, early dispositional criteria were defined vaguely in order to promote individualization. The Russell Sage Foundation's 1910 survey of state juvenile court laws identified twenty-five states that authorized juvenile courts to choose between commitment to an institution "having for its object the care of delinquent children" and probationary supervision in the child's own home or a foster home.[35] Although the NPA's 1914 model act followed this formulation,[36] the 1925 version was somewhat more systematic, authorizing juvenile courts to choose one of three possible dispositions: probation, institutional commitment, or "such further disposition as the court may deem to be for the best interests of the child."[37] Even the 1968 Uniform Juvenile Court Act allowed juvenile court judges to choose from among four types of dispositions the one deemed "best suited" to the "treatment, rehabilitation, and welfare" of delinquent juveniles.[38]

The purposes, broad jurisdiction, procedural informality, and dispositional practices of the juvenile court statutes modeled after the Illinois Juvenile Court Act were critical components of an attempt to approach juvenile crime and other childhood misbehavior according to a "rehabilitative ideal," whose central feature was rejection of traditional justifications for criminal sanctions like deterrence, retribution, and incapacitation. Instead, proponents of the rehabilitative ideal viewed the purpose of sanctions as being the transformation of the "characters, attitudes, and behavior of convicted offenders" in order to protect society and to enhance the offenders' own well-being.[39] The theoretical rationale for this approach was the highly deterministic causal explanation for juvenile crime adopted by the juvenile court movement and its corresponding faith in the behavioral malleability of children. The practical consequence of the rehabilitative ideal was a system of justice characterized by judicial discretion, procedural informality, and indeterminate dispositions. Eventually, deepening concern about these practical features would generate the conditions that triggered the Supreme Court's intervention in juvenile justice policy.

Second Thoughts

The implementation of the rehabilitative ideal in the context of juvenile justice was neither self-executing nor self-justifying; both its success and legitimacy required the development of accurate diagnostic tools and effective methods of treatment.[40] Although the Supreme Court's burst of activity in this field between 1966 and 1970 might suggest otherwise, skepticism about both the effectiveness and legitimacy of the rehabilitative ideal's implementation by juvenile courts did not suddenly emerge fully developed in the mid-1960s. Indeed, doubts about the wisdom of an informal, treatment-oriented approach to juvenile crime arose almost simultaneously with the juvenile court's founding. These doubts increased as it became apparent that conditions in juvenile institutions often belied their rehabilitative rhetoric and that behavioral experts seldom participated in juvenile court decision-making.[41] Early critics were especially concerned about the power of juvenile court judges, believing that it encouraged judicial arbitrariness.[42] This concern was understandable, since the founding principles of juvenile courts "made the personality of the judge, his likes and dislikes, attitudes and prejudices, consistencies and caprices, the decisive element in shaping the character of his courtroom."[43] As early as 1914, one critic speculated that judicial discretion in juvenile courts would "be just as unsafe as experience proved it to be in the criminal court."[44] These themes would be sounded again during the 1950s and 1960s.

Initially, however, the fear of judicial arbitrariness stemmed primarily from concerns about the absence of procedural safeguards for parents in proceedings where one potential consequence was the termination of parental custody rights and removal of the child from the home. As one critic expressed it, "In no single instance is so much of human rights at stake as is involved when the law . . . reaches out with an all-powerful arm and removes a child from his mother's arms."[45] The importance of such proceedings, critics contended, required the participation of clerks, court reporters, and probation officers. Other critics also believed that representation of parents and guardians by counsel, the provision of jury trials on demand, and the right to appeal to be necessary components of these proceedings.[46] Yet very little attention was directed toward the rights of children themselves during these proceedings. Even in the eyes of early critics, the juvenile court continued to project a protective and benevolent image with respect to children.

Attitudes changed in the mid-1940s, however, as the criticism became rhetorically sharper and substantively broader. In 1944, for example, the superintendent of the Los Angeles County Juvenile Hall argued that individualized treatment and procedural informality could no longer automatically be reconciled with the conventional principles of criminal justice and individual rights. In his view, some juvenile courts were taking advantage of the tension between these competing principles in order to pursue unauthorized objectives. Some juvenile courts ignored the substance of their authorizing statutes and dealt with juvenile offenses according to conventional principles of criminal justice (including inflicting punishment) without taking advantage of "the new techniques and principles of individualization," the use of which juvenile courts were designed to facilitate. Other courts adhered strictly to individualized treatment, disregarding altogether the conventional goals and procedures of criminal justice to the detriment of society and juveniles. A third group of juvenile courts simply used the rhetoric of rehabilitation to rationalize punitive intervention into juveniles' lives. What juvenile courts should practice, the superintendent argued, was "an enlightened 'justice' which will protect the rights of the community and yet leave scope for modern individualized treatment within the limits which the behavior of the individual permits."[47]

The rehabilitative ideal's hegemony over juvenile justice policy began to weaken significantly soon after World War II. Skepticism about the claims of the ideal's proponents during this period came from two sources. One was public concern about an apparent increase in both juvenile crime and juvenile court leniency. A second source was the legal profession, which had largely ignored juvenile courts and juvenile justice throughout the institution's early history. These two developments provided the critical mass necessary to make juvenile court reform possible.

JUVENILE CRIME AND THE DECLINE OF
THE REHABILITATIVE IDEAL

Although postwar Gallup polls usually found juvenile delinquency near the bottom of the list of "the most important problems" facing the United States as a whole, opinion shifted noticeably when respondents were asked about delinquency in their own communities. Throughout the mid-1950s and early 1960s, approximately 25 percent of Gallup poll respondents cited juvenile delinquency as the most serious problem in their community. As public concern over juvenile crime mounted, juvenile courts became the object of popular criticism.

Perhaps the most important factor contributing to public fears about juvenile crime was the release by the FBI of the annual statistics in its *Uniform Crime Reports* (UCR).[48] Although flawed in some respects, the UCR figures suggested to many observers that a steady and alarming increase in juvenile crime was occurring between 1950 and 1965.[49] In 1950 the FBI reported 34,559 arrests of juveniles, which accounted for 4.4 percent of all arrests in the nation. This figure included 3.7 percent of all arrests for serious crimes against persons and 14 percent of all arrests for serious property crimes.[50] By 1955 the number of juvenile arrests reported in the UCR statistics had risen to 195,626 (10.5 percent of the total), including 5,462 arrests for serious crimes against persons (12.4 percent of such arrests) and 76,782 arrests for serious property crimes (51 percent of such arrests). This number constituted a staggering 466 percent increase in total juvenile arrests, a 57 percent increase in juvenile arrests for serious crimes against persons, and a 331 percent increase in juvenile arrests for serious property crimes.

The increase in juvenile arrests continued unabated for the remainder of the decade. The numbers grew steadily from 234,474 (11.3 percent of total arrests) in 1956 to 526,905 (14.3 percent) in 1960, a 125 percent increase. The number of juveniles arrested for serious crimes against persons between 1956 and 1960 rose from 5,716 (13.4 percent of such arrests) to 15,947 (17 percent), an increase of 179 percent. Juvenile arrests for serious property crimes also increased dramatically: from 90,128 in 1956 to 191,872 in 1960, representing an increase of 113 percent.[51] In 1965, the FBI reported that local law enforcement agencies had arrested almost 1 million juveniles (21 percent of all arrests), including 27,762 for criminal homicide, forcible rape, robbery, and aggravated assault (21 percent of the total arrests for these crimes) and 332,410 for serious property crimes (56.3 percent of the total).

Given demographic changes, which included a 38 percent increase in the juvenile population between 1950 and 1960, one would expect some increase in the amount of juvenile crime.[52] This increase did not entirely explain the arrest statistics reported by the FBI, however, since these data indicated a 1,500 percent increase in juvenile arrests during the same period. This figure can be explained partly by such circumstances as changes in law enforcement practices (police may have implemented policies of arresting juveniles who had previously simply been warned and released), anomalies in the reporting system, and the tendency of juveniles to commit crimes in groups (which could lead to multiple arrests for a single criminal event). Influenced by such factors, the *Uniform Crime Reports* undoubtedly exaggerated the extent of juvenile crime in the United States during this period. Nevertheless, more accurate measures of delinquent activity during the late 1950s and early 1960s suggest that public concern over juvenile crime was not completely unfounded, at least in large urban centers.

For example, the average number of delinquency cases involving youth between the ages of ten and seventeen handled annually by juvenile courts increased by 123 percent between 1946 and 1965 (see data listed). More important, the average rate of cases per 1,000 of the juvenile population, which controls for demographic shifts, increased by 38 percent.

	Average Annual Caseload (in thousands)	Average Annual Case Rate (per 1,000 juveniles)
1941–1945	298.4	16.42
1946–1950	272.6	15.7
1951–1955	366.0	19.3
1956–1960	484.6	20.9
1961–1965	608.4	21.7

The increase after 1956 is particularly impressive, since traffic-related cases ceased to be included in the statistics after that year. By 1965 American juvenile courts were handling almost 700,000 delinquency cases annually, which meant that about 24 of every 1,000 juveniles between the ages of ten and seventeen were finding their way into a juvenile court. For whatever reason, increasing juvenile arrest rates were generating higher juvenile court caseloads, producing both public dissatisfaction and system overload. These results did not bode well for traditional juvenile court structures.

The nature of the problem is perhaps best understood by considering the snapshot of juvenile crime provided by researchers at the University of Pennsylvania, who studied the delinquent activity of all males born in 1945 who resided in Philadelphia between their tenth and eighteenth birthdays.[53] During this period, which covered the years between 1955 and 1963, 35 percent of the birth cohort's members (3,475) committed at least one delinquent act; and 1,862 of these offenders committed more than one offense. The aggregate total of offenses committed by the offenders among the cohort amounted to 10,214 delinquent acts, including 471 serious crimes against persons and 2,257 serious property crimes. The repeat offenders among this group committed an average of 4.6 offenses each and accounted for a total of 8,601 offenses. More striking is the fact that 627 of the repeat offenders committed five or more offenses and accounted for 5,305 delinquent acts (52 percent of the cohort total). These "chronic offenders" were responsible for 70 percent of the serious crimes against persons committed by the cohort and 62 percent of the serious property crimes. Despite this rate of delinquent activity among the cohort as a whole, and its most active offenders in particular, the researchers found that the juvenile court imposed a punitive sanction in only 17.5 percent of the 9,956 cases for which complete data were available. Dispositions in the other cases included arrest only, remedial action, or informal adjustment. The existing juvenile justice system did not appear to be performing the task for which it was created.

Whatever the actual change in the incidence of juvenile crime in the 1950s, or the explanation for that change, public fear of juvenile delinquency was sufficiently high to set in motion the investigative powers of the U.S. Senate. Between 1955 and 1957, a Senate subcommittee on juvenile delinquency chaired by Sen. Estes Kefauver investigated the link between the mass media and the nation's delinquency problem. Testimony given before the committee offered the theory that radio, movies, television, and (especially) comic books eroded parental control over adolescents and led to higher delinquency rates.[54] The hearings enhanced public concern over delinquency, and the theory presented to the Kefauver committee hearings struck a responsive chord among Americans. Indeed, most respondents to Gallup polls taken during the late 1950s blamed delinquency on inadequate discipline and parental supervision. By the end of the 1950s, therefore, both the general public and key policymakers seemed convinced that, despite fifty years of rehabilitative efforts by juvenile courts, the nation was in the midst of a vast juvenile crime wave that could not be entirely explained by absolute or relative increases in the juvenile population.

THE RISE OF LEGAL CRITICISM

For the group of juvenile court critics represented by the legal profession, the rapid increase in juvenile crime rates, and of recidivism rates in particular, suggested that the experiment with informal, nonadversarial juvenile proceedings could no longer be justified on rehabilitative grounds. Their response was to reevaluate the relationship between the procedural and substantive components of the rehabilitative ideal. This process eventually led to legal criticism of the juvenile court's procedural deficiencies and its alleged arbitrary treatment of children. Indeed, during the 1950s and early

1960s, juvenile courts became the subject of much greater attention in legal publications, which had largely ignored them earlier in the century. Between 1926 and 1952 the *Index to Legal Periodicals* listed on average only seventeen articles per year in the categories of "Juvenile Courts," "Juvenile Offenders," and "Juvenile Delinquency." Over the next fifteen years (1952–1967), however, the average number of annual entries in these categories was fifty-two, and between 1964 and 1967 the average reached seventy-five per year. The authors of these articles brought to the problems facing juvenile courts professional norms and methods of analysis quite different from those favored by the social reformers who had founded the juvenile court. Not surprisingly, many of these articles were highly critical of the assumptions underlying the implementation of the rehabilitative ideal in juvenile courts.

Typically, the writers of the legal commentaries argued that the rehabilitative ideal and its corresponding *parens patriae* doctrine impeded the juvenile court's legal functions, denied juveniles rights to which they were entitled, and encouraged the legal profession to abandon juvenile courts.[55] The critics who took this position were skeptical of behavioral scientists and the intentions of administrative decisionmakers; moreover, unlike prewar critics, they tended to emphasize the importance of protecting children's liberty interests against arbitrary state intervention.[56]

Paul Tappan, one of the most influential critics during this period, expressed this attitude in an important textbook on the subject published in 1949. Among the book's themes was the importance of "sav[ing] the child from his saviors."[57] At the core of Tappan's skepticism was his criticism of the juvenile court movement's interpretation and use of the *parens patriae* doctrine. He argued that the history of the English chancery courts, where the concept of *parens patriae* had first developed, did not support the juvenile court movement's assertion that the reliance on this doctrine required, or indeed justified, complete procedural informality.[58] He contended that the courts of chancery, although clearly civil in nature, had always been to some degree formal, official, and juridical. One of Tappan's principal concerns was that the juvenile court's peculiar use of the *parens patriae* concept violated the traditional presumption of innocence since it encouraged practices such as preparing and distributing social investigation reports prior to delinquency adjudication hearings.[59] Tappan suggested a number of procedural reforms to correct the abuses of the *parens patriae* doctrine, including limiting the juvenile court's jurisdiction, employing more consistent (but still largely informal) adjudicative procedures, and relying less frequently on commitment to custodial institutions as a dispositional alternative.[60]

Other critics repeated Tappan's concerns in various forms throughout the 1950s. Despite their skepticism, however, most of them shared a basic belief in the wisdom and necessity of a separate justice system for children. The authors of a 1950 article asked whether it was still possible "to justify the exclusion of juveniles from the protection of . . . constitutional safeguards."[61] Finding an answer to this question, they pointed out, was complicated by the difficulty of injecting procedural safeguards into juvenile courts without substantially altering their otherwise desirable features. Although some commentators suggested that juvenile court statutes should define delinquency more precisely (but still less precisely than the definitions given specific crimes), juvenile justice specialists remained reluctant to establish a direct link between dispositions and offenses.[62] Even the most critical commentators continued to be impressed by the potential benefits of individualization and rehabilitation, an attitude that did not change until the focus of attention among commentators turned to the functional similarity between juvenile courts and ordinary courts of criminal jurisdiction.

An early indication that this change in focus was occurring appeared in a 1952 article, which emphasized that the constitutionality of juvenile court laws "stands or falls . . . on whether the child within the jurisdiction of the court may be punished as a criminal."[63] If the principal consequence of juvenile proceedings is criminal punishment, Sol Rubin argued, then juveniles are entitled to the same procedural rights as criminal defendants, particularly in those instances where juvenile and criminal courts possessed concurrent jurisdiction. Rubin worried that in these cases the juvenile court, because of its lower procedural standards, would become the "recourse of a weak case" rather than "a refuge for the child."[64] Similar concerns emerged in an influential law review article published by Monrad Paulsen in 1957 in which he strongly challenged the view that juvenile courts were entirely benevolent institutions, arguing that "an adjudication of delinquency, in itself, is harmful and should not be capriciously imposed."[65] Paulsen took the position that any restraint of liberty by the state, however benevolently intended, must be justified on nonarbitrary grounds. He observed that juvenile courts frequently treated children in a summary manner and confined them in institutions similar to prisons. The remedy, he contended, was greater procedural rigor, including representation by counsel and defense access to the social investigation reports that judges relied on in making their dispositional decisions.[66] In Paulsen's view, the functional similarity between juvenile and criminal proceedings was sufficient to require procedural formalization of juvenile courts.

The notion of a functional similarity between juvenile and criminal proceedings gathered momentum throughout the 1960s. One commentator argued that "in practice, under the guise of 'personalized justice' the basic objectives in removing children from the criminal court system are often undermined both by depriving them of their civil liberties and by branding them as delinquent." He thus proposed "minimal constitutional safeguards at the fact-finding level" in order to "permit the development of a *reliable* juvenile court record."[67] Another observer went even further, arguing that "rehabilitation may be substituted for punishment, but a star chamber cannot be substituted for a trial." He charged juvenile courts with denying due process and equal protection, imposing cruel and unusual punishments, and interfering with the parent-child relationship. He concluded that states should repeal existing juvenile court laws and that private groups should mount test-case litigation to challenge the constitutionality of juvenile courts.[68]

An article in the *Cornell Law Quarterly* echoed these views one year later. "The time has come," its author wrote, "to seriously inquire if there are persuasive reasons why these young persons are to be denied constitutional rights." The article rejected the traditional justification for excluding criminal due process from juvenile proceedings and focused instead "on the effect of the proceedings conducted by the state."[69] Because juvenile courts impose punishment, its author argued, juveniles must be accorded the same rights enjoyed by defendants in criminal courts. The list of rights that the author insisted upon was extensive: grand jury indictment, bail, notice of charges, protection against double jeopardy, speedy and public trials, jury trials, confrontation of witnesses, representation by counsel, and the privilege against self-incrimination. The article represented an extreme view, however, and its sweeping proposals disturbed some critics who otherwise agreed with the necessity of imposing procedural safeguards, like the right to counsel, but who also wanted to avoid the complete transformation of juvenile hearings into adversary proceedings.[70]

This skepticism about the substantive accomplishments of juvenile courts became even more pronounced under the influence of critics such as Francis Allen and David Matza. Allen argued that the rehabilitative ideal's actual impact on juvenile court practices had not brought about the results that the court's founders intended. Instead, the ideal had allowed juvenile courts to use the language of rehabilitation to mask the reality of custodial institutions and to impose on juveniles increasingly severe punishments in pursuit of incapacitative rather than therapeutic objectives. The fact that the rehabilitative ideal also relieved juvenile courts of most of the procedural burdens imposed on criminal courts contributed to Allen's skepticism about its vitality.[71]

Matza attributed the phenomena Allen had observed to a fundamental misunderstanding of the distinction between the rehabilitative ideal's emphasis on the concept of individualized justice and the equity doctrine on which this concept rests. Equity, Matza contended, is not a principle in itself but merely "a qualification or legitimate exception to the principle of equality." According to Matza, the principle underlying formal equality—that like cases be treated alike—was inherently inconsistent with the notion of individualized justice. A court invokes its equity jurisdiction, he continued, only on those rare occasions when strict adherence to the formal equality principle would have unjust consequences. By relying exclusively on individualized justice, however, the juvenile court transformed this occasionally justified exception to the rule of formal equality into an overarching procedural rule by which all decisions must be made. The problem, according to Matza, is that such a rule "results in a frame of relevance so large, so all-inclusive, that any relation between the criteria of judgment and the disposition remains obscure."[72] The resulting absence of a significant relationship among individual acts, judgments, and dispositions meant that individualized justice could produce inequitable consequences and permit the rehabilitative ideal to serve purposes other than treatment.

The most comprehensive and influential critique of traditional juvenile court practices, however, was published in 1966 in the *Harvard Law Review*.[73] In this analysis and evaluation of prehearing decisionmaking and juvenile court proceedings in several jurisdictions, the legal critics could find empirical support for their arguments. The study found, for example, that the role of law enforcement agencies in juvenile justice had expanded far beyond their traditional discretionary arrest powers. The study attributed this expansion to inadequately staffed juvenile courts, which forced many judges to condone, and even to encourage, the settlement of cases by the police without referral to juvenile courts. The system of police hearings that emerged, the study found, was antagonistic toward the appearance of attorneys and tended to rely heavily on confessions. Although police hearing officers defended their practices on rehabilitative grounds, the Harvard study suggested that these practices also promoted the improper disposition of cases because of their extensive reliance on irrelevant criteria such as the juvenile's demeanor, physical appearance, and race.

The study noted similar problems in juvenile court proceedings themselves. It found that attorneys were only slightly more prevalent in juvenile court hearings than in police hearings, appearing on behalf of juveniles in no more than 5 percent of all cases examined in the study. This situation was the result of juvenile court judges' actively discouraging juveniles from retaining counsel and of the inability of attorneys to perform their traditional role in juvenile courts. The study warned attorneys who appeared in juvenile courts that their participation would depend largely on what the judge permitted, and it recommended that lawyers "maintain a healthy skepticism about the beneficence of the system." It suggested that counsel for juveniles participate actively in developing a rehabilitative program for their clients during the dispositional phase of proceedings.

This advice to lawyers was consistent with the harsh criticism that the study directed toward the dispositional experimentation undertaken by juvenile court judges: "The judge as amateur psychologist, experimenting upon the unfortunate children who must appear before him, is neither an attractive nor a convincing figure." In sharp contrast to the juvenile court's original rehabilitative thrust, it was argued that the "view of police and court contacts as themselves tools of psychological reform should be abandoned, except to the extent that such contacts serve, as they do in any criminal trial, as a means of communicating societal limitations on freedom of action to the offender."[74] The Harvard researchers acknowledged that confinement might be necessary in the interests of public safety but recommended that cases in which confinement appeared appropriate be waived to criminal courts in order to prevent juvenile court judges from resorting to punitive incarceration as a dispositional alternative. The authors implied that this would aid in preventing inappropriate institutionalization under the false pretense of rehabilitation.

The results of the Harvard survey of juvenile court practices offered additional evidence that the rehabilitative ideal was either fundamentally flawed or imperfectly implemented. In either case, juvenile courts functioned in a manner contrary to the ideal's spirit. The study recommended that certain constraints be imposed on the juvenile court's pursuit of rehabilitation in order to prevent the rhetoric of individualized justice from providing a rationale for unwarranted punishment. The study also suggested that unjustified punishment could be avoided altogether by recognizing the legitimacy of punishing some young offenders, thus reducing the incentive for juvenile court officials to use the rehabilitative ideal as a rhetorical cover for punitive purposes. The Harvard group combined these perspectives in calling for the participation of counsel at adjudication and disposition, the termination of uncontrolled dispositional experimentation by juvenile court judges, and the liberal use of waiver to impose punishment on deserving offenders.

The Harvard study's role in the future constitutional domestication of juvenile courts cannot be underestimated. Although critics such as Tappan, Paulsen, Allen, Matza, and Rubin had challenged the theoretical underpinnings of the juvenile court's immunity from constitutional standards of due process, the Harvard study provided the first synthesis of those critiques in the context of a comprehensive study of juvenile court practices throughout the nation. Sponsored and funded by the Walter E. Meyer Research Institute of Law, the Harvard study was cited extensively by the appellants in the *Gault* case. The use of law reviews to communicate new legal theories and policy information to the Supreme Court had started to come of age in the 1940s, when justices such as Felix Frankfurter, Charles Evans Hughes, and Robert Jackson acknowledged their utility and legitimacy as sources of information.[75] Historically rooted in the sociological and economic studies first introduced into constitutional jurisprudence by Louis Brandeis, the strategic and tactical use of law review and other publications was perfected by the NAACP in its constitutional struggle against racially restrictive covenants and segregated education.[76]

Law review articles, as well as statements of professional standards for the operation of juvenile courts, played an important role in the briefs submitted by all parties in *Kent, Gault,* and *Winship* (see Table 2.1). Not surprisingly, given the developing trends in the legal literature concerning juvenile justice and courts, most of this material found its way into the briefs submitted by the organizations seeking to constitutionalize juvenile court proceedings. With the prevailing law against these reformers, such extrinsic sources provided the authority necessary to support their program of legal change.

Not all law review articles, of course, were critical of the juvenile court ideal. For example, in an *American Bar Association Journal* article celebrating the fiftieth anniversary of the Illinois Juvenile Court Act, Judge Nochem Winnet of the Philadelphia juvenile court argued that any deficiencies in the court's performance of its child-welfare functions were the product of inadequate isolation from criminal courts rather than the absence of due process. Continued association with criminal courts, according to Winnet, detracted from the juvenile court's relationship with other social welfare agencies and prevented it from playing an active role in delinquency prevention. Judge Winnet did not doubt the soundness of the juvenile court's fun-

Table 2.1. Extrinsic Evidence Cited by Brief

	Brief	Articles Cited	Standards Cited
Kent	Petitioner	1	0
	United States	8	2
	Amicus	7	2
Gault	ACLU	22	5
	NLADA	1	0
	Legal Aid Society	8	0
	American Parents' Committee	9	4
	Arizona	4	1
	Ohio Juv. Ct. Judges Assoc.	11	0
Winship	Appellant	1	3
	Neighborhood Legal Services	13	3
	Appellee	6	3
	N.Y. Attorney General	1	0

damental principles, although he did concede that the optimistic expectations of the court's founders may have blinded them to some of the institution's limitations.[77] The dominant theme of post–World War II legal critiques, however, was that juvenile courts had strayed from their pursuit of the rehabilitative ideal to undertake functions more characteristic of ordinary criminal courts.

As reflected in the "good intentions gone awry" perspective articulated by critics such as Francis Allen, the loss of faith in the theoretical and empirical underpinnings of the rehabilitative ideal weakened the legitimacy of traditional juvenile jurisprudence and undermined support for the juvenile court's distinctive institutional character. The ideal suffered a further blow in the late 1960s when such scholars as Anthony Platt and Sanford Fox began to reinterpret juvenile court history.[78] Their review of the historical record suggested that the juvenile court's founders intended from the very beginning to use procedural informality as a mechanism for social control rather than to rehabilitate wayward youth. From this perspective, the juvenile court was not a benevolent enterprise gone awry but the effective execution of social coercion operating behind the veil of rehabilitative informality.

According to Platt and Fox, the actual motivation for the juvenile court movement included greater control of the urban poor, perpetuation of existing class structures, and state control over a wide range of children's behavior. Platt found these objectives embodied in the movement's overriding desire to perpetuate the dependent status of children, to disenfranchise juveniles of their legal rights, and to extend state control over previously unregulated behavior such as truancy, running away, and the omnibus (and indeterminate) offense of "incorrigibility."[79] Similarly, Fox criticized the 1899 Illinois act and its progeny for their questionable reliance on coercive predictions. Moreover, according to Fox, the Illinois statute perpetuated nineteenth-century summary trials, depended on flawed custodial institutions to replace and replicate family life, and reinforced private sectarian interests.[80]

Although some scholars disagreed with the reinterpretation of juvenile court history that Platt and Fox offered,[81] their work formed a significant part of the atmosphere in which the Supreme Court considered the constitutional status of nineteenth-century juvenile procedure throughout the 1970s. Although their influence was primarily indirect (they did not publish their studies until after the Court's decisions in *Kent* and *Gault*), every challenge to the "benevolent" assumptions that provided the justification for informal juvenile court procedures made it more difficult for traditionalists to defend their position. By debunking some of the myths surrounding the origins of the juvenile court movement, Platt and Fox strengthened the case for procedural reform.

In sum, the commentators of the 1950s and early 1960s began to suggest that the liberal democratic principles of individual liberty and voluntary consent, with which aspects of the rehabilitative ideal conflicted, should apply in juvenile justice as much as they did in the criminal justice system generally.[82] This reevaluation of juvenile justice was part of a broader reconsideration of the benefits of discretionary justice, of which juvenile courts were a prime example. Both the formal and effective limits on juvenile court judges' powers left them free to make relatively unconstrained choices among a wide range of possible courses of action and inaction. Moreover, not only did juvenile court judges possess the traditional element of discretion—the ability to decide the desirable course of action given a particular set of facts and legal principles—but they also controlled the process of finding facts and applying the law.[83] The purpose of this discretion, of course, was to permit individualized justice, and the relative absence of rules constraining judicial discretion was acceptable as long as juvenile court judges were perceived as dispensing individualized justice in the rehabilitative interests of children.

Once critics concluded that the effective goals of juvenile justice were at least partially if not completely punitive, however, the absence of rules drawn from the criminal justice tradition became anomalous. As support for the rehabilitative ideal declined in both theory and practice, critics came to see much of the discretion exercised in juvenile courts as unnecessary and in need of being confined, structured, and checked. In the context of juvenile courts, this view meant that, since juvenile hearings posed substantial risk to the liberty interests of children, the proceedings should be considered functionally similar to criminal proceedings and subject to the same due process limitations. During the early 1960s, therefore, the rehabilitative ideal gradually yielded its position of theoretical hegemony to a "procedural ideal," which embodied a different set of assumptions about the nature of childhood, the causes of crime, and the role of juvenile proceedings in the prevention of crime.

The impetus for this theoretical transformation came from a new group of legally oriented reformers who became concerned with juvenile justice in the mid-1950s. The social welfare orientation of the 1899 movement had discouraged participation by the legal profession in the development of juvenile courts, but as this original approach to juvenile justice lost some of its luster, lawyers felt more comfortable with juvenile justice issues, if not with juvenile court proceedings. The legal profession, with its attachment to due process and adversarial proceedings, paid increasing attention to the problems of juvenile court administration; and its concerns influenced the first significant legislative reforms of juvenile court proceedings in California (1961) and New York (1962).[84] The legal profession also played an important role in the national assessment of juvenile justice policy contained in the 1967 report of the President's Commission on Law Enforcement and Administration of Justice.

State Reforms and National Reassessment

The impetus for juvenile court reform in California came from three juvenile justice conferences sponsored by the governor in 1948, 1950, and 1954.[85] The principal topic of discussion at these conferences was the state's high juvenile detention rate, a phenomenon that conference participants linked to deeper flaws in the state's juvenile justice system. The conferences produced several resolutions blaming high detention rates on the absence of clear guidelines in the state's Welfare and Institutions Code for the apprehension and detention of juveniles. The primary actor in this movement was an Orange County attorney, Robert Fraser, who issued the first direct challenge to the code in 1956. Fraser successfully led an effort by the Orange County Bar Association to introduce a resolution at the 1958 conference of the state bar association calling for the introduction of full due process protections for both juveniles and their parents. Fraser's resolution averred that high detention rates were a direct consequence of inadequate procedural safeguards.[86]

Although local bar associations chose not to pursue Fraser's resolution, state policymakers did not ignore its criticism of juvenile justice administration. In 1958 the California Law Revision Commission recommended amending the Welfare and Institutions Code to require that alleged delinquent juveniles and their parents be advised of a right to be represented by retained or appointed counsel.[87] Shortly thereafter, a Special Study Commission on Juvenile Justice composed of two attorneys, a law school dean, a criminology professor, and the president of the state Parent Teacher Association introduced a series of recommendations that stressed "the rights of minors to fair treatment under formal guarantees of procedural law."[88] Probation officers, juvenile court judges, and law enforcement officials opposed the recommendations, the judges offering the most unified and adamant opposition. Ironically, the rather arrogant performance of a leading juvenile court judge before the State Senate Judiciary Committee played a large role in convincing the committee to accept the study commission's recommendations.[89]

The recommendations led to several amendments to the Welfare and Institutions Code. These amendments addressed excessive detention by specifying the juvenile court's jurisdiction more clearly and by encouraging the use of the least restrictive dispositional alternative.[90] Other important changes provided juveniles and their parents with a higher degree of procedural protection. The amended code required that parents be notified of their child's custody and that juveniles and their parents be granted the right to representation by retained or appointed counsel at most stages of juvenile court proceedings.[91] The amendments also provided the right to appeal judgments of the court and directed the court to make a stenographic record of its proceedings and to provide it to juveniles' attorneys at their request.[92] Despite these procedural changes, however, the amended code retained important elements of the rehabilitative orientation of earlier legislation. It specified, for example, that juvenile proceedings "shall be conducted in an informal nonadversary atmosphere with a view to obtaining the maximum co-operation of the minor on whose behalf the petition is brought."[93] Thus, although these amendments addressed many of the procedural criticisms leveled at juvenile courts, they left the nineteenth-century principles underlying California's juvenile courts relatively undisturbed.

The same assessment can be made with respect to New York's 1962 reforms. Beginning in 1904 delinquency matters in New York were the responsibility of a children's court whose structure and functions mirrored juvenile courts in other states.[94] Its jurisdiction covered a broad range of behavior and conditions—from improper guardianship and Sabbath-breaking to larceny and burglary—all under the rubric of juvenile delinquency.[95] The Family Court Act, which was the first major revision of family law in New York in almost three decades,[96] significantly altered many of the jurisdictional and procedural components of the children's court. As in California, the legal profession played an important part in the act's development. Indeed, its impetus was a pilot project conducted by the New York City Legal Aid Society, the city bar associations, and the Citizens' Committee for Children of New York to provide counsel—styled "law guardians"—to juveniles.[97]

The act formalized the law-guardian experiment by guaranteeing juveniles a statutory right to counsel, who could be appointed either at the juvenile's request or on the court's own motion.[98] The act also extended the application of this right to dependency and neglect proceedings. As in California, juveniles were granted the right to appeal and other due process rights in delinquency proceedings.[99] Despite providing juveniles with certain elements of criminal due process and protecting them from unwarranted state intervention, the Family Court Act did not completely abandon the *parens patriae* approach to delinquency proceedings.[100] Indeed, the legislative committee that drafted the act expressly endorsed a noncriminal approach to juvenile delinquency.[101] Moreover, since the act consolidated the jurisdictions of three domestic relations courts within the jurisdiction of a single court imbued with *parens patriae* ideals, some observers viewed the entire initiative as "an extension of the juvenile court's 'helping' approach to other proceedings."[102]

The Family Court Act, however, did offer two important innovations by virtue of its redefinition of delinquency and the restructuring of delinquency proceedings. The act narrowed the new court's jurisdiction by restricting the definition of delinquency to include only those acts that would be crimes if committed by an adult.[103] The act also established a new jurisdictional category, Persons in Need of Supervision (PINS), to replace the children's court's jurisdiction over noncriminal misbehavior.[104] Finally, it provided for bifurcated adjudication and disposition proceedings in order to separate factual questions from rehabilitative considerations.[105] The act permitted consideration of information about the juvenile's background only during disposition proceedings; the sole question of adjudication proceedings was whether the juvenile had committed the alleged act.

The legislative reforms undertaken by California and New York were a logical extension of the decline of the rehabilitative ideal. By defining delinquency more narrowly, by providing basic due process safeguards, and by separating factual determinations from treatment questions, the Family Court Act and the revised Welfare and Institutions Code acknowledged the rehabilitative ideal's limitations and sought to eliminate its more egregious features. The positive reaction to these legislative innovations, along with the animadversions of the juvenile court's critics in the scholarly and popular press, helped to place juvenile justice on the national policy agenda.

Its position on that agenda rose dramatically when the President's Commission on Law Enforcement and Administration of Justice reported its findings in 1967. The commission was established in July 1965 by Pres. Lyndon Johnson, who instructed its members to study the causes of crime and delinquency and to submit recommendations for preventing both phenomena and for improving law enforcement and the administration of criminal justice.[106] Chaired by Nicholas deB. Katzenbach, the commission met for the first time in September 1965 and eventually employed a full-time staff of more than forty professionals. The commission divided itself into nine task forces, one of which dealt specifically with juvenile delinquency and youth crime. The members of this task force included Genevieve Blatt, an attorney and member of the Pennsylvania Board of Pardons; Leon Jaworski, an attorney who had served as a special assistant to both the U.S. and Texas Attorneys General; and James Parsons, a federal judge who had served on the Cook County Superior Court. The task force benefited from the assistance of several consultants, including such well-known figures in the juvenile justice field as Edwin Lemert, Margaret Rosenheim, and Marvin Wolfgang.

The report of this task force, as well as the commission's general report, would be influential in forming the Supreme Court's views of the juvenile court's past accomplishments and future prospects. Relying on background papers prepared by consultants sympathetic to the postwar criticisms of the rehabilitative ideal, the task force criticized juvenile courts and the juvenile justice system for failing to rehabilitate delinquent youth, to reduce juvenile crime, and to provide justice and compassion to young offenders.[107] The task force attributed these failures to various theoretical and practical limitations of the rehabilitative ideal, and to the widespread public dissatisfaction with juvenile courts resulting from anxiety over rising juvenile crime rates.[108]

The failure of the rehabilitative ideal, the task force reported, caused a substantial gap between the public rationale for juvenile court dispositions and the actual purposes those dispositions served. Underlying its criticisms was the group's acceptance of the functional similarity argument advanced by juvenile court critics earlier in the decade. Its report averred that the standard objectives of criminal punishment, such as retribution, deterrence, and incapacitation, had become important considerations in dispositional decisionmaking despite language to the contrary in statutes, judicial pronouncements, and commentaries. As the full commission's report indicated, the task force attributed this gap between theory and practice to unrealistic assumptions about the goals that juvenile courts could accomplish. "The failure of the juvenile court to fulfill its rehabilitative and preventive promise," the commission explained, "stems in important measure from a grossly overoptimistic view of what is known about the phenomenon of juvenile criminality and of what even a fully equipped juvenile court could do about it."[109] The task force suggested that juvenile courts adopt a new institutional philosophy that recognized their limitations.

On the basis of these findings, the task force made five key recommendations for improving juvenile justice:

1. The formal sanctioning system and pronouncement of delinquency should be used only as a last resort.
2. In place of the formal system, dispositional alternatives to adjudication must be developed for dealing with juveniles, including agencies to provide and coordinate services and procedures to achieve necessary control without unnecessary stigma.
3. The range of conduct for which court intervention is authorized should be narrowed, with greater emphasis upon consensual and informal means of meeting the problems of difficult children.
4. The cases that fall within the narrowed jurisdiction of the court and filter through the screen of pre-judicial, informal disposition methods would largely involve offenders for whom more vigorous measures seem necessary.
5. Accordingly, the adjudication hearing should be consistent with basic principles of due process.[110]

In the task force's view, "what should distinguish the juvenile from the criminal court is greater emphasis on rehabilitation, not exclusive preoccupation with it."[111] The overall thrust of these proposals was to remove the responsibility for rehabilitation from the juvenile court itself and to give that task to other institutions within the social welfare system. The juvenile court's responsibilities would thereby become more like those of ordinary criminal courts, and they would include punishment and the pursuit of other public safety goals. The juvenile court, which had been conceived as the institutional focus of the rehabilitative ideal, would thus become a peripheral institution devoted to goals that its founders would have considered inappropriate in the treatment of juvenile delinquency.

The task force proposed to replace the rehabilitative functions of juvenile courts with community-based youth-service bureaus.[112] The bureaus would be part of local delinquency prevention programs and provide a broad range of services that juveniles and their families would take advantage of voluntarily. The ultimate goal was to rely on formal court processing and sanctioning as infrequently as possible. For the few cases requiring formal processing, the task force advocated improvements in the level of procedural safeguards available to juveniles.[113] Among the improvements listed as indispensable were the right to representation by retained or appointed counsel, tighter evidentiary standards, the right to adequate notice of charges, provision of transcripts, and the right to appellate review. The task force refused to insist on the total incorporation of criminal due process into juvenile proceedings, however, arguing that proof beyond a reasonable doubt and the rights to bail, public trial, and trial by jury were unnecessary in juvenile courts. Furthermore, it supported only a qualified privilege against self-incrimination. The task force did not regard these elements of criminal trials "as so essential to procedural justice as to warrant the risks their use would entail for the integrity of the juvenile court."[114] It attempted to accommodate the goals of both procedural justice and social welfare by "establishing procedures permitting the court effectively to pursue humane and rehabilitative aims within the framework of a system that recognizes the indispensability of justice in any coercive governmental venture into the lives of individuals."[115]

Both the task force and the law enforcement commission as a whole viewed procedural formality as more than simply a guarantee of fairness in juvenile proceedings. Indeed, the reports characterized due process as an integral and positive component of the rehabilitative process. Relying on a study conducted by two of its consultants, the task force reported to the commission that there was an "increasing feeling" among juvenile justice experts that the traditional procedural informality actually impeded, rather than advanced, rehabilitative efforts.[116] The full commission accepted this finding but in the process changed the task force's somewhat equivocal reference to expert *feeling* into a significantly stronger finding of increasing *evidence* that informal procedures affect rehabilitation negatively.[117] This finding added considerable authority to existing criticisms of the rehabilitative ideal's procedural framework.

The task force recognized that by the 1960s, and perhaps throughout their history, juvenile courts experienced difficulty reconciling the conflicting goals of social welfare and public protection. Moreover, the task force concluded that child welfare concerns had "been allowed to substantially interfere with the goals of fairness and reliability in the adjudicatory process." [118] Its proposed solution encompassed the establishment of specialized agencies to pursue the social welfare component of juvenile justice, the creation of procedurally stronger juvenile courts to treat juveniles more fairly, and the use of dispositions more sensitive to public safety. The task force's procedural recommendations viewed juvenile justice through the lens of the due process model of criminal justice, which placed a premium on adversary proceedings as a means of ensuring fair, equal, and accurate decisionmaking. [119] The procedural ideal embodied in the due process model, as well as the law enforcement commission's reflections on the relationship between procedural informality and rehabilitation, provided the Supreme Court with a theoretical framework for its own evaluation of juvenile court proceedings.

By the early 1960s it was clear that the juvenile court created in 1899 was on the verge of a fundamental transformation. The scholarly criticisms evident in the law journals had found their way into extensive legislative reforms in two influential states, and into the policy arguments articulated by the President's Task Force on Crime. Given the propensity of policy innovations enacted in one state to diffuse to other states, [120] especially when endorsed by an important national commission, it was probably inevitable that the traditional model of juvenile justice would be supplanted to some degree. Nevertheless, had the process of change remained in the state legislative arena, both its scope and speed would have been affected since reformers would have had to proceed incrementally, on a state-by-state basis. The vagaries of legislative calendars and differences in the availability of local resources that could be mobilized for reform would have ensured slow, uneven progress. As the authors of the due process revolution in ordinary criminal courts were learning, only one policymaking body was capable of articulating immediately applicable national standards in this area: the U.S. Supreme Court.

Although the idea of challenging the juvenile court's alleged procedural deficiencies in the national judicial arena had been suggested as early as 1960, [121] proponents of this strategy faced a large hurdle. Juvenile courts were explicitly designed to insulate them from the federal Constitution, and consequently no appeal from a decision of a juvenile court had ever reached the

Supreme Court. In 1964, however, juvenile court reformers received a signal from none other than Chief Justice Earl Warren that this hurdle could be overcome. Led by Warren, a former prosecutor and attorney general of California, the Court had already revolutionized criminal procedure through decisions such as *Mapp v. Ohio* (1961), *Gideon v. Wainwright* (1963), and *Escobedo v. Illinois* (1964). With these decisions—which extended the federal exclusionary rule to state criminal proceedings (*Mapp*), required states to provide counsel to indigent defendants (*Gideon*), and required that access to counsel during police interrogations not be impeded (*Escobedo*)—the Court had created new codes of conduct and procedure for local law enforcement agencies and state criminal courts.

Chief Justice Warren then indicated in 1964 that the Court would be willing to undertake similar reforms in juvenile justice. Speaking before the annual meeting of the National Council of Juvenile Court Judges, the chief justice observed that the juvenile court's "dual roles have given rise to vexing problems in defining its function and establishing appropriate limits upon its authority." He told his dismayed audience of juvenile court judges still attached to *parens patriae* ideals that juvenile courts "must function within the framework of law" and provide juveniles with due process protection against capricious decisionmaking. Although Warren did not identify which specific elements of due process juveniles should enjoy, he indicated that the Court would undertake the task of defining those elements when the "proper cases" came before it.[122] For all intents and purposes, the chief justice was inviting reformers to develop cases that the Court could use to constitutionalize juvenile court proceedings, which encouraged the juvenile court reform movement to raise its sights from achieving incremental change at the state legislative level to altering the constitutional status of juvenile courts. Warren's speech ensured that the seeds of reform planted in the 1950s and 1960s would blossom in the Supreme Court as well as in state legislatures.[123]

3. An Unexpected Opportunity:
Kent v. United States

Kent v. United States (1966) was the first in the trilogy of juvenile justice cases decided by the Supreme Court between 1966 and 1970.[1] Despite its close association with constitutional developments in juvenile law, however, the Court's decision in *Kent* was actually the result of an ordinary exercise in statutory interpretation. At issue was the manner in which juvenile courts in the District of Columbia exercised their statutory power to waive "original and exclusive" jurisdiction over criminal offenses committed by minors in order to transfer those cases to the jurisdiction of ordinary criminal courts. The District's Juvenile Court Act allowed juvenile court judges to waive jurisdiction after undertaking a "full investigation" of the necessity of ordinary criminal proceedings in individual cases. The Court held in *Kent* that no waiver investigation could be considered complete under the act unless the juvenile court held a "fair hearing" at which juveniles were represented by counsel who had access to all evidence pertaining to the waiver decision, including reports prepared by probation officers. The constitutional dimensions of the case emerged when the Court found it necessary during its consideration of the Juvenile Court Act to comment on the applicability of constitutional standards of due process to juvenile proceedings.

Juvenile Justice in the District of Columbia

Before a detailed examination of *Kent* itself is undertaken, a brief overview of the development of juvenile proceedings generally—and jurisdictional waiver in particular—in the District of Columbia is in order. Like most jurisdictions in the United States, the District adopted a special set of juvenile proceedings early in the twentieth century, with Congress establishing the District's first juvenile court in 1906.[2] Unlike legislatures in other jurisdictions, Congress' initial ambitions were relatively modest. The 1906 statute did not significantly augment judicial control over children's behavior but merely consolidated the existing powers exercised by several courts under the jurisdiction of a single court.[3] Although the law purported to give the newly established juvenile court "original and exclusive jurisdiction" over "all crimes and offenses of persons under seventeen years of age," this jurisdiction did not include capital offenses or many other serious crimes.[4] Moreover, in marked contrast to the broad, social welfare orientation of early state juvenile codes, the 1906 District of Columbia statute required that criminal charges be brought against a child prior to the juvenile court's exercising its jurisdiction. The effect of this requirement was twofold. First, the statute continued to treat juvenile offenders as criminals; second, it failed to provide any judicial mechanism for responding to noncriminal misbehavior.

The essential principles of *parens patriae* juvenile justice did not become a part of juvenile proceedings in the District until 1938. Motivated by concerns that the 1906 legislation constituted "the most antiquated . . . juvenile court procedure in the United States," Congress replaced it with a new juvenile court law largely based on the model legislation proposed by the National Probation Association in 1925.[5] According to the new act's congressional supporters, the most important substantive difference between it and its 1906 predecessor was that the earlier law understood the juvenile court's functions in terms of traditional criminal law principles, but the 1938 act considered the court's mission as "doing that thing for [children] which is best to be done to correct the thing that is making the child delinquent." As one of the sponsors of the 1938 statute explained, it was imperative that Congress change "the procedure of the juvenile court from a criminal procedure to one in chancery."[6]

Like the 1899 Illinois law, the aim of the new legislation was to "secure for each child under [the juvenile court's] jurisdiction such care and guidance, preferably in his own home, as will serve the child's welfare and the best interests of the State."[7] Congress extended the juvenile court's jurisdiction to encompass all criminal and noncriminal misbehavior by persons under the age of eighteen[8] but allowed the court to waive jurisdiction in felony cases and to transfer juveniles for trial in criminal courts after conducting a "full investigation" of the merits of waiver.[9] The noncriminal nature of juvenile proceedings under the new statute was evident in its requirement that delinquency hearings be conducted informally and preferably in private.[10] The sole exception to this general requirement of informality and privacy was the statute's provision for jury trials at the request of juveniles, their parents, or on the court's own motion.[11] Consistent with the promotion of individualized treatment, the act also required a prehearing investigation of the domestic and social environment of delinquent juveniles in order to guide disposition decisions.

Not surprisingly, the open-ended nature of the act's procedural provisions served as an invitation for judicial interpretation of the precise meaning of procedural informality in juvenile courts. Consequently, although the U.S. Court of Appeals eventually held in *Pee v. United States* (1959) that constitutional standards of due process were not directly applicable to the District's juvenile proceedings,[12] it nevertheless saw fit to circumscribe the scope of informality in decisions rendered both before and after *Pee.* In *Shioutakon v. District of Columbia* (1956), for example, the court held that juveniles were entitled to representation by appointed or retained counsel in juvenile proceedings. Although "recognizing and approving the laudable objectives" of the 1938 statute, Judge David Bazelon argued that "the right to be heard when personal liberty is at stake requires the effective assistance of counsel in a juvenile court quite as much as it does in a criminal court."[13] The court then held in *McBride v. Jacobs* (1957) that the right to counsel enunciated in *Shioutakon* could be effectively exercised only if juvenile court judges informed juveniles and their parents about the availability of this option during courtroom proceedings.[14]

Despite finding it necessary to control procedural informality to some degree, the court of appeals never questioned the basic principle that juvenile and criminal proceedings were qualitatively distinct in ways that benefited children. Indeed, the court even justified additional restrictions on procedural informality because of this very principle. In *Harling v. United States* (1961), for example, the court considered whether statements made by a juvenile while under the jurisdiction of the juvenile court were admissible in criminal proceedings. The court concluded that principles of "fundamental fairness" did not allow "admissions made by the child in the non-criminal and non-punitive setting of juvenile proceedings to be used later for the purpose of securing his criminal conviction and punishment." Judge Bazelon argued that, to permit such practices, "would destroy the Juvenile Court's *parens patriae* relation to the child and would violate the non-criminal philosophy which underlies the Juvenile Court Act."[15]

Like the act's provision for procedural informality, its waiver provision was sufficiently open-ended to require judicial and legislative clarification of several key points. Congress took one step in this direction in 1947 when it responded to a particularly violent juvenile crime by amending the waiver provision to authorize jurisdictional waiver of juveniles charged with any crime punishable by death or life imprisonment.[16] A more significant clarification occurred in 1959, when the juvenile court's chief judge established uniform rules to guide waiver decisions in specific cases, including

1. the seriousness of the alleged offense to the community and whether the protection of the community requires waiver;
2. whether the alleged offense was committed in an aggressive, violent, premeditated or willful manner;
3. whether the alleged offense was against persons or against property, greater weight being given to offenses against persons especially if personal injury resulted;
4. the prosecutive merit of the complaint, i.e., whether there is evidence upon which a Grand Jury may be expected to return an indictment (to be determined by consultation with the United States Attorney);
5. the desirability of trial and disposition of the entire offense in one court when the juvenile's associates in the alleged offense are adults who will be charged with a crime in the U.S. District Court for the District of Columbia;
6. the sophistication and maturity of the juvenile as determined by consideration of his home, environmental situation, emotional attitude and pattern of living;
7. the record and previous history of the juvenile, including previous contacts with the Youth Aid Division, other law enforcement agencies, juvenile courts and other jurisdictions, prior periods of probation to the Court, or prior commitments to juvenile institutions;
8. the prospects for adequate protection of the public and the likelihood of rehabilitation of the juvenile (if he is found to have committed the alleged offense) by the use of procedures, services and facilities currently available to the Juvenile Court.

The policy memorandum did not mention waiver hearings as a possible method for determining whether these criteria applied in specific cases. Instead, it assigned the task of collecting "all available information which may bear upon the criteria and factors set forth above" to juvenile court officers selected by the judge responsible for the case.[17]

The first significant decision concerning waiver proceedings occurred in *United States v. Dickerson* (1959).[18] Ironically, at issue in *Dickerson* was whether the juvenile court possessed the authority to hold a hearing prior to making its waiver decision. Dickerson admitted at a juvenile court preliminary hearing that he had held a toy gun during an attempted robbery; as a result of his admission, the juvenile court waived jurisdiction and transferred his case to the district court for trial on robbery charges. The district court dismissed the robbery indictment, however, on the grounds that a criminal trial held after a juvenile court hearing constitutes double jeopardy, even if the juvenile court had not yet made any disposition in the case. The court of appeals rejected this argument and held that informal hearings could be a legitimate component of the "full investigation" required by the act's waiver provision. The court ruled that it was not "improper for the Juvenile Court to conduct a hearing before determining whether or not to waive jurisdiction."[19] Although *Dickerson* established the legitimacy of waiver hearings, the court later held in *Wilhite v. United States* (1960) that such hearings were not mandatory.[20]

The attitude of the court of appeals toward waiver proceedings began to change during the early 1960s. In *Green v. United States* (1962), the court held that waiver decisions were substantively equivalent to findings of probable cause.[21] Two years later, in *Watkins v. United States* (1964), the court found that jurisdictional waiver constituted a "judicial determination that the child is beyond the rehabilitative philosophy of the [Juvenile Court] Act,"[22] a determination it described in *Black v. United States* (1965)[23] as "critically important" to the interests of juveniles. The principal procedural consequence of *Watkins* was that counsel for juveniles in disputed waiver proceedings could be denied access to juvenile court records only if there was a compelling "need for confidentiality."[24] In *Black,* the court determined that the critical importance of waiver meant that proper administration of juvenile justice requires the application of certain provisions of the Bill of Rights, such as the assistance of counsel, to waiver proceedings.[25] In neither case, however, did the court overturn its decision in *Wilhite* that mandatory waiver hearings did not constitute a due process requirement in juvenile proceedings.

The key idea underlying both *Watkins* and *Black* was that the waiver decision should be understood as a critically important step in juvenile proceedings through which juveniles were removed from the protective cocoon of rehabilitative treatment and made to endure the punitive atmosphere of criminal proceedings. Although this idea eventually played a crucial role in *Kent* at the Supreme Court level, it would be wrong to conclude that juvenile court reformers launched the case in a conscious effort to use this notion to alter waiver proceedings. Indeed, *Kent* began to wind its way through the judicial process some three years before the decisions in *Watkins* and *Black.* Nevertheless, *Kent* did originate in a conscious effort at legal reform, but it was legal reform far removed from juvenile justice.

The Genesis of a Supreme Court Case

Although *Kent's* contemporary importance stems from its contribution to developments in juvenile law, the case actually originated as part of an effort to reform the test used by District of Columbia courts to determine criminal responsibility. One part of the story begins in 1954, when the U.S. Court of Appeals for the District of Columbia decided *Durham v. United States,* a case in which it articulated a new test of criminal responsibility.[26] The second part of the story begins on September 5, 1961, when Washington police arrested sixteen-year-old Morris Kent Jr. after discovering his fingerprints in the apartment of a woman who had been raped and robbed. The connection between these two events is that Kent's arrest and subsequent conviction for housebreaking and robbery formed the basis of a test case designed to support and broaden the new test of criminal responsibility established in *Durham.*

Until 1954 the District of Columbia determined criminal responsibility according to a two-part standard. The first part consisted of the right-wrong test embodied in the common law M'Naghten Rule. According to this test, defendants could not be held criminally responsible if they suffered from a mental disease or defect that made it impossible for them either to know what they were doing or to understand the moral import of their actions. The second part, adopted in 1929, was an irresistible impulse test, which provided that defendants could also avoid culpability by showing that they acted under an uncontrollable or irresistible impulse, even if they were aware of what they were doing and understood that their actions were morally wrong.

Abe Fortas, the court-appointed attorney in *Durham,* argued for reversal of his client's conviction on both procedural and substantive grounds. Fortas's procedural argument was that the trial court had erred in its application of the District's rules governing the burden of proof in insanity defense cases. The prevailing rule in the District was that once the defendant showed "some evidence" of mental incapacity, the burden of proving the defendant's sanity beyond a reasonable doubt shifted to the prosecution.[27] According to Fortas, the trial court had erred when it refused to accept psychiatric testimony that Durham was of unsound mind at the time of committing his offense as prima facie evidence of his incapacity. Though the court of appeals eventually agreed with Fortas on this procedural point, the substantive component of Fortas's argument ultimately proved to be more important. Fortas urged the appeals court to look beyond the technical errors committed during Durham's trial and to adopt a test of criminal responsibility that recognized scientific advances in psychology and psychiatry. New knowledge about the relationship between rationality and action, he averred, rendered the existing tests of criminal responsibility obsolete.

Fortas had the good fortune of presenting these arguments before D.C. Circuit Court of Appeals Judge David Bazelon. A Democrat, Bazelon had come to Washington in 1946 as the assistant attorney general for the U.S. Lands Division, and three years later Pres. Harry Truman had appointed him to the D.C. Circuit Court of Appeals. Bazelon had a strong interest in mental health issues and would serve on several federal commissions and councils concerning mental health during the 1960s and 1970s while also lecturing on psychiatry at Johns Hopkins University. Throughout his judicial career, Bazelon established a reputation as one of the most staunchly liberal judges on the federal bench. Fortas could not have had a more sympathetic audience for his arguments.

Not surprisingly, Bazelon agreed with Fortas's assertion that advances in the behavioral sciences required a reassessment of traditional notions of criminal responsibility. Judge Bazelon found that the District's right-wrong and irresistible impulse tests were outdated and unreasonably narrow since they recognized only two conditions—absolute lack of knowledge of one's actions or an inability to understand the moral quality of action—as evidence of mental incapacity. The weakness of this standard was that "the science of psychiatry now recognizes . . . that reason is not the sole determinant . . . of conduct. The right-wrong test, which considers knowledge or reason alone, is therefore an inadequate guide to mental responsibility for criminal behavior."[28] According to Bazelon, there existed a wide variety of mental illnesses, each of which might affect behavior without necessarily impeding cognitive functions. He argued that such illnesses should be factors in determining criminal responsibility. Bazelon thus proposed to substitute for the District's allegedly obsolete tests the much broader rule that "an accused is not criminally responsible if his unlawful act was the product of mental disease or mental defect," regardless of the effect of the illness on cognitive functioning.[29]

Many members of the District's psychiatric and legal communities welcomed Judge Bazelon's redefinition of criminal responsibility as a progressive development. Richard Arens, a law professor at Catholic University in Washington, was one of the scholars most impressed by the opportunities that *Durham* offered to pursue and achieve additional legal reform. Arens's interest in the *Durham* decision was neither casual nor accidental. Considered one of the leading liberals in Washington's legal-psychiatric community, Arens knew most of its major figures. He had participated in forums at the Washington School of Psychiatry and had lectured at the Psychiatric Institute. Moreover, Arens had a close intellectual relationship with David

Bazelon, with whom he occasionally discussed the legal definition of insanity.

Arens believed that the "productivity rule" articulated in *Durham* could lead to a "civilized system of psychiatric sanction-equivalents in lieu of conventional punishment in any case in which the crime appeared to be a product of mental disorder."[30] In order to explore this possibility, Arens collaborated with the Washington School of Psychiatry in 1959 on a project designed to examine the impact of *Durham* on the frequency and success of insanity pleas in the District.[31] The project's central purpose was to determine whether professional attitudes toward insanity and criminal responsibility had changed in the aftermath of Judge Bazelon's ruling. In particular, the research team examined whether mental illnesses other than clearly defined psychoses with well-documented effects on cognitive functioning had become legally accepted indicators of diminished responsibility.

The core of the study consisted of interviews with thirty-five psychiatrists and twenty-seven criminal defense attorneys. Contrary to Arens's hopes and expectations, these interviews produced disappointing findings. According to Arens, the psychiatrists offered evasive responses to the interviewers' questions and appeared simply unaware of the doctrine enunciated in *Durham*. The attorneys, on the other hand, were more comfortable with, and remained attached to, the pre-*Durham* tests of criminal responsibility. The exception to this rule were those lawyers who fully understood the nature and implications of *Durham*'s productivity rule.[32] These findings suggested to Arens that Judge Bazelon's articulation of a new test for determining criminal responsibility was in itself insufficient to revolutionize the role of insanity pleas in the District. It became apparent that the realization of *Durham*'s potential required the actual use of the productivity defense in specific cases, an event that Arens's study suggested was an infrequent occurrence.

Arens's dissatisfaction with the results of his first project encouraged him to undertake a more ambitious study. In April 1961—again in collaboration with the Washington School of Psychiatry—Arens received a grant from the National Institute of Mental Health (NIMH) to continue his work. The second project's purpose was to gather data on the impact of the productivity rule during the course of live trials by initiating "actual litigation involving the insanity defense in which the cases selected . . . involve psychopathology of the nonpsychotic type and the defense could rationally and legally be based on a liberal interpretation of the local rule of criminal responsibility."[33] Arens used funds provided by NIMH to retain psychiatrists and attorneys in order to take selected cases to trial and further his research on the acceptability of the productivity rule among judges, jurors, and attorneys. In addition to satisfying Arens's research curiosity, this arrangement also gave him the opportunity to implement his law reform agenda by supporting test cases designed to expand *Durham's* conceptual reformulation of criminal responsibility.

The District of Columbia's legal aid office cooperated with Arens during the initial phases of the project by directing indigent clients to his staff. Arens's normal practice was to accept all clients referred to him by the legal aid office and then have his staff determine whether an insanity defense would be appropriate in specific cases.[34] On September 6, 1961, the legal aid office referred a light-skinned African American, Morris Kent Jr.—whom D.C. police had described as a "one-man crime wave"—to the project's attorneys. The attorneys retained two psychiatrists and a psychologist to determine whether Kent suffered from a "psychopathology of the nonpsychotic type" that could serve as the basis for a productivity rule defense.[35] In Kent's case, the diagnosis was positive, and his defense proceeded within the framework of the project. As a juvenile, however, Kent was under the jurisdiction of the District's juvenile court, which had been monitoring his behavior since placing him on probation in 1959 for committing several housebreakings and an attempted purse snatching.

Kent's status as a juvenile complicated the process of litigating his case within the framework of the *Durham* project. Although the productivity rule appeared to be especially relevant to Kent's circumstances, the 1938 juvenile court statute explicitly stipulated that delinquency adjudications were neither criminal convictions nor did they confer "criminal" status on juveniles.[36] Consequently, as in all juvenile proceedings based on the doctrine of *parens patriae,* criminal responsibility was not an issue usually considered by the District's juvenile court. This feature of juvenile proceedings traditionally meant that the insanity defense played no role in determining delinquency.[37] Kent's counsel thus faced the somewhat contradictory demands of advocating his client's interests in the juvenile court while simultaneously pursuing the matter as an insanity-defense test case. These competing demands became evident during lower court litigation in *Kent.*

One week after Morris Kent's arrest, and after reviewing his existing juvenile court file and a separate probation report prepared on September 8, the juvenile court determined that his case fell within the criteria established in the 1959 policy memorandum on waiver. The court thus waived its exclusive jurisdiction over Kent and transferred his case for trial in the District's criminal court. Although his counsel requested a hearing prior to the waiver decision and access to his juvenile court records, the court made its transfer decision without granting either request. Consequently, the juvenile court's announcement that Kent would be transferred for trial under the regular criminal jurisdiction of the D.C. district court led his counsel to appeal the waiver order in the Municipal Court of Appeals and to file an application for a writ of habeas corpus in the district court. The latter court quickly denied the habeas corpus petition, issuing its decision on September 19. The Municipal Court of Appeals, on the other hand, took seven months to deny Kent's appeal and affirm the waiver order. Kent's counsel persisted in challenging the waiver order, appealing both decisions to the District of Columbia Circuit Court of Appeals.

During the period that the juvenile court's jurisdictional waiver order was under appeal, Kent underwent two important psychiatric examinations.[38] On October 6, 1961, his counsel asked for a sixty-day psychiatric examination at the District of Columbia General Hospital. Two months later, the hospital reported that Kent suffered from a severe emotional illness that rendered him "incompetent to stand trial and to participate in a mature way in his own defense." The hospital also reported that Kent's illness, which it characterized as a type of schizophrenia, "interfered with his judgment and reasoning ability." Although the hospital did not reach a definitive conclusion, its report suggested that Kent might have been psychotic at the time of his alleged crimes. The report also stressed Kent's danger to himself and others but recommended that he be held in an institution other than a jail prior to trial.

After receiving the General Hospital's report, the prosecution requested that Kent be committed to the District's principal psychiatric facility, St. Elizabeth's Hospital, for further testing. The St. Elizabeth's doctors also found that Kent suffered from a mental disease of a "schizophrenic reaction, undifferentiated type," and that the criminal acts with which he was charged were probably the product of that disease. St. Elizabeth's found no evidence, however, to indicate that Kent suffered from a mental deficiency, nor did it find that he was incompetent to stand trial or incapable of understanding the nature of the proceedings against him. In contrast to the General Hospital's doctors, the superintendent of St. Elizabeth's recommended that Kent be "transferred to the District of Columbia Jail to await disposition of the charges pending against him."

On January 22, 1963, the court of appeals finally rendered its decision on Kent's appeals of the juvenile court's original waiver decision. It upheld the district court's September 1961 denial of habeas corpus on the grounds that it was "unnecessary to preserve appellant's rights, would interfere with and unnecessarily delay the orderly processes of the District Court, and would be inconsistent with the precedents developed in this court and the Supreme Court." The court also upheld the municipal court's decision not to overturn the waiver decision, holding that waiver did not constitute an appealable final order or judgment, and that the district court was "better equipped to determine whether a full investigation was had prior to waiver."[39] Thus, after more than a year of legal maneuvering, punctuated by two psychiatric examinations, Kent's trial on charges of housebreaking, rape, and robbery began in March 1963.

Consistent with the aims of the *Durham* project, the central issue during the trial became the degree to which Kent could be held criminally responsible for his alleged offenses. Defense counsel admitted that Kent had committed the criminal acts but called on the expert testimony of eight psychiatrists to persuade the jury that Kent's actions were the product of a mental disease. The prosecution responded by attempting to draw a distinction between the alleged rapes and the other offenses. Prosecution witnesses testified that Kent's principal motive for entering the women's apartments was robbery and that the rapes might have been an uncontrollable reaction to the circumstances surrounding the other crimes. Thus, though conceding that Kent might not be criminally responsible for the rapes, the prosecution stressed that the housebreakings and robberies were the products of free will for which Kent could be held responsible.[40] This strategy succeeded, and the jury convicted Kent of the housebreaking and robbery charges while acquitting him of the rape charges by reason of insanity. The court subsequently sentenced Kent to a term of thirty to ninety years in confinement.

The First Appeal

Although Kent's counsel engaged in extensive pretrial litigation to reverse the juvenile court's waiver decision, juvenile justice reform was at most a peripheral issue in the minds of Kent's attorneys. The idea of transforming the case from an insanity-defense test case to a juvenile procedure challenge first emerged during discussions between Kent's trial attorney, Mark B. Sandground, and Richard Arens.[41] Sandground had known Arens at the University of Michigan from 1948 to 1952 and had worked for a year in the criminal division of the Department of Justice before entering a prominent

District of Columbia law firm. Although a civil litigation specialist, Sandground was appointed chief counsel in Kent's case on Arens's recommendation, a duty his law firm permitted him to undertake pro bono.

Sandground viewed the jury's split verdict as an improper compromise with little legal justification, and he suggested that it should form the principal focus of an appeal. Upon further reflection, Arens decided that the appeal should also include a challenge to the procedures by which Kent's case had been transferred from the juvenile court to the district court. With this decision taken, Kent appealed his conviction to the D.C. Circuit Court of Appeals, which heard the argument on December 17, 1963.[42] A small problem arose, however, since Sandground had little experience in either due process or juvenile justice cases. Although Sandground knew that there had not been any meaningful hearing in the juvenile court prior to waiver, he had not devoted much attention to that issue during his defense of Kent in the district court.

Responsibility for conducting the appeal thus shifted from Sandground to Myron Ehrlich, who advanced two grounds to support the reversal of Kent's conviction. First, he argued that the district court had never acquired proper jurisdiction over the case and offered three reasons to support his contention: (1) the juvenile court's waiver of jurisdiction had not been preceded by the "full investigation" required by the district's juvenile court law; (2) there had been a general disregard for the standard requirements of due process in the proceedings that led to the juvenile court's jurisdictional waiver; and (3) the juvenile court had waived jurisdiction "in disregard of the *parens patriae* philosophy of the Juvenile Court system and in disregard of the Juvenile Court's own standards governing waiver."[43] In addition to these jurisdictional grounds for reversal, Ehrlich also asserted that the district court had committed several errors during the trial itself, the most significant being that the court had failed to apply the standard of criminal responsibility established in *Durham* when it refused to grant Kent's motion for a directed verdict of acquittal of all charges by reason of insanity.[44]

The court of appeals expended little energy rejecting Ehrlich's case against the procedures by which the trial itself had been conducted and his argument that the psychiatric evidence should have produced an acquittal without putting the question to the jury.[45] Dismissing Ehrlich's claim that the juvenile court had in general denied Kent due process, the appeals court noted that juveniles possessed only a statutory right to the protections of a specialized court and that the waiver provision in the District's statute limited this right in the case of juveniles accused of serious offenses.[46] The court thus concluded that constitutional standards of due process applicable in adult criminal proceedings did not apply to juvenile proceedings; the Constitution merely required that juveniles "be dealt with in a reasonable and decent manner which gives due regard to [their] claims upon society as well as to the latter's claims upon [them]."[47] The court found nothing to indicate "any treatment of appellant so unfair in nature as to constitute a denial of his right to due process of law." Indeed, it cited as evidence to the contrary the two psychiatric examinations with which Kent had been provided.

The court of appeals directed most of its attention to Ehrlich's contention that the district court had never acquired proper jurisdiction over Kent's case because of deficiencies in the waiver process.[48] The court began by rejecting the argument that the juvenile court's discretionary power to waive jurisdiction was inconsistent with the *parens patriae* philosophy of the Juvenile Court Act, arguing that judicial discretion to exclude certain juveniles from the protective atmosphere of juvenile courts was critically important for ensuring the effective implementation of the *parens patriae* ideal. Indeed, it declared that the realization of this ideal depended precisely on "the skill and experience of the specialist judge" and concluded that "revision of that trained judgment in a particular case by a non-specialist tribunal is a venture not to be undertaken lightly."[49] The court next turned to Ehrlich's assertion that the juvenile court's waiver decision had not been preceded by the "full investigation" required by the statute. Although the court found this to be the most serious challenge to the proceedings in Kent's case, it held that the criteria satisfying a full investigation "must be filled out in the first instance by the administering agency." Because the 1959 policy memorandum on waiver served this purpose, the court was left with determining whether the absence of a hearing requirement among the memorandum's criteria was a constitutional or statutory deficiency. It approached this question by weighing the knowledge of Kent acquired by the juvenile court through two years of contact against any additional information that might have been gained from testimony elicited during a waiver hearing. The court concluded that "the Juvenile Court had sufficient evidence to make an informed, intelligent decision" and declined to rule that waiver had occurred improperly in Morris Kent's case.[50]

The somewhat unsystematic fashion in which the procedural issues surrounding waiver were included in Kent's appeal raises a question: Why did the court of appeals find them to be more important and interesting than the insanity defense issues on which the case originally rested? Any answer is necessarily speculative, but at least three factors may have been instrumental in shaping the court's perception of the issues. First, subsequent appellate decisions had criticized *Durham's* productivity rule as ambiguous;[51] consequently, by the time Kent's case reached the court, *Durham's* value as a precedent had to some extent been reduced. Second, in cases like *Green, Watkins,* and *Black* the court had begun to lay the foundation for a close examination of procedural issues like those raised in Kent's appeal. Third, the jurisdictional question was logically prior to any question concerning the conduct of the trial itself; any errors committed during the trial were therefore moot if the district court had never obtained proper jurisdiction over the case.

Kent emerged from a context in which juvenile procedure was initially only a minor element. Although Kent's attorney had challenged the juvenile court's decision to waive jurisdiction in the case, he had done so largely out of a professional obligation to assist his client as fully as possible; juvenile justice reform was not high on his agenda. If Kent's counsel could be said to have had any objective other than simply securing his client's acquittal, it was to promote a particular defense against criminal responsibility. By largely ignoring the case's criminal responsibility aspects, however, the court of appeals undercut the importance of these issues in *Kent.* This interaction between litigation strategies and the lower trial and appellate court decisions served to shift the emphasis from the insanity defense to juvenile waiver proceedings by the time the case reached the Supreme Court.

Arguments Before the Supreme Court

THE CASE FOR KENT

Despite the court of appeals' lack of interest in the criminal responsibility issue, the brief filed in the Supreme Court on Kent's behalf by Myron Ehrlich and Richard Arens contained arguments drawn from both the insanity defense and juvenile procedure aspects of the case. The insanity defense component of the brief attacked the trial court's interpretation and application of the productivity rule set out in *Durham.* Ehrlich and Arens argued that the trial judge had committed plain error in his charge to the jury when he failed to stress that conviction required proof beyond a reasonable doubt that the defendant did not suffer from a mental disease or defect or that the accused's alleged offenses were not the product of such disease or defect. Failure by the prosecution to meet either of these evidentiary burdens, the brief asserted, should result in acquittal for lack of criminal responsibility. According to the brief, the charge to the jury did not accurately reflect this rule, resulting in the divided verdict on Kent's responsibility for the rapes and other offenses.

The brief made it clear, however, that the insanity defense questions had become largely peripheral to the main issue of the appeal. In fact, Ehrlich and Arens devoted only seven pages of their eighty-five page brief to insanity defense issues, most of which summarized the psychiatric testimony concerning Kent's mental state and its probable contribution to his criminal acts.[52] The brief claimed that the D.C. General Hospital had found Kent to be "a victim of schizophrenia and his crimes, if any, the probable products of his illness."[53] But the General Hospital's report did not mention productivity, nor did it reach a "definite opinion" about Kent's mental state when he committed the crimes.[54] Nevertheless, Ehrlich and Arens interpreted the report to mean that "a reasonable mind must necessarily have had a reasonable doubt as to the sanity of the accused at the times the alleged acts were committed, and that if the said acts were committed by him, they were the product of his mental disease." The only explanation for a contrary verdict, they asserted, was an improper charge to the jury.[55]

The main issue of the appeal, however, was the extent to which juvenile court waiver proceedings were subject to constitutional standards of administrative, civil, or criminal due process.[56] The brief argued that whatever the standard of due process applicable to waiver proceedings, it had been violated in Kent's case by "incommunicado interrogation," by the absence of a right to inspect social records and to have effective assistance of counsel prior to waiver, and by the absence of a hearing at which Kent's case against waiver could have been presented. The brief further maintained that it was improper for a criminal court to try a minor on capital charges where the juvenile court had waived its jurisdiction in violation of due process. Moreover, Ehrlich and Arens argued that fingerprints obtained while a defendant was under the juvenile court's jurisdiction could not be used in subsequent criminal proceedings.[57]

This part of the brief began by summarizing the case against waiver that could have been made on Kent's behalf had there been an opportunity to do so. The core of the argument against transferring him for trial in the criminal court was that he suffered from a mental illness that juvenile court officials had neglected and that could be treated more effectively in the rehabilitative atmosphere of the juvenile court than it could be in the punitive surroundings of the criminal justice system.[58] According to Ehrlich and Arens, the juvenile court's failure to hold a waiver hearing prevented the presentation of this argument, violating Kent's statutory right to a full investigation prior to waiver. Further, the brief contended that the absence of a waiver hearing violated Kent's constitutional right to fundamental fairness under the Fifth Amendment's due process clause and his Sixth Amendment right to effective assistance of counsel.[59]

In addition to these general charges, the brief catalogued a variety of other alleged violations of due process Kent had suffered.[60] The brief complained that a "shocking misuse of official power" had led to his "illegal arrest, detention, and coercive interrogation." It also asserted that Kent's interrogation had become accusatory soon after its initiation and that he had therefore been entitled to the assistance of counsel as required by *Escobedo v. Illinois* (1964).[61] The decision to include this argument constituted a somewhat questionable tactic, since in order to accept it the Court would have had to decide on the retroactive applicability of *Escobedo*. The Court was divided on the general issue of the retroactive application of procedural rights carved from the Bill of Rights through judicial construction; indeed, it did not finally resolve the issue until *Linkletter v. Walker* in 1965.[62] Finally, the brief reiterated its claim that the juvenile court's failure to hold a waiver hearing prevented the judge from gathering "*all* relevant factual information" necessary for an enlightened and fair waiver determination.

The brief's claim that juvenile proceedings in general, and waiver proceedings in particular, were subject to at least minimal constitutional standards of due process relied on two separate arguments. The first, which spoke to the brief's general claim about the applicability of due process to juvenile proceedings, was that the consequences of delinquency adjudications were largely indistinguishable from the punishment meted out by criminal courts.[63] The brief expressed this functional similarity argument:

> Although technically engaged in adjudication of "status" rather than "crime," Juvenile Courts inflict punishment. . . . Designation of their proceedings as "civil" rather than "criminal" in no way detracts from the consequences of Juvenile Court action in terms of the pain suffered by stigmatization as a juvenile delinquent, by loss of liberty or by exposure to adult punishment.[64]

Ehrlich and Arens urged the Court to ignore superficial terminological differences, to recognize the essential similarities between juvenile and criminal proceedings, and to terminate the juvenile court's immunity from constitutional scrutiny.

Their second argument focused on the specific similarity between the waiver decision and criminal proceedings, characterizing waiver as "the supreme penalty" available to juvenile courts since it deprived juveniles of the protection and rehabilitative services of the juvenile justice system. Indeed, according to the brief, "of all the sanctions meted out by the Juvenile Court, the most 'critically important . . . for the child' is waiver of Juvenile Court jurisdiction and the transfer of that child to adult court for trial under adult procedure."[65] Waiver was critical, Ehrlich and Arens asserted, because the severity of criminal sentences relative to juvenile court dispositions.[66] The brief concluded that the waiver decision

> should therefore be subject to constitutional safeguards of fundamental fairness commensurate with the gravity of the situation, and include a settled procedure for the apprehension and detention of the child. A hearing satisfying the minimal requirements of administrative due process in adversary matters and effective assistance of counsel is therefore essential. So is freedom from coercive interrogation.[67]

The brief's functional similarity and critical importance arguments unquestionably struck at the heart of the juvenile court's traditional waiver proceedings. Yet by citing the court of appeals' decisions in *Green v. United States* (1962), *Watkins v. United States* (1964), and *Black v. United States* (1965), the brief was able to soften the novelty of its argument.[68] Although in these decisions the court of appeals had limited judicial discretion to waive jurisdiction by comparing waiver to a probable cause finding, creating a presumption in favor of access to social records by a juvenile's counsel and defining waiver as a critically important determination, it had yet to require waiver hearings. Kent's brief simply asked the Court to take this small incremental step toward better waiver proceedings.

The brief's arguments were further strengthened by the manner in which it dealt with a paradox: If juvenile and criminal proceedings are functionally similar, then why is waiver so critically important that it must be circumscribed by additional procedural safeguards? The brief's answer was that, although the *qualitative* differences between the two types of proceedings might be minimal, there remained significant *quantitative* differences between them. These differences were such that waiver constituted a punitive disposition in itself and thus could be imposed only after careful consideration. The long period of confinement levied on Kent by the sentencing judge served to underscore this point and to provide support for the critical importance argument.

Additional support for the constitutional arguments came from the only amicus curiae brief filed in the case. Professor Nicholas Kittrie of American University prepared the brief on behalf of thirteen individuals who believed that it was necessary to undertake a careful review of the legal principles underlying juvenile courts.[69] Kittrie was well connected in Washington, having served as legal assistant to Sen. Alexander Wiley in 1959 and as counsel to Sen. Estes Kefauver from 1959 to 1962. Among the sponsors of his brief were Thurman Arnold, who had been an important figure in the Roosevelt administration and was one of Washington's most powerful lawyers, and Sol Rubin, a leading advocate of juvenile court reform. In addition to reiterating the major points of Kent's brief,[70] the attorneys urged the Court in their amicus brief to consider the broader constitutional issues raised by juvenile jurisprudence and the accomplishments of juvenile courts. In the view of Kittrie and his colleagues, *Kent* presented the Supreme Court with an opportunity to determine the extent to which "traditional constitutional [procedural] guarantees" apply to juvenile courts, as well as to establish uniform national "standards of fairness for juvenile courts."[71]

Citing many of the juvenile court's contemporary academic critics, including Chester Antieau, Mathew Beemsterboer, Monrad Paulsen, and Paul Tappan, they urged the Court to hold

> that the grant of discretionary power to the juvenile courts to waive jurisdiction, when unaccompanied by reasonable and ascertainable standards, is contrary to the due process and equal protection requirements of the Fifth Amendment, and . . . that the Sixth Amendment counsel guarantee applies to juvenile court and that there is a right to a hearing and counsel under the Fifth and Sixth Amendments in juvenile court proceedings where waiver is contemplated.[72]

The use of an equal protection argument to challenge the District's traditional waiver proceedings raised the constitutional stakes of *Kent* considerably. To argue that the juvenile court's procedural deficiencies might violate equal protection and due process implicitly brought into question the very constitutionality of maintaining separate proceedings for juveniles and adults. The amicus brief thus raised a difficult question: How could the substantive differences between juvenile and criminal proceedings be maintained once procedural differences were eliminated?

In terms of both its argument and overall objective, the amicus brief was far more reform-minded than the brief filed on Kent's behalf. Kent's counsel attacked the juvenile court's waiver proceedings and the district court trial to advance their client's own interests rather than to initiate widespread juvenile justice reform, but the amicus brief presented a broader view and stressed the national significance of the case as a potential turning point in the development of juvenile courts. It therefore invited the Court to use *Kent* as a vehicle for reevaluating the constitutional status of juvenile proceedings and for imposing national standards of juvenile due process. Although undoubtedly concerned with the outcome in the specific case, the amicus participants defined the success of their endeavor mostly in terms of its wider impact.

The task of defending the District's waiver proceedings against Kent's petition and the amicus brief fell to Theodore Gilinsky, an attorney in the U.S. Justice Department who had argued five cases before the Supreme Court but otherwise possessed no special expertise in juvenile justice. Gilinsky's response to the position staked out in the two opposing briefs consisted of two separate arguments. The first, which covered less than eight pages of the government's fifty-six page brief, dealt with the alleged errors committed during Kent's trial. Gilinsky argued that none of these errors could form the basis of an appeal since Kent's counsel had not objected to them during the trial itself. According to Gilinsky, this lack of interest in procedural matters was due entirely to Sandground's "strategic decision to rest [his case] solely on proof of insanity."[73] Although necessary to respond to one component of Kent's challenge of his conviction, this argument was clearly less important or critical than Gilinsky's treatment of the issues surrounding waiver.

Gilinsky insisted that the only significant juvenile court procedural question raised by *Kent* was whether jurisdiction had been waived in compliance with statutory requirements and "without fundamental unfairness to petitioner."[74] He presented his main argument in three parts. First he argued that, although Kent's case raised significant questions about the statutory rights to which juveniles were entitled under the District's juvenile court statute, it did not implicate any of their constitutional rights. Gilinsky continued in the second part of his argument to assert that these statutory rights could be adequately protected by administrative investigations such as the one conducted prior to Kent's transfer to the criminal court. Third, Gilinsky averred that the administrative investigation conducted in Kent's case was adequate to protect his statutory rights and to satisfy the criteria established in the 1959 waiver memorandum. The essence of this argument was that neither the District's juvenile court statute, nor the Constitution, contained any provision specifically requiring waiver hearings. According to Gilinsky, the necessity of waiver hearings should be left to the judgment of juvenile justice specialists.[75]

Gilinsky construed the District's juvenile court law as establishing a "statutory presumption that society is better served if youthful offenders are treated by a social service agency rather than by judicial criminal process."[76] The statute's waiver provision, however, recognized that there were exceptions to this general rule. The decision to waive jurisdiction, in other words, did not directly deprive juveniles of constitutionally guaranteed rights to life, liberty, or property; it simply transferred them to a judicial proceeding that was public, permitted longer periods of treatment, and provided for the possibility of criminal sanctions where appropriate.[77] Although waiver did not affect any of the constitutional rights of juveniles, Gilinsky conceded that the statutory rights at stake were sufficiently important that waiver could not be imposed arbitrarily. Consistent with this construction of the statute, Gilinsky concluded that the main issue of the case was "whether procedures short of those followed in criminal trials may be used in determining whether an accused is entitled to a *statutory,* rather than *constitutional,* right."[78]

Gilinsky argued that, in the absence of any direct threat to constitutional rights, the waiver decision was not "the type of determination which requires all the safeguards of a criminal trial."[79] Instead, the principal requirement was that waiver proceedings allow for "an informed and intelligent decision" with a "minimum of formality and delay."[80] Gilinsky urged the Court to refrain from articulating a national standard to govern such proceedings, particularly in view of the relative underdevelopment of juvenile courts as institutions. "In an area such as this one, where the frontiers of knowledge are expanding," Gilinsky argued, "it was and remains desirable for the legislature to delegate the enumeration of specific criteria to those who daily encounter the problems which gave rise to the legislation."[81] He thus asked the Court to defer to Congress' judgment that the desirability of waiver could properly be determined by an administrative investigation.[82]

Gilinsky devoted the remainder of his brief to showing that the "administrative investigation" preceding the juvenile court's waiver of jurisdiction over Kent had been conducted properly. The court had acted reasonably, Gilinsky argued, in relying on Kent's social record to evaluate his amenability to treatment, one of the important criteria for waiver articulated in 1959.[83] Gilinsky also cited the various procedural maneuvers conducted prior to Kent's trial to attack opposing counsel's assertion that there had not been an adequate opportunity to challenge the waiver decision. In concluding, Gilinsky defended the substantive conclusion of the juvenile court's waiver investigation by arguing that the seriousness and frequency of Kent's alleged offenses, despite probationary supervision by the court, indicated its limited capacity to rehabilitate Kent.[84] According to Gilinsky, therefore, the administrative investigation offered ample evidence of Kent's "dangerousness" and "unamenability to treatment."

SUMMARY

Neither side's argument in *Kent* was free from difficulty. The main weakness of Gilinsky's argument for traditional waiver was its reliance on a view that was rapidly becoming an outmoded understanding of the differences between juvenile and criminal proceedings. He conceptualized waiver as a bridge between juvenile courts—where constitutional rights to life, liberty, and property are not at stake—and criminal courts—where those rights are jeopardized. Although this made waiver an important aspect of juvenile proceedings, it did not make it the type of decision circumscribed by constitutional standards of due process. Gilinsky offered no real evidence to support this proposition, however; he simply repeated the original theory underlying juvenile courts and cited authorities who were under attack in the scholarly literature.

The difficulty with the argument advanced on behalf of Kent was that it did not entirely resolve the tension between the functional similarity and critical importance arguments. It failed, for example, to take account of the fact that certain qualitative differences between juvenile and criminal proceedings—such as full due process protection and the availability of various defenses otherwise excluded from juvenile proceedings—might actually make criminal proceedings superior to juvenile proceedings in cases like Kent's. Moreover, it did not offer any evidence that the severity of Kent's sentence was typical of the treatment juveniles received from criminal courts after juvenile courts waived jurisdiction. Overall, however, the argument on behalf of Kent had the advantage of being consistent with emerging theoretical developments in juvenile jurisprudence and with the trio of cases decided by the court of appeals during the period between the juvenile court's waiver of jurisdiction over Kent and the case's appearance on the Supreme Court's docket.

The Supreme Court Decides

When the Supreme Court delivered its decision in Morris Kent Jr.'s appeal in March 1966, it was fully engaged in the nationalization of criminal due process that is one of the distinguishing features of its jurisprudence between

1961 and 1972. Indeed, 1966 marked the precise midpoint in the series of decisions extending Bill of Rights protections to state criminal accused, defendants, or both; the Court issued six of the decisions in its "due process revolution" between 1961 and 1966 and five decisions between 1967 and 1972. Kent's appeal thus arrived before a Court that was instinctively suspicious of the procedures used by states to deny their citizens' liberty. No justice harbored this suspicion more than its newest member, Abe Fortas. A partner in one of Washington's leading law firms before joining the Court, Fortas had been indirectly involved in the "revolution" as the court-appointed attorney in *Gideon v. Wainwright* (1963). He had also been responsible for leading Judge Bazelon to a new doctrine of criminal responsibility in *Durham*. *Kent* was Fortas's first real opportunity to contribute to the Court's growing due process jurisprudence.

The opportunity was almost lost, however. Ironically, the court of appeals' 1964 and 1965 decisions in *Watkins* and *Black*, on which much of the strength of Kent's argument for waiver hearings depended, almost caused the Court to avoid the issue altogether. Four justices, including Potter Stewart, Hugo Black, John Harlan, and Byron White, argued on jurisdictional grounds that the case simply should be remanded to the court of appeals for reconsideration in light of its decisions in *Watkins* and *Black*. Justice Stewart argued that the court of appeals should have the first opportunity to determine whether its acknowledgment in those decisions that waiver constitutes a critically important decision meant that the lower court modify its earlier view that the Juvenile Court Act's waiver provision did not require waiver hearings. According to Stewart, this response would be consistent with the Court's "general practice" of "leav[ing] undisturbed decisions of the Court of Appeals for the District of Columbia Circuit concerning the import of legislation governing the affairs of the District."[85]

A bare majority of the Court decided, however, that it was unnecessary to wait for a new decision from the court of appeals, and it proceeded to consider the case on its substantive merits. In an opinion authored by Fortas, the majority focused its entire attention on Kent's challenge to the proceedings by which the juvenile court had waived jurisdiction and transferred him for trial in the criminal court. Despite Fortas's prior association with the doctrine of criminal responsibility that Kent's attorneys had initially hoped to advance with the case, he merely noted in passing that Kent's defense at trial "was wholly directed toward proving that he was not criminally responsible" under the productivity rule established in *Durham*.[86] Indeed, Fortas dispensed with the insanity defense aspects of the case in a single footnote.[87] The bulk of his opinion consisted of conclusions drawn from three separate observations. The first was that the theory underlying the District's juvenile court statute was "rooted in social welfare philosophy rather than in the *corpus juris.*" Thus, according to Fortas, the juvenile court was "theoretically engaged in determining the needs of the child and of society rather than adjudicating criminal conduct." The juvenile court's objective in making this determination was to provide "guidance and rehabilitation for the child and protection for society, not to fix criminal responsibility, guilt and punishment." In order to pursue these objectives, the state functioned as *parens patriae* in juvenile courts rather than as prosecutor and judge. Fortas concluded, however, that the "admonition to function in a 'parental' relationship is not an invitation to procedural arbitrariness."[88]

Fortas's second observation was that, although there could be "no doubt of the original laudable purpose of juvenile courts," the reliance on procedural informality was now questionable because of doubts about "whether actual performance [of juvenile courts] measures well enough against theoretical purpose to make tolerable the immunity of the process from the reach of constitutional guaranties applicable to adults." Fortas based this observation on a 1965 article in the *Wisconsin Law Review* and the 1966 Harvard study of juvenile court practices, which served as his primary source of information about the actual operation of juvenile court systems.[89] These "studies and critiques" led Fortas to conclude that there were "grounds for concern that the child receives the worst of both worlds: that he gets neither the protections accorded to adults nor the solicitous care and regenerative treatment postulated for children." This concern was not enough, however, to induce Fortas to follow the amicus brief's recommendation and to declare that the criminal procedure provisions of the Bill of Rights should apply in their entirety to juvenile proceedings.[90] This analysis was consistent with a context-sensitive approach to due process, which seeks to structure and confine discretion when its exercise permits outcomes that are inconsistent with the initial purpose of the institution in question.

Fortas's final observation was that it "is clear beyond dispute that the waiver of jurisdiction is a 'critically important' action determining vitally important statutory rights of the juvenile." In addition to denying juveniles their "statutory right to the 'exclusive' jurisdiction of the juvenile court," Fortas noted that, in Kent's case at least, the waiver decision "was potentially as important to petitioner as the difference between five years' confinement and a death sentence." Fortas concluded from these observations that no investigation of the appropriateness of waiver could be complete without a hearing; that this hearing must comport with at least the fundamental fairness notion of due process; and that, given the nature of the rights at stake in waiver hearings, fundamental fairness required representation by counsel and access to social reports.[91] In reaching this conclusion, Fortas relied on *Watkins* and *Black* to modify the court of appeals' construction of the "full investigation" requirement in the District's waiver provision. Although these decisions had granted juveniles a right to counsel during waiver proceedings (*Black*) and given counsel the right to inspect social reports (*Watkins*), Fortas argued that both of these rights are "meaningless—an illusion, a mockery—unless counsel is given an opportunity to function."[92] According to Fortas, this opportunity fully exists only where there is a hearing at which counsel may challenge the juvenile court's waiver decision. Consequently, if a "full investigation" requires the assistance of counsel and access to social reports, then a hearing is necessary to give these requirements substance.

Underlying Fortas's review of the questions surrounding waiver was a set of broader issues about the general nature of juvenile proceedings. One such issue was "the adequacy of custodial and treatment facilities and policies" available to juvenile courts.[93] Even more basic, however, was the "justifiability of affording a juvenile less protection than is accorded to adults suspected of criminal offenses."[94] Fortas was particularly skeptical about the "quid pro quo" justification for procedural informality, in which the denial of constitutional rights to due process was offset by the special treatment accorded to juveniles. The potentially punitive consequences of waiver made this issue particularly salient since juveniles could be denied special treatment altogether through informal proceedings. Although Fortas found it unnecessary to address either of these issues directly in deciding *Kent*, the similar concerns expressed in the scholarly literature acquired added legitimacy through Fortas's recognition that problems existed in the basic structure of juvenile proceedings.

Fortas's concern with broader issues of juvenile justice administration also led him to view the critical importance issue somewhat differently from the court of appeals' view in *Black*. Judge Bazelon's opinion in *Black* appeared to emphasize that waiver denied juveniles the benefits of rehabilitation, but Fortas's acknowledgment of two serious deficiencies in the structure of juvenile proceedings—the lack of due process and an apparent lack of rehabilitative success—implied that the critical importance of waiver had little to do with the benefits emanating from juvenile proceedings. Instead, Fortas's perception of critical importance was largely a function of the potentially negative consequences of criminal proceedings, which included longer terms of confinement in possibly less benign institutions. Although perhaps a subtle difference, this shift in perception was indicative of the increasingly hostile atmosphere in which traditional concepts of juvenile jurisprudence found themselves operating.

As in Kent's brief, however, Fortas's emphasis on the punitive consequences of criminal proceedings led him to overlook some of the positive elements of those proceedings. In particular, the opinion failed to mention either the procedural safeguards or the variety of defenses available in criminal proceedings that might reduce the probability of criminal conviction. Moreover, Fortas did not consider the possibility that Kent's sentence was an anomaly and that criminal courts might actually be lenient in their treatment of juveniles transferred from juvenile courts. Fortas simply assumed, on the basis of Kent's long sentence, that all juveniles tried in criminal courts receive significantly more severe punishments than those that juvenile courts might impose. If later studies are any indication of conditions prevalent in the early 1960s, however, this assumption may have been unwarranted. One study, for example, found that only 4 percent of serious juvenile offenders tried in criminal courts received longer sentences than could have been imposed by the juvenile court.[95] Faced with such data, Fortas might have reached the radically different conclusion that juveniles are actually better off in criminal courts, where they enjoy the full range of criminal due process protection and, in practice, often receive less severe punishments.

By the early 1960s, the loss of faith in the rehabilitative ideal and its corresponding institutional framework had generated significant demands for juvenile justice reform. The circumstances surrounding Morris Kent Jr.'s case provided the legal dispute necessary to push those demands into the adjudicative arena of Supreme Court decisionmaking for the first time in juvenile court history. However, *Kent* was not a pure test case in the sense that a law was deliberately violated in order to test its constitutionality. Nor was the case the product of a systematic strategy to advance the interests of juvenile defendants as a class through litigation. *Kent's* impact on juvenile procedure was the unexpected outcome of a campaign to advance a particular theory of criminal responsibility. Richard Arens's ability to control both the law reform and client service aspects of the *Durham* project allowed him to redefine the case as a juvenile procedure challenge, which proved instrumental in ensuring the success of the appeal.

Arens's effort was obviously aided by the extremely severe sentence that

Kent received from the trial court, which had the effect of underscoring the alleged "critical importance" of the waiver decision. Yet the legislative facts necessary to determine this characteristic of waiver in a general way were never really developed in either the lower court record or in the arguments presented to the Supreme Court. For example, the Court did not receive any aggregate data on the frequency with which juveniles transferred to criminal courts in the District of Columbia or any other jurisdictions received harsher sentences than those imposed by juvenile courts. The majority was forced simply to assume on the basis of Kent's own sentence that juveniles must be disadvandaged in criminal courts. More important, *Kent*'s initial development as an insanity-defense reform case did not lend itself to developing the broader juvenile justice issues raised by the case, such as the "adequacy of custodial treatment facilities and policies."[96] In this respect, *Kent* foreshadowed the policymaking hurdles that the Court would be forced to confront in *Gault* and *Winship*. As a result of its internal deficiencies, *Kent* did not allow for extensive judicial reform of juvenile courts. Nevertheless, given the origins of the case, even the original reforms the decision contained were impressive.

Although *Kent* did not fulfill the promise of juvenile justice reform that Chief Justice Warren had hinted was on its way in his 1964 speech to the National Council of Juvenile Court Judges, the decision moved the Court significantly in that direction. Without any opposition within the Court on the merits, the majority opinion acknowledged procedural and substantive deficiencies in juvenile proceedings, agreed that certain aspects of juvenile proceedings should be subject to constitutional review on due process grounds, and suggested a standard to apply in that review—the "essentials of due process and fair treatment."[97] The transition from constitutional neglect to constitutional review that began in *Kent* was made easier because jurisdictional waiver represented the point of intersection between juvenile and criminal proceedings. By strengthening procedural formality at the waiver stage, the Court's decision could be presented as being supportive of the traditional aims of juvenile justice. Presumably, the purpose of introducing waiver hearings in *Kent* was to make it more difficult to transfer cases from juvenile to criminal courts, and thus fewer juveniles would be expelled from the juvenile justice system's rehabilitative embrace. Another way to view the situation, however, is to see jurisdictional waiver as an important safeguard of traditional juvenile justice. Without waiver, the juvenile justice system faced the threat of collapse under the weight of excessive demand on its scarce resources and because of the problems of legitimacy arising from the use of noncriminal proceedings for potentially serious and violent offenders. These different visions of the purposes of jurisdictional waiver underlying the conflict in *Kent* illustrate the difficulties inherent in judicial reform of juvenile justice, difficulties that would become even more evident in *Gault.*

4. *Gault:* The Road to Washington

Like many of the pivotal cases in American legal history, the *Gault* case encompassed several different settings and a changing cast of characters, ranging from the unlikely to the obvious. Also like other cases, the nature of *Gault* continuously evolved to reflect these changes. In Arizona, the physical setting was an old mining town surrounded by the ugly reminders of its former industry. The characters were the harried parents of two boys, local juvenile court officials of dubious qualifications and judgment, a refugee from New York's cold winters, and a state supreme court, some of whose judges had achieved surprising prominence in national affairs. In this setting, and guided by these characters, the principal issue raised by the case concerned parental custody rights, which Gerald Gault's parents argued had been taken from them without due process. From Arizona the setting moved to New York and Washington, where the cast of characters included prominent members of the national juvenile court reform movement and highly visible organizations such as the American Civil Liberties Union. For these individuals and organizations the important issue was to determine the rights and liberty interests of juveniles themselves.

Set against the background of three mountain ranges, Globe, Arizona, sits on the western edge of the San Carlos Indian Reservation, seventy-five miles east of Phoenix. By the late 1950s, Globe was no longer a prosperous western mining town but the quiet administrative seat of Gila County. With the local economy suffering, Paul Gault often sought employment away from Globe, and during summer 1964 he was working near the Grand Canyon. His wife, Marjorie, worked as a babysitter in Globe to help support their family. Although far from financially secure, the Gaults were not destitute. They lived in a relatively new mobile home park and were white, which put them at a distinct advantage relative to the residents of Globe's Mexican barrio or to the Apache Indians who lived on the nearby reservation.

The Gaults had two sons, Louis and his younger brother Gerald (who was born on January 23, 1949). In 1962, at the age of thirteen, Gerald came to the attention of the Gila County Juvenile Court for the first time when another boy accused him of taking his baseball glove. Two years later, in February 1964, the court asserted its jurisdiction over Gerald after the police found him in the company of another boy who had allegedly stolen a woman's wallet. On that occasion, the court ordered Gerald to "stay out of trouble" and placed him on six months' probation. In June, two months before the end of this probationary period, Gerald again found himself in trouble with court authorities. One of the Gaults' neighbors complained to authorities that Gerald had placed an obscene telephone call to her.

No one connected with Gerald Gault's case in summer 1964 could have known that they would become participants in an important episode of constitutional history. In June 1964, Morris Kent Jr.'s attorneys were still waiting for a decision from the D.C. Circuit Court of Appeals, and it was not until May 3, 1965, that their case was accepted for consideration by the Supreme Court. Chief Justice Warren did not articulate his concerns about juvenile court procedure until two weeks after Gerald's detention. To the law enforcement and juvenile court authorities of Gila County, their actions were perfectly consistent with the standard operating procedures of Arizona, and as far as they knew, with most other states in the nation.

That Arizona remained firmly attached to the nineteenth century juvenile court ideal, while states such as California and New York were undertaking important reforms of their juvenile court statutes, is not unusual. The final territory on the continental United States to acquire statehood, Arizona has never included policy innovation as one of its defining characteristics during its history as a territory or a state.[1] Nevertheless, Arizona did abandon its usual caution between 1900 and 1929 when populism, progressivism, and the drive to statehood dominated its political life.[2] Not surprisingly, it was during this period that Arizona's territorial government joined the nascent juvenile court movement, and it is with this legislative act that the story of *Gault* begins.

The Legal Framework of Juvenile Justice in Arizona

Arizona instituted special procedures for the treatment of juvenile offenders in 1907, when the Territorial Assembly passed Arizona's first juvenile court act. The statute was part of a longer list of social reform legislation passed by the twenty-fourth legislature, which included prison reform and stricter control of gambling and alcohol. In advancing the reforms, the proponents of these laws were pursuing a complicated agenda. Although agitation by social reformers was partly responsible for the legislation, the assembly's desire to demonstrate that the territory was civilized enough for statehood was even more important.[3] To this end, the juvenile court law followed the early twentieth-century consensus that the appropriate approach to "children lacking proper care or guardianship" was to house them separately and treat them differently from criminals.[4] Consequently, it provided that courts with responsibility for these children should exercise powers clearly distinguishable from those "exercised in the administration of the criminal law." After achieving statehood, Arizona took the important step of vesting its superior courts with explicit constitutional authority to exercise the special *parens patriae* powers over young offenders contained in the 1907 statute.[5]

The 1907 legislation remained in force until 1955, when Arizona enacted the Juvenile Code whose constitutionality would be challenged in *Gault*.[6] Under this statute, juvenile courts did not constitute courts of separate record but were established as divisions of the superior court of each county. Instead of creating a unique court system, the Juvenile Code established a special set of procedures for superior courts to follow when exercising their jurisdiction over dependent, neglected, and delinquent children. In smaller counties, superior court judges heard both juvenile and adult cases, adjusting their procedures accordingly. The code required that superior courts in larger counties designate one judge each year to serve exclusively as judge of the juvenile court.

Like its 1907 predecessor and other state juvenile codes, the 1955 code dispensed with the formalities of criminal procedure in order to create a nonadversarial setting in which judges could act in the best interests of the juveniles who appeared in their courtrooms. The code promoted this objective by providing for unrecorded, informal hearings conducted without juries in the privacy of judges' chambers. The statute gave probation officers, rather than legal counsel, the responsibility of representing and articulating the interests of juveniles who found themselves the subject of delinquency petitions. Judges were responsible for ascertaining facts, determining delinquency, and ordering dispositions. The code did not associate dispositions with specific acts but simply listed ten possible dispositions from which judges were free to choose, according to their perception of the "child's welfare and the interests of the state." Finally, the code provided that delinquency adjudications did not constitute criminal convictions, nor could they be used prejudicially in subsequent criminal proceedings against the juvenile.

In contrast to the systems in other states, Arizona's juvenile proceedings were relatively free from major criticism during the 1950s and early 1960s. Prior to Gerald Gault's case, the state's major law review had published only two items concerning juvenile procedure, one of which was a case note about an Arizona Supreme Court decision.[7] The only substantive article appeared in 1962, and in stark contrast to other law review writers of the era its author argued that the presence of legal counsel was unnecessary in juvenile hearings. Although the author—himself a juvenile court judge—conceded that judicial discretion unsupervised by legal counsel might in some cases lead to abuse, he asserted that nonadversarial hearings provided the best opportunity for determining the proper response to delinquent activity in specific instances. He argued that the success of juvenile courts depended on establishing a positive relationship among juveniles, their parents, and the court. "The concept of the State 'versus' the child," he wrote, "is the epitome of what the court is seeking to avoid."[8] The juvenile court was there to help, not to confront.

The noncriminal nature of proceedings under both the Juvenile Code and its 1907 predecessor constituted an important theme in the development of the case law surrounding Arizona's approach to juvenile justice. As construed by the state's appellate court, neither the 1955 nor the 1907 statute jeopardized any liberty interest held by minors. Instead, the case law recognized that these laws existed to protect and promote the welfare of children, which were goals best achieved by preserving the family unit. In 1931, for example, the Arizona Supreme Court described the 1907 statute as a measure designed to provide distinctive treatment procedures and programs for juveniles.[9] In 1942 the court upheld the requirement of confidentiality of juvenile records on the grounds that it was a necessary component of the state's policy of hiding "youthful errors from the full gaze of the public and bury[ing] them in the graveyard of the forgotten past."[10] In these cases and others, the court reached its decision by emphasizing the social welfare orientation of the juvenile courts established in 1907.

This mode of analysis continued unaltered into the 1960s. In 1963 the state supreme court overturned a juvenile's conviction as an adult in the superior court because the police had failed to contact a probation officer before interrogating the juvenile suspect. The police had used the lack of access to counsel in the informal atmosphere of the juvenile system to justify the interrogation, but the court held that this procedure contradicted the very rationale of that system. Procedural informality and the denial of certain rights to juveniles, the court ruled, aimed at promoting rehabilitation and at protecting children's welfare interests rather than at facilitating police interrogations.[11] Both procedural informality and any limits on its use derived from the same source: the state's concern with children's welfare. The notion that these limitations emanated from the constitutional rights of juveniles themselves, as was the case in ordinary criminal courts, simply did not exist. Indeed, in 1965 the supreme court denied that juveniles could claim a right to appeal juvenile court orders, since this right was not crucial to protect their welfare.[12]

To Arizona's Supreme Court judges, the ultimate objective of the state's juvenile court law was to protect children's welfare, which could be achieved without (and, perhaps, only without) applying the standard rules of criminal due process to juvenile proceedings. Child welfare was also advanced, however, by protecting parental custody rights, which, ironically, depended on guaranteeing parents some access to the usual trappings of adversarial proceedings. Two cases from the pre-1955 period—*Harper v. Tipple* and *Ex parte Winn*—are good examples of this feature of juvenile jurisprudence in Arizona. In *Harper* the supreme court considered an appeal from a superior court decision that had granted custody of a young girl to her maternal grandfather instead of to her father. On the one hand, the court recognized the necessity of judicial discretion in custody matters, since a judge's "paramount consideration" in such cases must be the child's welfare rather than the technical legal rights of parents. On the other hand, the appellate court warned that this discretion must be exercised cautiously, since "the court should not invade the natural right of the parent to the custody and care of an infant child, except upon a clear showing of delinquency on the part of the parent."[13] The supreme court upheld this ruling seventeen years later in *Winn,* arguing that in custody matters "it is not the personal liberty of the child but its welfare only that is involved, because the infant, for obvious reasons, is presumed to be in the custody of someone during its minority."[14] State courts were deeply concerned with safeguarding parental custody rights because of their relationship to the integrity of the family unit, which the Juvenile Code recognized as key in the promotion of children's welfare.

This concern with parental custody rights was most clearly articulated in *Arizona State Department of Public Welfare v. Barlow.*[15] Decided in 1956, *Barlow* involved applications for writs of habeas corpus filed by the parents of seventeen juveniles who had been placed in the Department of Public Welfare's custody following dependency and neglect proceedings in various juvenile courts. The writs had been filed in the Maricopa County Superior Court, which eventually ordered the department to return the children to the custody of their parents. The department appealed this order to the Arizona Supreme Court, which upheld the lower court's ruling and vacated the original commitment orders placing the children in the custody of state welfare authorities.

According to the supreme court, deficiencies in the original dependency and neglect hearings had violated the fundamental rights of the juveniles' parents. The court argued that, given the importance of the family unit, any party seeking to remove a child from parental custody bears the burden of proving "that it is not to the best interest and welfare of the child for the parents to retain custody." Therefore, the court concluded, juvenile courts cannot be entirely immune from due process requirements. Although affirming the distinctive, noncriminal character of juvenile courts, the supreme court held that the Juvenile Code's reliance on procedural informality merely constituted "legislative authorization for the court to disregard technical matters of procedure which do not affect the fundamental rights of litigants to due process of law." However, parental interest in the custody of their children, the court averred, is sufficiently important to prohibit juvenile courts from denying parents their fundamental due process right to representation by counsel in dependency and neglect proceedings. Yet the court stressed that its holding was "limited to a consideration of the rights of other persons who may be affected by the determination of custody" and did not "embrace the rights of minors in juvenile hearings."[16]

As interpreted by the Arizona court in *Barlow* and in other decisions, the state's Juvenile Code granted juveniles a right to special treatment, protected them from criminal proceedings, and restricted the types of action that the state could take against them. The court also confirmed that the principal right that juveniles possess is to protective custody rather than to liberty. The purpose of juvenile court hearings, in the court's view, was to determine what form of custody—parental or state (both directly and through probationary supervision)—would serve the child's best interest, a determination that could be made without interfering with any other rights possessed by juveniles. Moreover, since the statute permitted the state to remove juveniles from their parents' custody, the court ruled that juvenile proceedings did affect the fundamental natural rights of parents, which had to be protected through such devices as representation by counsel. This is where matters stood when the Gila County Juvenile Court committed Gerald Gault to the State Industrial School in 1964.

From Committal to Habeas Corpus

When Marjorie Gault returned home from work at 6:00 P.M. on June 8, 1964, she learned from neighbors that Gerald and his friend Ronnie Lewis had been taken away by sheriff's deputies. Mrs. Gault went immediately to the juvenile detention home, where she was told that there would be a hearing on Gerald's case at 3:00 P.M. the next day. The Gaults' legal odyssey thus began on June 9, 1964, when the Gila County Juvenile Court heard a petition filed by the county's probation officer, Charles D. Flagg. The petition asked that Gerald be found delinquent and that an order be made regarding his care and custody. The hearing took place in the chambers of superior court judge Robert McGhee (acting in his capacity as juvenile court judge) and in the presence of Gerald, his mother and older brother (Paul Gault was still away working), and Probation Officer Flagg (another probation officer was also present). Judge McGhee did not reach a decision on the petition during this initial hearing, and Gerald remained in custody for three additional days.

Gerald was finally released to his parents on Friday, June 12, and later that afternoon Mrs. Gault received a short, handwritten note from Probation Officer Flagg informing her that Judge McGhee would hold a second hearing on Gerald's delinquency at 11:00 A.M. on the following Monday (June 15). In attendance at this hearing were both of Gerald's parents (Mr. Gault had returned home over the weekend), Probation Officer Flagg, and Ronnie Lewis and his father. At the conclusion of this hearing, Judge McGhee upheld the facts alleged in the petition and ordered Gerald committed to the Arizona Industrial School at Fort Grant for an indeterminate period. In Gerald's case, this meant the possibility of six years confinement in an institution of questionable rehabilitative value. Located ninety miles southeast of Globe, Fort Grant had been established in 1859 by the federal government as a military base to protect settlers in the area. Abandoned in 1905, the fort became the site of the Industrial School in 1912 when the existing facilities at Benson were declared too dangerous for occupancy. Gerald would eventually spend six months in this century-old army barracks. An adult found guilty of a similar offense, which Judge McGhee later identified as consisting of uttering an obscenity in the presence of women or children, would have faced a maximum penalty of two months in jail or a fine of fifty dollars.

As required by the Juvenile Code, both the June 9 and June 15 hearings were conducted informally, in the judge's chambers, and without any participation by counsel acting on behalf of Gerald or his parents. Further, the juvenile court did not require the presence of or testimony from the complainant, Mrs. Cook, nor did the court keep a written record of its proceedings in either hearing. The only information about what occurred at the hearings is found in testimony elicited during later habeas corpus proceedings.

The testimony from these proceedings suggests that the delinquency hearings may have suffered from at least three flaws, even by the existing standards of Arizona law. First, the nature of Gerald's participation in the call was never firmly established. Although Judge McGhee testified during the habeas corpus proceedings that Gerald had admitted asking at least one of the questions at the June 9 hearing, Gerald himself claimed that he had only admitted dialing the woman's telephone number but had denied asking any of the questions. This factual ambiguity was relatively insignificant, however. Because Gerald was on probation and had been ordered to "stay out of trouble," any participation in the call, however peripheral, was probably sufficient to find him delinquent under the Arizona code. The second flaw in the hearings was more significant. The absence of the complainant from the hearings meant that the court did not hear the testimony necessary for establishing the factual basis of the petition, for determining the seriousness of the misbehavior, or for guiding the judge's disposition of the case. The third and most important deficiency was the fact that Gerald's parents had not benefited from the assistance of counsel in hearings, the potential consequence of which was the loss of parental custody. This fact raised the possibility that the hearings were at odds with the requirements established in *Barlow*.

This third deficiency became the focus of the initial efforts by Gerald's parents to regain custody of their son. Six weeks after the juvenile court issued its commitment order they traveled to Phoenix and contacted Philip Haggerty, the chief criminal trial lawyer in the Arizona attorney general's office, in order to obtain advice about securing Gerald's release from the Industrial School. A thirty-two-year-old lawyer with five years experience, Haggerty called Amelia Lewis, an experienced attorney who had moved to Arizona and been admitted to the state bar in 1958 after retiring from her law practice in New York City. An active member of the American Civil Liberties Union, first in New York and then in northern Arizona, Lewis met with the Gaults in her office on August 1 and agreed to assist them despite her limited background in juvenile law. Meeting Lewis and persuading her to participate in the case was a stroke of luck for the Gaults; not only was she an experienced and dedicated civil rights lawyer, but her son had been a Columbia University classmate of Norman Dorsen, who taught constitutional law at New York University and served on the national executive of the ACLU. This informal personal contact would later prove invaluable in securing the ACLU's participation in the case at the Supreme Court level.

Lewis's initial response to the Gaults' situation was that she should pursue an appeal through the usual Arizona appellate process. When she discovered that the Juvenile Code precluded this course of action, Lewis contacted Arizona Supreme Court justice Lorna Lockwood about the possibility of filing a petition for habeas corpus. A graduate of the Arizona Law School in Tucson, Justice Lockwood had amassed an impressive record of public service by 1964. It included five years in the Arizona House of Representatives, service on the legal staff of the Office of Price Administration during World War II, service as assistant attorney general of Arizona, and a position as a superior court judge in Maricopa County. In 1961 Lockwood was elected to the Arizona Supreme Court, and in 1965 her male colleagues unanimously elected her chief justice, making her the first woman in the United States to hold such a post. She would be reelected to the position in 1969.

Lewis met with Lockwood on August 3, and with the justice's help, filed the petition for habeas corpus the same day. The writ of habeas corpus is one of the most important components of the common law, and access to it is explicitly guaranteed by the federal and state constitutions. In its usual form, a habeas corpus writ commands any person detaining another to produce the detained person in order to test the legality of the detention or imprisonment. Although limited to determining whether someone has been detained according to due process, rather than to determining the person's guilt or innocence, habeas corpus was described by Sir William Blackstone as "the most celebrated writ in the English Law."[17] With no formal appeal procedure available under the state's juvenile court statute, it was the only means of reviewing Gerald's committal to Fort Grant.

When Lewis met Justice Lockwood, she had not yet prepared a formal petition for habeas corpus; Lewis had only an affidavit from the Gaults setting forth the facts of the case as they remembered them. Lockwood suggested that Lewis simply add a caption to the affidavit, which she would accept as a "petition in the form of affidavit." Lockwood then called the chief judge of the Maricopa County Superior Court to ask for his assistance in arranging a hearing on the petition, which eventually took place on August 17 before superior court judge Fred Hyder. The petition challenged Gerald's commitment on two grounds. First, Lewis argued that the juvenile court had failed to follow even the minimal procedural requirements of the Juvenile Code. She carefully avoided a direct attack against the constitutionality of these requirements, however. Her petition praised the code for promoting the care and protection of children, and she conceded that informal proceedings should be the norm in juvenile courts and that counsel could be excluded in most cases.[18] Her principal complaint was that the judge in Gerald's case had transformed informality into arbitrariness by ignoring the statutory requirements of the code and by denying Gerald's parents due process.

The petition's second complaint was that Gerald's parents had not been represented by counsel, a complaint based on the parental right to counsel granted in *Barlow*. This was a difficult argument to make, since *Barlow*'s applicability to the circumstances of Gerald's commitment was somewhat ambiguous. There was no evidence, for example, that the juvenile court had expressly denied the Gaults representation by counsel, as had been the case in *Barlow*. Lewis attempted to meet this objection by arguing that the juvenile court's failure to inquire specifically whether the Gaults were appearing knowingly and voluntarily without counsel amounted to an outright denial of representation. Because the "natural and legal rights of these parents to their minor child's custody" were at stake, Lewis argued, the juvenile court should have exercised greater care in protecting those rights.[19] This argument failed to resolve the ambiguity entirely, however, because of *Barlow*'s association with dependency and neglect proceedings where parental fitness was in question and where loss of custody was as much a sanction against unfit parents as a form of protective intervention. Under these circumstances it made sense to grant parents procedural protection. Whether *Barlow* mandated similar protections in delinquency proceedings, where parental fitness was not so directly at issue, was unclear.

Neither Lewis's legal arguments nor the testimony she elicited during the habeas corpus hearing impressed Judge Hyder, however, and he dismissed the petition immediately after the hearing with a three-line order remanding Gerald to the custody of the Industrial School. Although the order meant that Gerald had to return to Fort Grant, the outcome was not entirely negative, since under Arizona law it provided the opportunity for a direct appeal to the state supreme court. With this shift in venue came the first significant signs that Gerald's case might grow in importance to overshadow its origins as a desperate attempt by two parents to regain custody of their son.

Appeal to the Arizona Supreme Court

The first indication of this growing importance was the interest in the case displayed by the Arizona Civil Liberties Union, which responded positively to Amelia Lewis's request for legal and financial assistance with the appeal. As might be expected of the state chapter of the ACLU, its interest in the case extended beyond Gerald's own plight. The organization participated "not only to assist the petitioners here, but because it presents a clear opportunity for this court further to delineate the standards of due process to be maintained in the juvenile courts of the state." It thereby urged the Arizona court "to take a second look at the Juvenile Code of Arizona and how the children of this state are faring under it, to the end that just and consistent procedures be established."[20] In support of this request, the organization quoted Roscoe Pound's statement to a U.S. Senate committee that the "powers of the Star Chamber were a trifle in comparison with those of our juvenile courts and courts of domestic relations."[21]

A second sign of the case's growing importance could be found in the nature of the argument made to the Arizona court itself. Lewis broadened her attack on Gerald's detention from a narrow focus on the procedural irregularities of his delinquency hearings to the constitutional status of the statutory framework that permitted those alleged irregularities. Indeed, Lewis asked the court whether the Juvenile Code was unconstitutional in failing to provide for "timely and adequate notice to children and parents of the charges made, to provide a record of the proceedings be made and of findings of fact, and for an appeal."[22] Nevertheless, the principal issue on which the case turned remained whether delinquency hearings deprived parents of rightful custody through improper proceedings rather than whether they deprived juveniles of liberty in violation of the due process requirements of the federal Constitution.

Amelia Lewis submitted her brief to the Arizona Supreme Court on November 17, 1964. After summarizing the sequence of events as revealed by the habeas corpus hearing, the brief listed six sets of errors that had corrupted the process through which the state had committed Gerald to the Industrial School.[23] At the top of the list was the unconstitutionality of the Juvenile Code itself, whose failure to provide adequate notice of the nature of the charges and the timing of hearings constituted a failure of due process. Next on the list came twelve separate procedural errors committed by the juvenile court, ranging from the court's failure to advise Gerald's parents of their right to counsel to its decision to suspend parental custody without any showing that Gerald's parents were incompetent. The third set of errors was aimed at the manner in which the lower court had conducted the habeas corpus hearing. Most of these errors concerned rulings by the lower court that had allegedly limited the scope of the petitioners' examination of the juvenile court judge. Fourth on the list of errors was an attack on the failure to require proof beyond a reasonable doubt in juvenile court proceedings.

Fifth, the brief alleged that the probation officers erred by taking Gerald into custody without receiving prior approval from the juvenile court. The sixth assignment of error alleged that the absence of any provision for appeal from the final decisions of juvenile courts constituted a failure of due process.

These assignments of error rested on five important propositions of law that Lewis advanced. The first of these propositions asserted that two conditions had to be met before the state could sustain a commitment of delinquency and remove a child from his or her parents' custody. It is important to note that Lewis linked delinquency commitments to loss of parental custody rather than to the child's loss of liberty. This approach stands in stark contrast, of course, to the relationship between incarceration and loss of personal freedom posited in ordinary criminal proceedings. To a large degree, Lewis was content to work within the general framework of traditional approaches to juvenile justice.

According to Lewis, in order to suspend parental custody, the state had to show both that the juvenile had engaged in delinquent behavior and that the delinquent behavior occurred because "the parent or legal guardian is incompetent or has neglected and failed to care and provide for the child or is unable to handle the child."[24] Lewis asserted that the parental incompetence test developed for dependency and neglect proceedings in earlier cases should also apply to delinquency proceedings. She buttressed this argument by playing on the anticommunist sympathies of the era and the state. Quoting from the Communist Manifesto, she argued that communism, unlike democracy, aims at destroying the "bourgeois" family; consequently, legal procedures designed to prevent the state from invading and breaking down family life are an important safeguard of democracy.[25] Similar arguments had been used successfully in the NAACP's battle against racial segregation, with the LDF asserting that the continuing existence of Jim Crow legislation hampered the United States in its ideological and political struggle with the Soviet Union.[26]

The second legal proposition to which Lewis directed the court's attention was simply that due process of law requires, at a minimum, fair hearings. According to Lewis, the procedural deficiencies of Gerald's delinquency hearings, which the testimony elicited during the habeas corpus proceedings allegedly revealed, clearly demonstrated that the Gila County Juvenile Court had failed to meet this simple requirement.[27] These deficiencies included the juvenile court's failure to notify Gerald's parents of the charges against him, to provide for confrontation and cross-examination of witnesses, to advise either Gerald or his parents of their rights to call witnesses and to retain counsel, to guarantee the privilege against self-incrimination, to warn of the possible consequences of the hearings, and to make findings of fact and to record the proceedings.[28] In Lewis's view, these deficiencies made it impossible for the juvenile court to determine fairly or accurately either Gerald's delinquency or his parents' incompetence. These errors were exacerbated by the absence of a right to appeal the court's findings directly.[29]

The third, fourth, and fifth propositions of law that Lewis advanced were less central to her argument but were important, nevertheless.[30] The third proposition asserted that law enforcement authorities must receive prior authorization from the juvenile court itself before taking any child into custody, a circumstance that clearly had not occurred in Gerald's case. Fourth, Lewis argued that in habeas corpus proceedings the burden of proof shifts to the respondent to show the legality of detention, once the petitioner makes a prima facie case of illegality. In her view, the Maricopa County Superior Court had not followed this rule in the proceedings against juvenile court judge McGhee. In the fifth instance, Lewis proposed that the law provided for witnesses to be cross-examined on any matter relevant to a petition, leading her to complain that her examination of Judge McGhee during habeas corpus proceedings had been unduly circumscribed.

In addition to Lorna Lockwood, the five-member court that deliberated on these arguments contained two other judges of some distinction: Ernest W. McFarland and Levi Udall. Born in 1894, Justice McFarland had graduated from Stanford Law School in 1922. He served as a judge of the Pima County Superior Court from 1935 until 1941, when he was elected to the U.S. Senate, where he served for twelve years, including two (1951–1953) as Senate Majority Leader. McFarland returned to Arizona and became governor in 1955, a position he held until 1959. Not content to leave public life altogether, he was elected to the Arizona Supreme Court in 1964. For his part, Justice Udall belonged to one of Arizona's leading Mormon families and producers of national politicians. United by their common drive to public service, Justices Lockwood, McFarland, and Udall would also be united in their support for traditional juvenile procedures.

The Arizona Supreme Court unanimously rejected Lewis's claim that her clients had been denied due process, and it affirmed the superior court's denial of habeas corpus.[31] In constructing its decision, the court adopted an approach to juvenile due process that focused on the specific interests at stake in the proceedings and the type of hearing under consideration. Thus, although the court agreed that juvenile courts were not entirely exempt from due process requirements, it ruled that the applicable procedural standards must be derived from, and be consistent with, the unique nature and function of juvenile proceedings. "Our task," it declared, "is to determine the procedural due process elements to which an infant and his parents are entitled in a juvenile hearing and decide whether our statute may be construed to include them."[32] The court declined the invitation to set new procedural standards against which to judge the Juvenile Code but did clarify standards relating to notice, sworn testimony, and evidence. It found, however, that none of these standards had been violated in the proceedings against Gerald.

The court's opinion began by noting that juvenile court laws in every state provided "for less than the full set of due process guarantees available in a criminal proceeding" and that "the overwhelming majority of courts have expressly or impliedly recognized the statutes to be constitutional." It attributed this state of the law to the underlying theory of juvenile justice policy that the "delinquent is the child of, rather than the enemy of society and their interests coincide." Juvenile court laws, the court continued, recognize a special relationship between the child and society and authorize the state to act "*in loco parentis* to the child." Juvenile proceedings, the court averred, represent "an effort to substitute protection and guidance for punishment, to withdraw the child from criminal jurisdiction and use social sciences regarding the study of human behaviour which permit flexibilities within the procedures."[33] The court agreed, however, that procedural flexibility could not justify unrestrained judicial discretion. Relying on *Barlow,* it affirmed that only "technical matters of procedure not affecting the fundamental right to due process of law" could be abandoned in the interests of informality and flexibility. Moreover, the court extended the *Barlow* principle in an unexpected direction by applying it to the rights of juveniles in delinquency proceedings. "Good intentions," it wrote, "do not justify depriving a child of due process of law. Fairness is not inimical to the proper treatment of juveniles. Fairness is as good for them as it is for adults."[34] Thus, the court recognized that juveniles have interests at stake in delinquency proceedings that are distinguishable from those of both their parents and the state.

Although the court's recognition of this principle was an unexpected victory for the Gaults and the Arizona Civil Liberties Union, the application of that principle offered mixed results. The court's evaluation of the steps that "fairness" required in delinquency proceedings was driven by its desire to maintain the confidentiality of juvenile proceedings and to avoid creating excessively adversarial hearings. The court declared that fairness did not require that juveniles be granted the rights to appeal and confrontation, the privilege against self-incrimination, or the right to verbatim transcripts and records of the proceedings.[35] Yet it ruled that juvenile courts must provide reasonable prior notice before conducting a hearing and an oral statement during the hearing of the facts supporting the petition.[36] The court also ruled that delinquency petitions must be supported by clear and convincing evidence and that all witnesses "who are part of or officially related to the juvenile court structure" must be sworn before providing testimony.[37] Finally, although the court affirmed its *Barlow* rule that parents could not be denied counsel, it refused to extend the same protection to juveniles.[38] The court ruled that juvenile court judges were in the best position to determine on a case-by-case basis whether a juvenile would benefit from counsel.

For Gerald Gault and his parents, the immediate effect of the decision was defeat. The court found as matters of fact that Gerald's parents knew the nature of the charges against their son; were aware of their rights to retain counsel, call witnesses, and cross-examine the probation officer; and understood that the juvenile court appearance could result in commitment to the State Industrial School. The court also found that the Gaults had voluntarily appeared at the two July hearings without counsel. It thus determined that due process had not been denied prior to Gerald's commitment, even under the newly articulated standards of juvenile due process.

It has often been observed that in landmark constitutional cases defeat in the lower court points the way toward possible victory in the Supreme Court by providing pegs on which to hang future appeals. The most famous example of this is *Brown v. Board of Education* (1954).[39] In 1951 the U.S. District Court in Kansas ruled against the petitioners in *Brown*, but in so doing it made an important finding of fact: Segregated education affects African-American children detrimentally by inflicting on them a psychological sense of inferiority.[40] Although the district court refused to overrule the separate-but-equal doctrine established in *Plessy v. Ferguson* (1896)[41] on its own initiative, its finding of fact pointed out the doctrine's most vulnerable element. In making its 1896 decision, the Supreme Court had concluded that there was no objective basis for any feelings of inferiority associated with segregation.[42] The legal basis for the *Plessy* doctrine, in other words, was grounded in psychology rather than in the Constitution. The district court's finding of fact in *Brown* directly contradicted the psychological dimensions of the *Plessy* decision and thereby undermined its legal conclusions. The key to overturning the *Plessy* doctrine, therefore, was to persuade the Supreme Court to accept new psychological evidence. The nature of its lower court defeat led the NAACP to concentrate its efforts at the Supreme Court level on elaborating the district court's psychological finding, which it did successfully. The *Brown* Court accepted the argument that segregation denotes the inferiority of African Americans, that this sense of inferiority reduces African American children's motivation to learn, and that this lack of motivation impedes the intellectual development of African American children and perpetuates inequality.

As in *Brown,* therefore, a negative decision by a lower court offered the possibility of future relief by suggesting to Lewis and the Gaults possible strategies for an appeal to the U.S. Supreme Court. One avenue was to accept the Arizona court's use of the fairness doctrine and then challenge its specific application of that doctrine in the juvenile court context. Another possibility was to ask the Court to review delinquency proceedings according to a different standard altogether. Moreover, the state court's unexpected extension of *Barlow* suggested that an appeal focusing on the liberty interests of juveniles might bear better fruit than one stressing parental custody rights. Ultimately, Gerald's attorneys combined the latter two strategies to attack the Juvenile Code in the Supreme Court. The litigation strategy consequently shifted from seeking fundamental fairness protection for parental custody rights to demanding the protection of juveniles' liberty interests by selectively incorporating the Bill of Rights into state juvenile proceedings through the Fourteenth Amendment.

Preparations for the U.S. Supreme Court

After her defeat in Arizona, Amelia Lewis wrote to Melvin Wulf, the ACLU's national legal director, to solicit his advice and aid in challenging the Arizona court's ruling in the U.S. Supreme Court.[43] Lewis's letter arrived at an opportune moment. Although the ACLU's founder, Roger Baldwin, had coauthored one of the early leading texts on juvenile justice,[44] the issue had not been an active part of the ACLU's agenda before the mid-1950s.[45] The first reference to procedural deficiencies in juvenile courts appeared in the ACLU's 1956 *Annual Report,* in which the organization summarized a study conducted by its Philadelphia chapter concerning the civil liberties issues raised by juvenile procedures in Pennsylvania. Although the study recognized the "worthy motivations" behind those procedures, it criticized juvenile court statutes for failing to separate fact-finding (adjudication) proceedings from the determination of appropriate treatment (dispositions).[46] Drawing this distinction between adjudication and dispositional decisions was significant since it implied that the court's jurisdiction to intervene should be triggered by the commission of a specific offense, even though the purpose of juvenile court intervention might be to ameliorate a destructive behavioral pattern. In 1959 the ACLU's Pennsylvania state chapter recommended that the same rules of evidence should apply in disputed adjudication proceedings in juvenile courts as applied in the state's criminal courts. The chapter also recommended that juveniles be accorded the right to confront and cross-examine witnesses in such proceedings.[47] Within five years of the Pennsylvania reports, ACLU chapters in twelve states and the District of Columbia were engaged in similar activity on behalf of juvenile court reform. By the time the *Gault* case was ready for the Supreme Court, the ACLU's national due process committee had itself begun to develop an interest in juvenile rights and had asked its Florida affiliate to prepare a discussion paper on the constitutional rights of juvenile defendants.[48]

Wulf agreed to provide technical and financial support for the appeal, beginning with his own revision of Lewis's proposed notice of appeal to the Arizona court. His principal suggestion was that Lewis reformulate her "natural rights" argument for procedural protection of parental custody as a "right to privacy" matter, on the assumption that the latter would be received more favorably by the Supreme Court.[49] First articulated in an 1890 article by Samuel Warren and Louis Brandeis,[50] the right to privacy had been powerfully expanded in the Court's 1965 decision in *Griswold v. Connecticut*.[51] In *Griswold*, the Court had struck down a Connecticut statute prohibiting the use of contraceptives on the grounds that the law violated an implicit constitutional right to privacy that the Court purported to discover in the "penumbral emanations" of several provisions of the Bill of Rights.[52] According to the Court, these amendments each protected an aspect of personal privacy that, when viewed in their entirety, pointed to a general right to privacy protected by the Constitution. The specific context in which Justice William Douglas had applied the right in *Griswold* must have made it appear particularly relevant to Lewis's case, since the justice had placed tremendous emphasis on the sanctity of the marital relationship. If the right to privacy protected the marriage relationship from undue state interference, it was only a small step to argue that the right should similarly protect the family unit more broadly understood.

Lewis filed the revised notice in February 1966 and sent her case file to Wulf, along with a draft jurisdictional statement. She asked the ACLU to take primary responsibility for the appeal, and by spring 1966 Wulf's staff controlled the litigation.[53] Lewis participated infrequently in the case's preparation thereafter, later complaining mildly to Wulf that she had not been consulted more frequently about the brief prepared on her clients' be-half.[54]

Wulf forwarded Lewis's file to Gertrude Mainzer of the Project on Social Welfare Law at New York University. Established in 1966, this project was engaged in research and litigation designed to advance the rights of persons entitled to public benefits and protections. The project existed as part of the Arthur Garfield Hays Civil Liberties Program at NYU. Founded in 1958 to advance civil liberties and public interest law, the Hays Program provided the ACLU with high-level research skills and litigation expertise. Indeed, the program served as the focus for much of the ACLU's public interest litiga-tion activity.[55] In 1963, for example, the ACLU, operating through the Hays Program, filed an amicus brief in *Gideon v. Wainwright* to support the right to appointed counsel. Two years later, the program exhibited its wider con-cerns by cosponsoring a symposium on poverty and civil liberties with the Office of Economic Opportunity, which eventually led to the ACLU's suc-cessful litigation against statutes imposing disadvantages on illegitimate children. Although not directly connected in a formal way, the close links and strong overlap between the objectives and personnel of the Hays Pro-gram and the ACLU made their relationship something less than arm's length.

Wulf asked Mainzer to review the file and to examine the adequacy of Lewis's statement of facts.[56] Mainzer's reaction was surprisingly negative; she did not think that *Gault* was the best case in which to resolve successfully most of the issues that Lewis had raised.[57] Wulf concurred, agreeing with Mainzer that the case's greatest strength was its argument for granting juve-niles the constitutional right to counsel in delinquency proceedings. Wulf based this judgment in part on a decision rendered by the Mississippi Su-preme Court on April 4, 1966. The Mississippi court had pointed out that the state's juvenile code recognized the possibility that delinquency proceedings could be adversarial in nature and thereby provided for appearances by counsel on behalf of both the state and juveniles. Therefore, the court ar-gued, juvenile courts had an obligation to advise minors and their parents of the statutory right to representation by counsel.[58] Wulf's reaction to the Mississippi decision was obvious in a short letter he wrote to Mainzer: "If Mississippi holds that juveniles are entitled to counsel, I would think that every other state in the Union would be ashamed to do otherwise."[59]

Despite concerns about the case's overall suitability, the ACLU filed a wide-ranging jurisdictional statement on May 2, 1966, asking the Supreme Court to entertain a direct appeal of the Arizona decision.[60] Proceeding by direct appeal, the method that Wulf had recommended to Lewis in November 1965,[61] is one of two ways by which cases may come before the Supreme Court. In theory, the Court's mandatory appellate jurisdiction includes cases in which (1) federal courts rule congressional acts unconstitutional and where the federal government is a party to the dispute; (2) federal courts find conflicts between state laws and the U.S. Constitution or a federal law; (3) state supreme courts hold acts of Congress unconstitutional; and (4) state supreme courts uphold the validity of state laws against claims that they violate the federal Constitution or a federal law.[62] In practice, since direct appellants from state courts must still demonstrate that their cases raise "a substantial federal question," the Court exercises significant discretion even where it is supposedly required to consider an appeal. This discretion is even greater with respect to certiorari, the device through which the Court exercises its discretionary jurisdiction over other cases decided by federal appellate courts and those decided by state supreme courts involving issues of federal law. The distinction between the Court's mandatory and discretionary appellate jurisdiction is therefore more apparent than real, and motions for direct appeal are usually considered automatically as petitions for certiorari as well. In effect, the Court exercises virtually complete control over its own docket, with more than 95 percent of its docket coming on certiorari.[63] Persuading the Court to hear Gerald's appeal was thus a critical step.

The ACLU's jurisdictional statement listed Norman Dorsen, a colleague of Mainzer's at NYU Law School, as Gerald Gault's principal attorney. A graduate of Columbia and Harvard, Dorsen had served as a law clerk to Justice John Marshall Harlan during the Supreme Court's 1957–1958 term. After a short time in private practice, Dorsen started his teaching career at NYU in 1961, where he also served as director of the Hays Civil Liberties Program. He then became the ACLU's general counsel (1969–1976) before serving as its president for fifteen years (1976–1991).

Dorsen's jurisdictional statement presented a single question for the Court's consideration:

> Whether the Juvenile Code of Arizona . . . on its face or as construed and applied, is invalid under the Due Process Clause of the Fourteenth Amendment to the [U.S.] Constitution because it authorizes a juvenile to be taken from the custody of his parents and to be committed to a state institution by a judicial proceeding which confers unlimited discretion upon the Juvenile Court.[64]

The statement continued by arguing that the "unlimited discretion" of juvenile courts led to six specific abuses of process, including (1) denial of the right to adequate notice of the charges constituting the child's delinquency;

(2) denial of the right to counsel; (3) denial of the right to confront and cross-examine witnesses; (4) denial of the privilege against self-incrimination; (5) denial of the right to a transcript of proceedings; and (6) denial of the right to appellate review of the juvenile court's decision. Dorsen had wanted to omit the fifth and sixth issues, but Amelia Lewis asserted her privilege as Gerald's first attorney to insist that they be included.[65]

Dorsen argued that the federal constitutional issue raised in *Gault* was substantial because it questioned "the extent to which fundamental requirements of procedural fairness guaranteed by the Due Process Clause of the Fourteenth Amendment are applicable to juvenile court proceedings."[66] Deciding this question, Dorsen asserted, was important for two reasons. First, it would clarify the Court's ruling in *Kent*, where Justice Fortas had criticized state juvenile courts for their lack of procedural rigor but had not decided whether the constitutional guarantees of due process applicable to criminal proceedings also govern juvenile proceedings.[67] Second, the number of juveniles placed at jeopardy through delinquency hearings was increasing; therefore, the Court could use *Gault* to clarify the "basic rights of large numbers of individuals who are being deprived of their liberty without due process of law."[68] Following the Arizona Supreme Court's lead, Dorsen advanced fundamental fairness as the appropriate standard of due process review in the juvenile court context.

The jurisdictional statement forced the Court to face squarely the constitutional issue it had been able to avoid in *Kent*. By accepting jurisdiction on the ACLU's terms, the Court clearly committed itself to making a decision with substantial constitutional impact, whether it upheld or undercut traditional juvenile court procedures. The statement also revealed the manner in which the ACLU had reshaped *Gault* to make the case consistent with its own aims and interests. The ACLU played down some of the issues raised by Lewis in Arizona and instead emphasized the threat that delinquency committals posed to the liberty interests of juveniles; Lewis had stressed parental custody rights. The organization also alerted the Court to the national importance of the deficiencies in juvenile proceedings allegedly exposed by Gerald's case. The statement's reference to the "large numbers of individuals" subjected to proceedings similar to those Gerald had suffered served to underscore this importance.

The Supreme Court added *In re Gault* to its docket on June 20, 1966—the last day of its 1965 term and barely three months after its decision in *Kent*.[69] Given Chief Justice Warren's 1964 speech and Justice Fortas's remarks in *Kent*, it is hardly surprising that a case involving the constitutionality of traditional juvenile proceedings would eventually be accepted for review by the

Court. Indeed, only ten weeks earlier (April 4), the Court had granted certiorari in a case from Washington State, *Miller v. Rhay*.[70] Miller had been transferred from juvenile court to criminal court jurisdiction, convicted, and subsequently incarcerated. He was seeking release from custody on a writ of habeas corpus on the grounds that the juvenile court had improperly transferred jurisdiction over his case. The *Miller* case thus provided the Supreme Court with an opportunity to upgrade the waiver standards articulated in *Kent* from statutory to constitutional rules. On April 28, however, the Washington Supreme Court delivered its decision in *Dillenburg v. Maxwell,* in which it nullified a transfer order on the grounds that no hearing had taken place prior to the jurisdictional waiver decision.[71] Thus, the Supreme Court did not address the substantive issues raised in *Miller;* it simply vacated the lower court decision and remanded the case for rehearing in Washington in light of the *Dillenburg* decision.[72]

The turn of events in the *Miller* case left the Court temporarily without a vehicle for its first journey into the previously unexplored constitutional territory of juvenile justice. As it turned out, this development was only a momentary setback for juvenile court reformers. The loss of the *Miller* case prompted the Court to look closely at *Gault,* a case that raised broader constitutional questions and presented an even more sympathetic set of facts. Unlike *Kent,* which involved a particularly brutal set of crimes and where the defendant at least had been given the opportunity to defend himself according to the relatively rigorous procedures of a criminal trial, both the absence of procedural regularity in Gerald's hearings and the disproportionality of his punishment to his offense were blatantly obvious. As one commentator later argued, *Gault* presented the Court with an "easy" case from which it could conclude that procedural rights would improve the performance of juvenile courts without inhibiting their "child welfare mission."[73] Thus, the Supreme Court substituted *Gault* for the Washington case over which it had previously noted jurisdiction. With probable jurisdiction noted by the Court, work began almost immediately on the ACLU's brief.

5. *Gault* in the Supreme Court

Once Gerald Gault's case left Arizona, it took on national importance and ceased to be a matter of merely local interest. The case fit perfectly with the ACLU's agenda of the early 1960s and with its approach to public interest litigation. Beginning in 1932 the ACLU had played a leading role in the development of new constitutional standards for the administration of criminal justice, and its arguments had been pivotal in the Supreme Court's landmark decisions in *Mapp* (1961), *Escobedo* (1964), and *Miranda* (1966).[1] Further, lawyers associated with the ACLU participated in other litigation campaigns, such as the NAACP LDF's campaign against the death penalty. As the organization's principal historian has commented, "The combination of an activist Court and the popular pressure of the civil rights movement created a unique moment in the history of civil liberties. Lawyers responded with fresh ideas and found in the ACLU a channel for their energies."[2] The ACLU's position in *Gault* epitomized the organization's growing skepticism of the social welfare programs developed during the Progressive Era, including those—such as the juvenile court and its accompanying philosophy—that had been created through the efforts of the ACLU's own founders. The thread connecting this general skepticism with the campaign against police misconduct and the absence of due process in judicial proceedings was the ACLU's growing concern about the potential for abuse latent in the discretionary power exercised by the professionals who administered those programs.[3] Nevertheless, the organization was not engaged in a systematic litigation campaign to reform juvenile courts, nor was it actively looking for a case in which to raise the issue. When the proper case presented itself, however, the ACLU embraced it enthusiastically.

The Case Against *Parens Patriae*

THE ACLU'S BRIEF

During July and August, James Murray, a New York attorney whom Wulf had recruited in June to assist with the case, prepared an initial draft of the ACLU's position. Murray argued in his draft that the procedural means used by juvenile courts were counterproductive to realizing their desired ends of individualized justice and benevolent treatment. "Begun as non-criminal treatment for the sake of protection of the child," Murray wrote with reference to the procedural informality of juvenile courts, "juvenile court proceedings have led in many cases to non-criminal treatment *without* protection of the child."[4] The procedures employed in juvenile courts, Murray argued, often produced results contrary to those intended by the institution's founders. He cited several authorities as proof of the proposition that standards of fair procedure would promote the original intentions of the juvenile court movement, including such sources as the New York and California legislatures, the National Probation and Parole Association,[5] and the U.S. Department of Health, Education, and Welfare. The procedural standards advocated by these authorities, Murray claimed, did not depreciate individualized justice but merely revitalized it "in accordance with the general development of adult criminal procedure." Indeed, he argued that "application of the highest due process requirements in juvenile courts" might serve rehabilitation by offering juveniles a lesson in fair and civilized conduct.[6] At the core of Murray's draft brief was the functional similarity concept first employed in *Kent*.

At the end of August, Norman Dorsen engaged Daniel Rezneck, a Washington, D.C. lawyer with experience in criminal justice and due process matters, as both a defense attorney and federal prosecutor, to assist in rewriting the brief for final submission to the Court. Like Mainzer and Wulf, Rezneck was initially skeptical about seeking the extensive list of procedural rights enumerated by Amelia Lewis. Arguing that additional safeguards would follow at the insistence of attorneys who appeared in juvenile courts, Rezneck suggested that the brief focus exclusively on the right to counsel.[7] Dorsen believed that the ACLU had nothing to lose by advancing a broader set of claims, and ultimately he and Rezneck decided to argue a number of different constitutional issues on the assumption that at least some would resonate positively within the Court.[8]

The construction of Dorsen and Rezneck's argument proceeded in two stages, each one presenting its own strategic problems. In the first stage, they sought to persuade the Court to subject juvenile proceedings to Bill of Rights scrutiny through the Fourteenth Amendment's due process clause. The major obstacle was that most appellate courts had rejected similar claims on the grounds that juvenile courts were civil courts and hence not subject to the constitutional provisions governing criminal matters. To overcome this obstacle, the ACLU had to demonstrate that juveniles possessed independent interests that were jeopardized by juvenile court proceedings and required the protection of the Bill of Rights. This issue had not been argued in the Arizona courts, and arguing it before the Supreme Court forced the ACLU to recharacterize juvenile proceedings. It did so by comparing the actual consequences of juvenile court intervention with state rhetoric about the juvenile court's *parens patriae* jurisdiction and use of protective intervention.

As in the draft brief, Dorsen and Rezneck's strategy here was to emphasize the functional similarity between juvenile and criminal courts, despite the rhetoric of state legislatures to the contrary. Their argument was straightforward: The specialists who warned against formalized proceedings, and the judicial authorities who supported them, ignored the real consequences of juvenile court hearings. Contrary to conventional wisdom, juvenile proceedings, like criminal trials, affected the vital interests of alleged delinquents; procedural informality thus prevented juveniles from protecting these interests. States were simply mistaken in believing that, by acting "as a prudent parent treats his child," they could avoid adversely affecting juveniles' personal interests.[9] Exhibiting sensitivity to the support enjoyed by juvenile courts in some quarters, the ACLU did not impugn the motives of the state legislators who had adopted the *parens patriae* approach. It suggested instead that these motives were ill-served by procedural informality; the laudable objectives underlying *parens patriae* had been corrupted by proceedings "that lack the most elemental protections of due process."[10] The means by which states had implemented this ideal meant that "juvenile court proceedings, which were instituted to protect the young, led in many jurisdictions to *findings* of delinquency in proceedings that conspicuously failed to protect the child."[11] Dorsen and Rezneck urged the Court to ignore precedents based on the "theoretical comforts" of *parens patriae;* instead, the Court was asked to decide *Gault* in a manner consistent with "the hard realities of a proceeding in which the vital interests of a child are engaged."[12]

Dorsen and Rezneck were not content, however, to rely exclusively on this straightforward formulation of the functional similarity argument. They added a twist, designed to address the counterargument that procedural formality might undermine efforts at rehabilitation. According to traditional conceptions of juvenile justice, the procedural differences between juvenile hearings and criminal trials reflected the distinction between the rehabilitative objectives of juvenile courts and the punitive nature of criminal law. The simple functional similarity argument challenged the relevance of this distinction by stressing the often punitive nature of juvenile proceedings. Dorsen and Rezneck's twist was to note that the criminal justice system itself had become more concerned with rehabilitation. This shift in purpose had occurred, moreover, without diminishing the due process safeguards available to criminal defendants; indeed, precisely the opposite had occurred.[13] This development clearly indicated, Dorsen and Rezneck argued, that criminal due process was not incompatible with rehabilitation, a point that Dorsen would stress during oral argument.[14]

The second stage of the brief's argument provided the legal justification for its specific procedural claims. The major strategic problem at this stage was to select the theory of incorporation most likely to support those claims. Dorsen and Rezneck were well aware that the Court would be divided in *Gault*, as it had been in many of the criminal procedure decisions of the 1960s, over the question of the principles that should govern federal review of state criminal proceedings. Several factors led Dorsen and Rezneck to abandon the jurisdictional statement's reliance on fundamental fairness and to adopt instead the selective incorporation approach. Fundamental fairness had not produced the desired result when applied by the Arizona Supreme Court, largely because its emphasis on the context of procedural claims resulted in excessive deference to the traditional characterization of juvenile proceedings that Dorsen and Rezneck had already rejected in the brief's first section. Total incorporation, on the other hand, implicitly required that juvenile proceedings be shown to be not merely similar to criminal proceedings but virtually identical to them. Total incorporation, moreover, provided no support for the transcript and appellate review claims. Selective incorporation had the dual advantage of neither requiring the rejection of all distinctions between juvenile and criminal proceedings nor of automatically excluding procedural claims not expressly supported by the Bill of Rights. Perhaps most important, Dorsen believed that at least four justices were sympathetic to the selective incorporation argument.[15]

The selective incorporation component of the ACLU's case was evident in the arguments supporting each of its specific procedural claims. "The first essential of due process, where an individual's liberty is in jeopardy," Dorsen and Rezneck wrote, "is that he be clearly informed of the nature of the charge against him so that he can prepare his defense."[16] In juvenile proceedings, the brief continued, such notice should state the specific misconduct underlying the delinquency petition, the statute or rule of law the misconduct violates, and the consequences of the petition's being upheld.[17] To serve its purpose effectively, notice must also be followed by "reasonable time" for "appraisal of all facts" necessary "to prepare and contest the charges."[18] Because the Arizona Juvenile Code required none of these steps, Gerald's parents had been denied the opportunity "to make an intelligent decision on how best to proceed in their son's interest."[19]

The opportunity to confront and cross-examine witnesses, along with the privilege against self-incrimination, constituted additional elements of due process that were essential in juvenile proceedings. Dorsen and Rezneck characterized the right to confrontation and cross-examination as "one of the most vital and lasting contributions of Anglo-American law to the attainment of a reliable fact-finding proceeding."[20] Because the Court had imposed this requirement on other noncriminal adjudicatory proceedings, its absence from Gerald's delinquency hearings represented an extraordinary breach of due process, even if those hearings were characterized as purely civil in nature.[21] Again consistent with the selective incorporation approach, Dorsen and Rezneck argued that the necessity of confrontation and cross-examination should be determined by the individual's exposure to harm from government action.[22]

The brief employed similar reasoning with respect to self-incrimination: "The relevant inquiry in determining the applicability of the privilege is not the nature of the proceeding, but whether the witness may in any way incriminate himself by testifying or making a statement."[23] Because statements made by Gerald to the juvenile court judge appeared to have been decisive in his eventual commitment to the Arizona Industrial School,[24] the ACLU urged the Court to hold that "if a state allows the risk of self-incrimination to arise in its juvenile proceedings, it must afford the privilege to the juvenile."[25]

The self-incrimination issue presented Dorsen and Rezneck with one of the more difficult tactical problems of the case. In proposing that juveniles be warned against making incriminating statements, they challenged a core principle of traditional juvenile jurisprudence, that admissions of wrongdoing are an indispensable element of the rehabilitation process. Dorsen and Rezneck's response to this potential conflict between due process and rehabilitation was critical to the success of their case. "There is ample scope for individualized treatment," they argued, "when the court comes to decide the proper disposition of a juvenile it has adjudged delinquent. But the adjudicatory process in juvenile court cannot be allowed to serve, however inadvertently, as a means of compelled self-incrimination."[26]

The importance of this argument was its conceptualization of the juvenile process as a combination of several distinct elements rather than as the organic whole advocated by the nineteenth-century ideal. To be sure, this idea was not entirely original—it had appeared in the 1962 New York Family Court Act[27]—but the ACLU was able to use it to separate adjudication from the rehabilitation-oriented disposition phase of juvenile proceedings and to focus the Court's attention on the integrity of the fact-finding process. Once the Court accepted the proposition that adjudication had little to do with rehabilitation, it could impose constitutional requirements of due process on that stage of juvenile proceedings while declaring its continued fidelity to the traditional rehabilitative doctrines of juvenile justice.

As one might expect, the assertion of a right to counsel in juvenile proceedings was a crucial part of the brief because of the likelihood that without it, "all other procedures in juvenile courts and all other rights ostensibly given in such proceedings are unsubstantiated and incapable of effective implementation."[28] Dorsen and Rezneck explicitly argued that state juvenile proceedings were bound by the Court's earlier rulings that "the right to counsel in criminal proceedings is an essential part of the Fourteenth Amendment's due process clause" and that "no distinction may constitutionally be drawn between the right to appear by retained counsel and the right to have counsel appointed."[29] This argument went furthest in equating juvenile and criminal proceedings, which the ACLU underscored by arguing that "the fact that a juvenile may be deprived of his liberty through an adjudicatory process in which the aid of counsel would be indispensable to him requires the application of the *Powell* and *Gideon* principles."[30]

This argument linked the constitutional deficiencies of juvenile proceedings to deficiencies that the Court had discovered in earlier cases involving serious criminal offenses. The 1932 *Powell* decision, for example, had initiated the Court's nationalization of the Bill of Rights by extending the federal rights to fair trial and counsel into state proceedings for capital offenses. In *Gideon*, of course, the Warren Court had taken the *Powell* doctrine a step further by extending the right to counsel into all state felony prosecutions. Lest this argument appear too extreme, however, the two attorneys suggested that a right to counsel was equally consistent with a fundamental fairness evaluation of due process that deferred to *parens patriae* ideals. Juvenile court judges, they asserted, were simply too inexperienced and lacked the necessary legal training to protect the interests of juveniles as proficiently as counsel.[31]

In contrast to the other four procedural claims, selective incorporation offered weak support for the appellate review and transcript claims. Dorsen and Rezneck thus resorted to arguments more consistent with the context-driven approach to due process characteristic of the fundamental fairness doctrine. They conceded that nothing in the Fourteenth Amendment expressly required states to provide a right to appeal juvenile court orders. They asserted, however, that a right to appellate review is extremely important where a legal process permits wide judicial discretion; its absence from juvenile proceedings thus offended an important ideal of American law.[32] Offering a slightly stronger argument for the right to transcripts, they contended that whether review of juvenile court decisions is by appeal or habeas corpus, a transcript is indispensable.[33] The "most elemental notions of due process," Dorsen and Rezneck suggested, "require that a transcript of the juvenile court proceedings be made, in order to provide an adequate basis for whatever mode of review is deemed appropriate."[34]

Dorsen and Rezneck supported their arguments throughout the brief with a variety of extralegal material, most of it necessary to establish the functional similarity proposition. It included law review articles, social science materials, historical studies, and reports from the Department of Health, Education, and Welfare and the U.S. Commission on Civil Rights. The right to counsel section, for example, quoted extensively from an article by Charles Schinitsky about the role of attorneys under the New York Family Court Act. Schinitsky's article was valuable in countering the claim that counsel would render juvenile hearings overly legalistic and would thus undermine rehabilitation efforts.[35] Articles by Chester Antieau, Monrad Paulsen, and Orman Ketcham and studies by the National Probation and Parole Association were also cited frequently.

The ACLU's brief advanced a modified theory of selective incorporation, which balanced its most important due process claims with the necessity of maintaining distinctions between juvenile and criminal proceedings. The ACLU's desire to strike this balance was evident in its decision not to challenge the Arizona Code on equal protection grounds. Dorsen and Rezneck could have relied on the functional similarity between juvenile and criminal proceedings to argue that the absence from juvenile hearings of due process standards already held applicable to state criminal proceedings denied juveniles equal protection of the law solely on the basis of age. There were two problems inherent in making this claim, however. First, it would have challenged the very constitutionality of separate juvenile proceedings. Second, it would have forced the Court to consider whether age was a suspect classification under the equal protection clause. Making an equal protection claim, therefore, would have unnecessarily complicated the questions at issue and might have been sufficiently radical to frighten the Court away from granting any of the ACLU's claims.

AMICUS BRIEFS

Dorsen and Rezneck perhaps felt somewhat constrained in how far they could push their position, but this was not the case with some of the organizations who participated in the litigation on their behalf as friends of the court. On June 30, 1966, Dorsen and Melvin Wulf met with Gertrude Mainzer, Charles Ares (then dean of the University of Arizona Law School), and Leon Polsky of the National Legal Aid and Defender Association (NLADA) to discuss amicus participation in the case. The association was ultimately one of three organizations to file amicus briefs in support of the ACLU's position. The others were the New York Legal Aid Society (NYLAS), on behalf of itself and the Citizens' Committee for Children of New York (CCNY), and the now defunct American Parents' Committee. There was almost no coordination of strategy either between the ACLU and amici, or among the amicus participants themselves. In fact, Nanette Dembitz of the Legal Aid Society decided to file a separate brief on behalf of her organization, despite the similarity of its concerns with those of the NLADA.[36]

In addition to these private organizations, the ACLU also sought the federal government's support. In July 1966, Dorsen wrote to Solicitor General Thurgood Marshall and Attorney General Nicholas deB. Katzenbach to seek the government's participation in the case as amicus on behalf of Gerald Gault.[37] Often referred to as the Court's "tenth justice," the solicitor general is responsible for representing the federal government's interests in any case before the Court. As a result, the solicitor general enjoys certain advantages relative to other parties. For example, only the solicitor general can assert an automatic right to participate through both written and oral arguments as amicus curiae in constitutional cases. Whether due to litigation experience and expertise or because of the justices' respect for the office, the Court adopts the solicitor general's position in about 70 percent of cases decided on their merits.[38] Consequently, the solicitor general's support and participation can be crucial, as it was for the NAACP in its constitutional battles against segregation. Neither Marshall nor Katzenbach, however, thought the federal government's interest in the juvenile justice issue sufficiently important to accept the invitation to participate in *Gault.*

After the June 30 meeting among potential amicus participants, Leon Polsky wrote to Michael Getty, director of Defender Services for the NLADA, to express his concern that the ACLU was not taking its argument far enough. He suggested that the NLADA file an amicus brief to argue the point that "the whole bundle of criminal process should attach to [juvenile] proceedings and that where an act otherwise criminal is the basis for the juvenile court proceedings the standards of proof should be the criminal one." He warned Getty that the Court would not look favorably on a " 'me too' *amicus* brief" and advised that the NLADA brief cover "matters falling within our particular expertise."[39] The brief eventually filed by the NLADA had a narrow focus, which was, however, in an area of the association's special expertise—the provision of legal representation to indigent juveniles. "The outcome of the instant matter," the association argued in its brief, "will directly affect the continuing validity of such representation and its growth and vitality."[40] Thus, the NLADA urged the Court to grant juveniles both the general right to counsel and the right to court-appointed counsel paid by the state. Toward this end, the association suggested that the Court adopt the 1966 recommendation of its Defender Standards Committee that indigent juveniles whose liberty is at stake be informed upon being arrested or taken into custody that the state would provide competent counsel to represent them.[41] This conclusion, the NLADA asserted, reflected the "growing concern of the legal profession for protection of rights of children in juvenile court proceedings."[42]

The NLADA's legal argument in support of this proposition was that the "right of counsel in any proceeding in which personal liberty is at stake is a basic requirement of the Sixth Amendment and the Due Process Clause of the 14th, regardless of the forum."[43] The association also argued that *Gideon v. Wainwright*'s holding that indigent defendants are "entitled to court appointed counsel in all felony cases" should be broadened to include any proceeding in which liberty is at stake.[44] It cited the findings of a survey of its member offices in eighteen states, the District of Columbia, and Puerto Rico, as well as one other study, to show that adoption of these standards would not significantly alter existing practices in most states.[45] According to the NLADA's own survey, in every jurisdiction where its offices handled juvenile cases, parents were given notice of the charges against their children. Moreover, in 78 percent of these jurisdictions, juveniles were advised of their right to counsel; and in 70 percent of the jurisdictions, they received notice of their privilege against self-incrimination. Ironically, the survey had the potential to function as a double-edged sword. On the one hand, it could be used to soften the novelty of what the Court was being asked to do. On the other hand, relying on these data to argue that the Court would merely be constitutionalizing existing state practices potentially undermined the ACLU's constitutional case, which rested on the assumption that the arbitrary practices and egregious results permitted by Arizona's juvenile court law typically occurred in the juvenile courts of other states.

Although the NLADA argued strongly for the right to counsel, it carefully avoided specifying the precise role that counsel should play in juvenile proceedings.[46] In a memorandum to the association's deputy director, an

NLADA research assistant had warned that "any suggested change in the juvenile court system should recognize both the values inherent to the court and the concerns of the lawyer for procedural fairness."[47] The impact of extremely adversarial proceedings on the juvenile court's therapeutic objectives, the memorandum continued, was still an uncertain matter to be determined empirically by the "social and psychological sciences."[48] The association's caution in this respect may have reflected the influence of the National Council of Juvenile Court Judges, which was located in the same office building as the NLADA and had missed an opportunity to file a brief generally supportive of the ACLU's position. The NLADA's brief suggested that the Court wait for the results of a study on the role of attorneys in juvenile courts then being conducted by the council before establishing guidelines for the participation of counsel in juvenile hearings.[49]

Like the NLADA, the New York Legal Aid Society focused its attention on the necessity of legal representation for juveniles. The society had been the sole provider of counsel to indigent juveniles and their parents in New York since passage of the 1962 Family Court Act, and in one twelve-month period NYLAS attorneys had represented 80 percent of all juveniles processed by the family courts. The society was not satisfied, however, with the statutory right to counsel and other components of due process enjoyed by juveniles under New York's Family Court Act. It entered the litigation to establish "the requirements of fair procedures [in juvenile courts] as a matter of constitutional right."[50] The society argued that juvenile proceedings involving violations of the law or other misconduct, because they carry the risk that liberty will be restrained, are "so similar in substance and import to a criminal prosecution that the fundamental safeguards of justice afforded to adults charged with crime must be observed."[51] The NYLAS urged the Court to abandon the view that an adjudication of delinquency "merely establishes the court's authority over the child; that a juvenile commitment is based on the child's need rather than the violation; and that its purpose is to rehabilitate him."[52] Instead, it argued that the Court should recognize the punitive aspect of delinquency adjudications.

In one sense, the society's brief added few new arguments to support the ACLU's specific procedural claims, except to comment on its experience with the privilege against self-incrimination[53] and the right to counsel. On the latter point, the NYLAS argued that counsel was necessary in delinquency proceedings to exercise the traditional function of attorneys in adversarial hearings, namely, "to promote accurate fact-finding by examining and cross-examining witnesses and to promote issues of law." This function was particularly important in delinquency hearings, the argument continued, because the facts in such cases are often unclear. Counsel was also important, the NYLAS argued, during the dispositional component of delinquency proceedings in order to challenge probation and psychiatric reports, to present additional background information, and to suggest alternative treatments. Finally, the society argued that the poverty of most juveniles made the right to appointed counsel crucially important.[54]

The most original portions of the NYLAS brief concerned dispositions and the definition of delinquency. Although other participants in the case were reluctant to suggest formalization of the dispositional phase of juvenile proceedings, the NYLAS argued in favor of a constitutional right to a disposition hearing. Such a hearing, it asserted, would have allowed Gerald and his parents the opportunity "to try to refute or explain whatever adverse facts the judge was considering, and to urge countervailing facts and reasons against his commitment. Due process guarantees a hearing, to avert arbitrariness or false surmises in the crucial determination of whether to remove a child from his parents and confine him in a State institution."[55] The NYLAS explained that disposition hearings were necessary for three reasons. First, judges possess enormous discretion to set dispositions. Second, "the evaluation of the child, his relationships and his environment goes to the very heart of a juvenile proceeding," and disposition hearings could ensure that these evaluations serve rehabilitative goals. Third, unlike criminal sentences, where only the defendant's liberty is affected, juvenile dispositions affect "the parent's legally cognizable interest in the child's development and in retaining custody."[56] Thus, while the ACLU was attempting to soften the implications of its argument by distinguishing between adjudication and disposition, the NYLAS was urging formalization of this crucial aspect of the rehabilitative process.

The NYLAS also asked the Court to remove "immoral or unhealthful conduct" from Arizona's definition of delinquency. This provision, the society argued, was unconstitutionally vague. As a result, it gave juvenile court judges "broad and unchanneled power . . . to impose [their] subjective standards, and to assert authority to commit a child on the basis of [their] personal values and individual interpretation of the statute."[57] Although already accomplished in New York, this redefinition of delinquency struck a blow against the traditional view of juvenile court intervention. It also focused attention on the point that might have been the fundamental reason for the outcome in Gerald's hearings: unlimited judicial discretion to impose a variety of dispositions.

The third amicus participant in the *Gault* litigation was the American Parents' Committee (APC). It believed that a "review of standards and proceedings will aid, rather than weaken, the public role of the juvenile court."[58] In its view, the issue raised by *Gault* was whether a system of social control "parallel but distinct from criminal law" could exist "free from the traditional formalities and safeguards made applicable to the latter."[59] Not surprisingly the APC answered this question in the negative, concluding that only the introduction of an adversary system of justice into juvenile courts could maintain the proper balance between social and individual interests and provide protection against "inequity and the abuse of discretion."[60] The absence of adversary proceedings had transformed "the parens patriae doctrine into an oppressive tool."[61] Better procedures and better-trained personnel, the APC believed, would "give the juvenile court a more effective role in protecting both children and society."[62]

Thus, the case against *parens patriae* advanced by the ACLU and its allies rested on an allegedly more realistic understanding of the nature of delinquency proceedings. According to this understanding, there was no operational difference between these proceedings and criminal trials; both aimed at depriving individuals of their liberty. The failure of the juvenile justice system to rehabilitate the individuals placed in its custody contributed to the perception that both sets of proceedings were functionally similar. The original justification for exempting juvenile courts from constitutional standards of due process, therefore, could no longer be sustained. (For the arguments advanced by the ACLU and its amicus supporters and the response by Arizona and its sole supporter, see Tables 5.1 and 5.2).

The Case for *Parens Patriae*

ARIZONA'S BRIEF

Arizona assigned the task of defending its Juvenile Code to Frank A. Parks, a thirty-year-old graduate of George Washington University Law School who worked in the state attorney general's office. Born in New Jersey, Parks had received his law degree in 1964 and been admitted to the bar in 1965, making him one of the least experienced attorneys in his office. Parks shared his oral argument time with counsel for the Ohio Association of Juvenile Court Judges, who selected for this task Merrit W. Green, a Cleveland lawyer with extensive trial and appellate court experience. Assisting Green on his brief was Don J. Young, a federal district court judge who had served

Table 5.1. Comparison of Arguments on the Merits

	Appellant	Appellee
Juvenile court history	History reveals high purposes perverted by proceedings lacking "most elemental protections of due process." (5 pages)	Benevolent intentions; therapeutic functions will be destroyed by injecting criminal due process. (4 pages)
Juvenile proceedings in Arizona	Boundless discretion of Arizona Juvenile Court denies due process contrary to "growing recognition of the importance of providing juveniles with the protection of the Constitution." (10 pages)	Arizona juvenile proceedings satisfy "fundamental fairness concept" of due process. (4 pages)
Constitutional arguments		
Notice	First essential of due process; must be communicated prior to hearings. (5 pages)	Fair hearing does require adequate notice; Arizona Juvenile Court law provides for such notice; requirement met in case. (3 pages)
Counsel	Denial of right "inconsistent with minimal standards of procedural fairness"; true even if proceedings are considered civil; judges cannot adequately protect rights. (9 pages)	Presence of counsel will destroy nonadversary nature of proceedings and relegate juvenile court to a "junior criminal court." (4 pages)
Confrontation and cross-examination	Vital for reliable fact-finding; also applies in adjudicatory administrative proceedings. (6 pages)	Relevant only where charges are denied. (3 pages)
Self-incrimination	Juvenile at risk of criminal prosecution; privilege required. (8 pages)	Undermines therapeutic purposes of juvenile proceedings. (3 pages)
Appellate review and transcripts	Review necessary to constrain discretion; transcripts necessary for adequate review. (5 pages)	Review matter of grace rather than of right; Arizona proceedings provide adequate access to review. (2 pages)

Table 5.2. Comparison of Amicus Curiae Briefs in *Gault*

For Appellants	For Appellees
NLADA	*Ohio Association of Juvenile Court Judges*
Arizona Juvenile Court procedure does not follow NLADA's "Standards for a Defender System"; it violates due process clause of 14th Amendment.	Juvenile court must recognize the differences between children and adults.
Arizona procedure is contrary to national trends in dealing with juvenile matters.	Dispositional powers should be restricted only by requirements of child's welfare.
Absence of right to counsel violates juveniles' 6th and 14th Amendment rights.	Mere procedural errors in a single case should not be the basis for a holding that due process is denied.
LAS/CCNY	
Constitutional requirements for delinquency proceedings must be determined on the basis of its similarities to a criminal prosecution.	
Rights essential for fairness and equal justice must be accorded in delinquency proceedings.	
Constitutional right to a hearing must be recognized in a juvenile disposition.	
Arizona provisions as to conduct endangering morals or health is excessively broad and vague.	
APC	
All sanctioning systems authorized to deprive liberty must be subject to the Constitution.	
The Constitution does not allow for two systems for dispensing justice.	
The Adversary system is the best protection against inequity and abuse of discretion.	
Absence of counsel deprives child of needed protection while denying society protection against wasteful dispositions.	
Deprivation of legal safeguards from children hinders development toward responsible adult citizenship.	
Justice requires procedural control over human discretion.	
Juvenile court is an unproven social experiment that requires fresh public assessment.	

on the juvenile court bench. Young had once been chairman of the National Council of Juvenile Court Judges (NCJCJ) Appellate Law Committee, and he was intent on preserving the nineteenth-century philosophical underpinnings of juvenile justice.[63] In contrast to the position advocated by the ACLU and its amicus allies, the argument against direct application of the Fourteenth Amendment's due process clause to juvenile proceedings made by Arizona and its amicus supporter relied entirely on the principles to which Young was attached.

The Arizona brief had two objectives. First, it sought to establish that the philosophy underlying the state's Juvenile Code justified its characterization of delinquency hearings as noncriminal proceedings to which only fundamental fairness standards of due process apply. Arizona therefore conceded that "the child in a juvenile court proceeding is entitled to due process of law" but argued that "the question necessarily posed is what constitutes due process in such a proceeding." The proper standard for determining this issue, Arizona averred, was fundamental fairness, since that standard considers "the nature of the proceeding" and avoids an "[adversary] approach to juvenile proceedings." Fundamental fairness, understood in the unique context of *parens patriae* juvenile proceedings, protects "the child of tender years and provides him with due process of law."[64] The brief's second objective was to persuade the Court that Gerald's hearings had been consistent with these standards of fundamental fairness.

Arizona's argument brought clearly into focus the necessity of choosing between two distinct visions of juvenile justice. The state left little doubt about the vision it advocated; its brief characterized juvenile courts as shielding juveniles "from the stigma of criminality when the acts performed would otherwise subject children to the criminal system."[65] Juvenile courts functioned "on a socio-legal basis, where the purpose is therapeutic and preventive, rather than retributive and punitive."[66] This function was incompatible with the adversary atmosphere characteristic of criminal proceedings, requiring instead proceedings based on the "sound and purposeful doctrine" of *parens patriae*.[67] In its brief Arizona urged the Court to acknowledge the widely recognized right of state legislatures to "say that an act done by a child shall not be a crime or punishable as such" and to establish special courts to respond to those acts.[68] Since juvenile courts were qualitatively distinct in their concern for children's welfare, "the 'fundamental fairness concept' embodied in the Fourteenth Amendment is satisfied in juvenile courts, even though the constitutional safeguards of criminal jurisprudence are not applied in them."[69] To the state of Arizona, in other words, the context and objectives of juvenile court proceedings permitted substantial departures from the procedural rules governing criminal courts.

Arizona devoted the remainder of its brief to defending the procedures followed in Gerald's hearings against the six due process claims raised by the ACLU. The state argued that the ACLU's claims exhibited a fundamental misunderstanding of its juvenile proceedings. Gerald's first hearing, the brief explained, dealt with the juvenile court's jurisdiction and the facts alleged in the delinquency petition. The jurisdictional question presented little difficulty because Gerald was still on probation for earlier transgressions and therefore already subject to the court's jurisdiction. Similarly, Gerald's admission of the facts alleged in the petition meant that there was no need to examine witnesses or to schedule a more formal adjudicatory hearing. Had Gerald denied the alleged acts, Arizona admitted, both he and his parents would have been entitled to "reasonable time to prepare a defense for the subsequent full-scale adjudicatory hearing."[70]

In Arizona's view, these aspects of Gerald's hearings adequately answered the ACLU's notice and confrontation claims, leaving the issues of counsel, self-incrimination, appellate review, and transcripts. Because Dorsen and Rezneck had not really pressed the latter two claims, the brief dealt with them in rather perfunctory fashion. Parks dismissed the claim for appellate review by noting the availability of habeas corpus review and the fact that appellate courts had held that "a right to review is not essential to due process, but is a matter of grace only."[71] The state further argued that the desirability of keeping juvenile hearings confidential meant that leaving the question of transcripts to the discretion of juvenile court judges in individual cases was both good law and sound policy.

The right to counsel and self-incrimination claims required a more complex response. The best Arizona could do, however, was to rely on the nineteenth-century vision of juvenile courts about which the Court was already skeptical. It argued that the principal consideration in deciding these claims should be the importance of creating a nonadversarial atmosphere in which the state could properly perform its *parens patriae* function. Rigid adherence to the adversary system, the state argued, "would undermine the informal approach to juvenile problems."[72] It asserted that the "philosophy of shielding children from traditional criminal court procedures, their atmosphere and concomitants is still an admirable approach of juvenile jurisprudence."[73] The state refused to concede the ACLU's characterization of juvenile proceedings or the relevance to those proceedings of Supreme Court decisions concerning criminal due process.[74] Dogmatic application of the right to counsel and the privilege against self-incrimination to juvenile proceedings, Arizona concluded, threatened to destroy juvenile courts by transforming them into junior criminal courts.[75]

The Arizona court's ruling on each of the six due process claims, the state concluded in its brief, satisfied the requirements of fairness in noncriminal, nonadversarial hearings. The lower court had not ruled, the state stressed, that juvenile courts were entirely exempt from procedural standards or that juvenile court judges could exercise unlimited discretion. It had ruled (as had the D.C. Circuit Court of Appeals in *Pee v. United States*[76]) that the substantive requirements of those standards should not be determined by direct application of the Bill of Rights to juvenile court statutes. According to Arizona, this approach was the best way to balance the desire for procedural regularity with the need for rehabilitative flexibility.

AMICUS BRIEF

The Ohio Association of Juvenile Court Judges entered the case as a friend of the court not only in the technical sense but in a literal sense as the defender of traditional juvenile court procedures and practices. The association took the theme of Arizona's argument a step further and denied outright any basis for due process review of juvenile proceedings. In language strikingly similar to that used by Judge Julian Mack almost sixty years earlier,[77] the association argued that juvenile courts are not concerned "so much with what a child did as with why he did it, and how he can be helped to avoid getting into further or more serious difficulties." The judges argued that the Gila County Juvenile Court's actions should be viewed as a judgment that Gerald's participation in the obscene call indicated "much worse trouble to follow" without court intervention. Underlying this argument was the judges' conviction that the "basic right of a juvenile is not to liberty but to custody."[78] Neither "the pressures of urbanization on the vastly increased numbers of children in our society" nor the "upsurge of interest in civil liberty" changed this basic feature of childhood.[79] The judges also directed a significant portion of their brief against what they perceived to be the more damaging aspect of the ACLU's argument: its attack—"rather by innuendo than with honest force"—on judicial discretion at the dispositional phase of juvenile proceedings.[80] Creating a direct link between specific law violations and juvenile court dispositions, they claimed, would deny juveniles "the treatment which offers the greatest prospect of rehabilitation."[81]

To deny juveniles this treatment would subject them to the "horrible practical results of legislative action relating dispositions in juvenile cases to the specific wrongful action of the child."[82]

Formalization of adjudicative and dispositional procedures, the association asserted, would destroy the juvenile court's "flexibility and freedom to act in the child's best interests."[83] "Because children are not adults," the judges concluded,

> their problems require treatment different from that afforded adults. Informality in procedure and flexibility of disposition are essential to the concept of individualized justice. Departure from the civil and equitable character of juvenile court actions by blanket application of constitutional guarantees designed to protect adult defendants in criminal proceedings would vitiate our juvenile court laws.[84]

It would be difficult to imagine a clearer statement of traditional juvenile justice principles. According to the Ohio judges, informal procedures and flexible dispositional standards were simply exempt from due process review, even under the most deferential fundamental fairness standard. Occasional errors in applying these procedures and standards, the judges argued, should not "wipe out or revise" juvenile court statutes.[85]

Given the growing criticism of traditional juvenile jurisprudence and the timing of the case's emergence in the midst of the Warren Court's expansive use of the due process clause, it is difficult to understand how the state of Arizona or the Ohio judges expected to win their case by simply restating arguments developed during the previous century. Their procedural arguments rested on a vision of juvenile courts that, the ACLU's brief had persuasively claimed, did not comport with reality; and neither Arizona nor the Ohio judges offered solid evidence to dispute this key claim of the *parens patriae* doctrine's opponents. Thus the actual outcome was almost a foregone conclusion when Norman Dorsen and Frank Parks took their positions at the attorneys' tables in the courtroom of the Supreme Court building on December 6, 1966; for both of them, it was the first opportunity to argue a case before the nation's highest court. As they prepared themselves for oral argument, Dorsen and Parks undoubtedly understood that this was no longer really about Gerald Gault's "lewd phone calls" or his commitment to Fort Grant. It was, as would become apparent when Justice Fortas quickly interrupted Parks's recitation of traditional juvenile court philosophy, an inquiry into the constitutional status of every juvenile court statute in the nation.

The Court Decides: "Being a boy does not justify a kangaroo court"

On May 15, 1967, more than five months after oral argument, the Supreme Court delivered its decision, voting by a significant margin to bring juvenile court proceedings under the protective umbrella of the Fourteenth Amendment's due process clause. To say that the *Gault* Court was inherently sympathetic to the type of claims raised by the case would not be an exaggeration. The Court included the core members of the so-called Warren Court, including four of the justices who had decided *Brown v. Board of Education* (Warren, Douglas, Clark, and Black). On criminal due process matters, it was a Court that favored defendants' rights. Indeed, if *Mapp v. Ohio* (1961) marks the beginning of the Warren Court's due process revolution, then seven of the justices (Warren, Douglas, Clark, Black, Brennan, Harlan, and Stewart) had been part of the revolution from its outset. The chief justice exerted considerable influence on the *Gault* Court, carrying the other members with him approximately 70 percent of the time (only Harlan—at 52.2 percent—agreed with Warren less than 60 percent of the time). Warren generated this rate of agreement despite presiding over a relatively experienced Court (the average length of service was about fifteen years, ranging from Black's thirty-year tenure to Fortas's two years of service), one that was evenly divided between Democratic (five) and Republican (four) appointees. This record suggests that, despite other differences, there was a remarkable level of consensus among the justices on key issues.

THE MAJORITY VIEW

As in *Kent,* the majority opinion in *Gault* came from the Court's most junior member—Justice Abe Fortas. Once again, the importance of Fortas's prior views on criminal procedure issues and his emergence as the Court's juvenile justice expert played a decisive role in the case's outcome. Indeed, one of his biographers has written that the decision "best illustrates Fortas's personal approach to judging and his identification with those left out of society."[86] Nevertheless, the decision had to overcome the doubts expressed by his own law clerk and survive a conference in which two justices who eventually joined the majority initially did not support the full range of procedural protections that Fortas wanted to extend to juveniles.[87] His decision in *Gault* generated concurring opinions from Justices Hugo Black and Byron White and a strong dissenting opinion from Justice Potter Stewart. Justice

John Harlan concurred in part and dissented in part. Although Fortas's review of juvenile proceedings on behalf of the majority rested on his conclusion that both the Fourteenth Amendment and the Bill of Rights were relevant for determining the procedural rights available to children in juvenile proceedings, he did not want to leave the impression that he aimed at transforming the "totality of the relationship" between children and the state.[88] This cautious approach produced a relatively narrow ruling in which Fortas restrictively applied his decision to delinquency hearings, excluding both dependency and neglect proceedings from the decision's requirements. Furthermore, the decision did not apply to the preadjudication or disposition phases of delinquency proceedings or to proceedings in which juveniles' liberty was not at stake. Fortas's incorporation of the Bill of Rights into juvenile proceedings was thus selective both in terms of specific provisions and the proceedings to which they applied (see Table 5.3).

Like the ACLU, Fortas undertook two principal tasks in his opinion. His first was to establish the relevance of the Bill of Rights to the questions at issue, which he did by discrediting the historic basis for the distinction between delinquency hearings and criminal trials. Fortas described the *parens patriae* ideal as a "murky" doctrine whose "historic credentials" were of "dubious relevance" for determining the procedural standards juvenile courts were required to meet.[89] He argued further that the juvenile court's experiment with procedural informality had not produced substantial improvements in rehabilitation. Instead, the experiment merely "demonstrated that unbridled discretion, however benevolently motivated, is frequently a poor substitute for principle and procedure."[90] "The absence of rigorous procedural standards," Fortas argued,

> has not necessarily meant that children receive careful, compassionate, individualized treatment. The absence of procedural rules based upon constitutional principle has not always produced fair, efficient, and effective procedures. Departures from established principles of due process have frequently resulted not in enlightened procedure, but in arbitrariness.[91]

Fortas offered two explanations for the failure of procedural informality to produce "careful, compassionate, individualized treatment."[92] One stumbling block was inaccurate fact-finding, which made identification of appropriate rehabilitative responses difficult. The second explanation was that arbitrary proceedings encouraged a lack of trust in juvenile courts among its "clients," which caused juveniles to be unresponsive to the courts' rehabilitative interventions. Fortas argued that proceedings consistent with constitutional principles of due process would solve both problems. On the one

Table 5.3. Justice Fortas's Opinion

Argument	Support
1. CONSTITUTION APPLIES TO JUVENILE PROCEEDINGS	
A. "Neither the 14th Amendment nor the Bill of Rights is for adults alone."	
B. Limitations of holding	
1. Not concerned with totality of juvenile-state relationship	
2. Not applicable to intake or dispositional stages	
C. Widespread agreement that due process clause applies to juvenile proceedings	Cites to president's commission report; articles by Gardner, Paulsen, Ketcham, Allen; *Harvard Law Review* Note
2. HISTORY AND THEORY	
A. Establish therapeutic procedures; abandon idea of crime and punishment	
B. *Parens patriae* theory a "murky doctrine of dubious relevance"	Cites to articles by Paulsen, Mack, and others
C. Absence of substantive standards has not produced desired outcome.	Cites to article by Handler; *Harvard Law Review* Note; comments by chairman of Pennsylvania Council of Juvenile Court Judges
D. Due process of law primary and indispensable foundation of individual freedom	Quoting Felix Frankfurter
3. IMPACT OF CONSTITUTIONAL DOMESTICATION	
A. No impairment of uniquely beneficial features	Cites to *Columbia Law Review* Note; president's commission report
B. Will enhance therapeutic objectives	Cites to Wheeler and Cottrell's study for president's commission report
4. SPECIFIC ISSUES	
A. Notice: must provide adequate preparation time and set forth particularities of misconduct	Cites to president's commission report; cases on adequate notice in criminal context
B. Counsel: juvenile requires assistance to cope with problems of law, to inquire skillfully into facts, to insist upon procedural regularity, to prepare and submit defense.	Cites to court decisions, expert opinion, legislative developments
C. Confrontation, self-incrimination, and cross-examination: confessions by children unreliable; necessary to prevent state psychological domination	
D. Appellate review and transcripts: not required to satisfy requirements of due process	

hand, due process would separate "essential facts from the conflicting welter of data that life and our adversary methods present," thereby ensuring that "truth will emerge from the confrontation of opposing versions and conflicting data."[93] Fortas implied that this process would enhance the diagnostic accuracy of juvenile proceedings. On the other hand, as "the primary and indispensable foundation of individual freedom" and "essential term in the social compact which defines the rights of the individual and delimits the powers which the state may exercise," due process legitimates state intervention into individuals' lives.[94] Fortas suggested that use of due process would promote trust in the system and make juveniles more amenable to rehabilitation.

Fortas's final criticism of the protective rhetoric surrounding traditional juvenile jurisprudence was that delinquency proceedings interfered with the liberty interests of juveniles. Consequently, the fact that delinquency adjudications could lead to institutional confinement became key in his rejection of traditional juvenile court practices. He found that the possibility of confinement required the "exercise of care implied in the phrase 'due process,' " regardless of the purposes of confinement or the name given to juvenile institutions.[95] The discrepancy between the statutory penalty for Gerald's offense and the length of his commitment was especially influential in this respect: "So wide a gulf between the State's treatment of the adult and of the child requires a bridge sturdier than mere verbiage and reasons more persuasive than cliché can provide."[96] "The condition of being a boy," Fortas declared, "does not justify a kangaroo court." Delinquency hearings must therefore "measure up to the essentials of due process and fair treatment."[97]

Fortas thus concluded that proceedings based on constitutional principles of due process would improve those aspects of juvenile courts that were weakest. More important, he suggested that this change could be accomplished without undermining the successful and valuable innovations of juvenile courts. "The observance of due process standards," he wrote, "will not compel the States to abandon or displace any of the substantive benefits of the juvenile process."[98] He expressed confidence that "the features of the juvenile system which its proponents have asserted are of unique benefit will not be impaired by constitutional domestication."[99] Indeed, Fortas stressed the positive impact of due process on the juvenile system's uniquely beneficial features, a conclusion that he found supported by the 1967 report of the President's Commission on Law Enforcement and Administration of Justice. Fortas's decision to take judicial notice of the report, which none of the briefs cited, can be viewed as a natural consequence of the judicial philosophy that he had forged out of legal realism and sociological jurisprudence. From the perspective of that philosophy, the report summarized the experience from which a living constitutional law should emerge. Fortas thus relied on the report to conclude that there was "surprising unanimity" among juvenile court experts that the "essentials of due process may be a more impressive and more therapeutic attitude so far as the juvenile is concerned."[100]

In order to reach this conclusion, however, Fortas engaged in a rather selective reading of the commission's report. To begin with, Fortas purported to discover in it evidence of a positive relationship between due process and successful rehabilitation of juvenile offenders, but the report presented its findings in terms of a negative impact of procedural informality on rehabilitation. Second, the "surprising unanimity" to which Fortas referred was expressed in the commission's report as "increasing evidence." This phrase, moreover, was a generous interpretation of a similar finding by the Commission's Task Force on Juvenile Delinquency and Youth Crime, which had merely noted an "increasing feeling" among experts that procedural informality impedes rehabilitation. Fortas furthermore overlooked the commission's rather pessimistic conclusion that there might not be anything that juvenile courts could do to rehabilitate young offenders. To reiterate a point made in chapter 2, the commission suggested that juvenile court authorities were operating according to "grossly overoptimistic" assumptions about "what is known about the phenomenon of juvenile criminality and of what even a fully equipped juvenile court could do about it."[101] By ignoring this crucial sentence and by taking another out of context, Fortas was able to imbue an important component of his ruling with the authority of a presidential commission's findings.[102]

After presenting both his legal and policy reasons for formalizing juvenile procedure, Fortas used the remainder of his opinion to specify the essentials of juvenile due process. He accepted the Arizona court's finding that appellate review and written transcripts were not constitutionally required, largely because the Bill of Rights itself is silent about them. He rejected the lower court's holding on the right to notice, however, since it posed little threat to the substantive benefits of juvenile proceedings and had long been recognized as an integral part of the "scheme of ordered liberty" protected by the Bill of Rights.[103] The rights to counsel, confrontation, and cross-examination and the privilege against self-incrimination received most of Fortas's attention.

The application of these provisions to juvenile courts challenged the core premise of juvenile justice that delinquency proceedings should be nonadversarial. Moreover, since the Court had only recently decided that they applied to state criminal proceedings, the wisdom of applying them to juvenile proceedings was unclear. What convinced Fortas that these rights should be incorporated into at least the delinquency adjudication phase of juvenile proceedings was his conclusion that juveniles possess interests separate and distinct from those of the state. He conceptualized delinquency adjudication hearings as adversary confrontations between the state and individuals whose interests could not be adequately represented by either probation officers or juvenile court judges. Indeed, he suggested that in many instances delinquency hearings were equivalent to felony prosecutions. Under these circumstances it was crucial that juveniles have the assistance of counsel and that judges notify juveniles of their right both to retained and appointed counsel.[104]

Fortas's reliance on principles firmly anchored in criminal due process reached its apex, however, in his discussion of the privilege against self-incrimination. This issue had raised the most controversy in conference as the justices discussed the case. Indeed, Chief Justice Warren was unsure whether it was a good idea to extend this right to juveniles.[105] In the end, Fortas convinced Warren and most of his other colleagues that juvenile confessions were inherently unreliable and therefore had to be constrained by the privilege against self-incrimination. Moreover, Fortas explained in his opinion, "the roots of the privilege tap the basic stream of religious and political principle because [it] reflects the limits of the individual's attornment to the state . . . and insists upon the equality of the individual and the state."[106] This view of the privilege's purpose was taken directly from the decision in *Miranda,* in which the Court had stressed the privilege's importance in equalizing the relationship between the state and the individual.[107] In applying this approach to juvenile proceedings, Fortas blurred the distinction between children and adults, at least with respect to their relationship to the state. The privilege against self-incrimination served the same equalizing function for children as it did for adults, regardless of the nature of juvenile proceedings. Indeed, according to Fortas, the privilege's function was even more important where juveniles are concerned because of their immaturity.[108]

Thus, in extending the rights to notice, counsel, confrontation, and cross-examination and the privilege against self-incrimination to respondents in juvenile proceedings, Fortas also imported into juvenile proceedings the principles embedded in the decisions that originally incorporated these rights into state criminal proceedings. In those decisions, the Court determined the fundamental importance of each of these rights on the basis of their relationship to the "adversarial" and "accusatory" system of criminal justice established by the Bill of Rights.[109] This implicit application of principles intimately associated with adversary criminal proceedings eventually led to a conceptual shift in juvenile justice. The Bill of Rights established an adversarial, accusatory system of criminal justice for a reason: to employ the rule of law to limit government attempts to punish individuals. By giving delinquency hearings at least some of the procedural trappings of adversary proceedings, the Court invited states to incorporate explicitly the substantive objective of such proceedings—punishment—into their juvenile court statutes.

DISSENTS AND CONCURRENCES

The possibility that criminal procedure might lead to criminal sanctions as a result of the *Gault* decision did not go unnoticed or unremarked upon by other members of the Court. The possibility that selective incorporation might erode the distinction between children and adults bothered both Justices Stewart and Harlan. In contrast to Fortas's approach, Stewart's unequivocal dissent and Harlan's mixed dissent and concurrence reflected an adherence to fundamental fairness standards of due process. For both Stewart and Harlan the crucial question in *Gault* was whether Arizona's delinquency proceedings were potentially so prejudicial that they violated the fundamental right of juveniles to a fair hearing.[110] The fundamental fairness approach allowed them to consider this point without questioning the non-criminal nature of juvenile proceedings. The precise requirements of a "fair hearing" in juvenile courts flowed directly from the distinctive nature of delinquency proceedings.

In Stewart's view, delinquency hearings were "simply not adversary proceedings," and it was inappropriate to analyze them according to the norms of either civil or criminal procedure.[111] He vigorously criticized the majority's decision to use "an obscure Arizona case as a vehicle to impose upon thousands of juvenile courts throughout the Nation restrictions that the Constitution made applicable to adversary criminal trials." He found this course of action "wholly unsound as a matter of constitutional law, and sadly unwise as a matter of judicial policy."[112] Although Stewart shared the majority's disappointment with the accomplishments of juvenile courts, he argued that remedying this failure required more than due process review under the Fourteenth Amendment.[113] "I possess neither the specialized experience nor the expert knowledge," he wrote, "to predict with any certainty where may lie the brightest hope for progress in dealing with the serious problems of juvenile delinquency."[114] Like the juvenile court's nineteenth-century founders, however, he was certain the answer did not lie in exposing children to adversary proceedings.

Justice Harlan agreed that the majority had approached the question of juvenile due process incorrectly by not taking seriously the state's own characterization of juvenile proceedings. Unlike Stewart, however, Harlan did not think that delinquency proceedings were entirely beyond constitutional scrutiny. The weakness of the majority opinion, he argued, was that the standard it provided for elaborating juvenile due process was based on criminal due process.[115] As a result, the majority opinion left the impression that it was questioning "the wisdom of having such courts at all."[116] In a succinct summary of the fundamental fairness approach, Harlan argued that the Court should instead "determine what forms of procedural protection are necessary to guarantee the fundamental fairness of juvenile proceedings, and not which of the procedures now employed in criminal trials should be transplanted intact to proceedings in these specialized courts."[117]

Fundamental fairness, Harlan continued, provides four criteria for defining due process: the problems confronting the state, the actual character of the state's procedural system, the interests affected by the proceedings, and the circumstances of the particular case.[118] These criteria should be applied cautiously, especially in juvenile proceedings where the "procedural framework is . . . a principal element of the substantive legislative system."[119] Harlan further suggested that the Court should also be guided by the desirability of preserving the essential purpose of juvenile court laws and of maintaining flexibility for future constitutional development.[120] These criteria, he averred, would permit the Court to establish procedural requirements that both protect juveniles and permit the states "to pursue without unnecessary hindrance the purposes which they believe imperative in this field."[121] In the longest of the separate opinions, Harlan concluded that juveniles should be protected by the rights to timely notice, counsel, and a written record.

Gault's facts and legal issues also produced separate concurrences from Justices Byron White and Hugo Black. White, a supporter of selective incorporation, filed a concurring opinion to register his disagreement with the majority's decision on the self-incrimination issue. He argued that the privilege could be violated only if the state compelled a suspect to confess, and he found no evidence in the record to suggest that this had occurred in Gerald's case. White thus considered Gault an inappropriate case in which to decide whether confessions were an unnecessary part of the rehabilitative process.[122] Justice Black, on the other hand, wrote a separate concurring opinion in order to stress that Stewart was correct in pointing out that the majority opinion had struck "a well-nigh fatal blow to much that is unique about the juvenile courts in the Nation."[123] Unlike Stewart, who was moved by this observation to dissent, Black viewed this aspect of Fortas's opinion to mean that, without the total incorporation of every criminal procedure provision of the Bill of Rights into juvenile proceedings, juveniles would be denied equal protection as well as due process.

Black's decision to add his voice to the debate rather than simply to allow Fortas's opinion to speak for him was symptomatic of the deteriorating relationship between the two men. Black had always been critical of judges who believed themselves capable of interpreting the spirit of the Constitution, which was something that Fortas was apt to do with respect to the Fourteenth Amendment's due process clause. Partly because of this dispute over judicial philosophy, and partly because of their mutual desire for leadership on the Warren Court, the Fortas-Black relationship was bitterly conflictual in several cases, including *Gault*.[124]

Although Fortas believed that the similar form, consequences, and interests at stake in juvenile and criminal proceedings required that the Court abandon the deference to traditional juvenile procedure implied by the fundamental fairness standard of review, he rejected Black's view that every procedural difference between the two types of proceedings should fall. Indeed, the Fortas-led majority made an effort to ensure that selective incorporation would not harm integral aspects of the rehabilitative process. It sought to do so by confining its holding to that part of juvenile proceedings—delinquency adjudication—that was most like criminal proceedings and by suggesting that procedural formality consistent with due process norms would actually enhance the rehabilitative objectives of juvenile justice. Both of these qualifications allowed the majority to soften the impact of its rejection of almost seventy years of legal orthodoxy about the nature and structure of juvenile proceedings.

The concurring and dissenting opinions in *Gault* can thus be summarized:

Black (concurring)
1. The holding "strikes a well-nigh fatal blow to much that is unique" about juvenile courts.
2. Where conviction and confinement for crimes is possible, the Constitution requires that both children and adults benefit from *all* provisions of the Bill of Rights.

3. The procedural distinction between children and adults denies equal protection.

White (concurring)
1. *Gault* is a "poor vehicle for resolving a difficult problem."
2. Although agreeing with Fortas, Justice White takes exception to the holding with respect to privilege against self-incrimination.

Harlan (concurring/dissenting)
1. States may create separate court systems for juveniles.
2. The Court should measure requirements of due process according to standards of "fundamental fairness."
3. Only three requirements are necessary: notice, counsel, and written record.

Stewart (dissenting)
1. The Court's decision is unsound constitutional law and unwise judicial policy.
2. Juvenile proceedings are neither criminal trials nor adversary proceedings.
3. Inflexible restrictions of the Constitution are not the answer to the problems of juvenile justice.

The central disputes resolved by the Court in *Gault* involved questions concerning the nature of juvenile proceedings and the nature of childhood. According to the traditional view espoused by Arizona, the status of children was such that whatever rights they possessed were not those explicitly protected by the Constitution and the Bill of Rights. Consequently, although Arizona admitted that juvenile proceedings were governed by the Fourteenth Amendment's due process clause, the state argued that this meant that children are entitled to a standard of fundamental fairness consistent with the noncriminal, nonadversarial nature of juvenile proceedings in which constitutional rights are not at stake. The ACLU, on the other hand, perceived confinement in terms of its impact on the independent right of children to liberty rather than in terms of its contribution to their welfare. Therefore juvenile proceedings were functionally similar to criminal proceedings and juvenile due process should be determined by selective incorporation of the Bill of Rights. Tactical considerations caused the ACLU to moderate its claims, but its argument still encompassed almost the entire panoply of due process rights available to defendants in ordinary criminal trials. The consummate legal realist, Justice Abe Fortas, accepted the ACLU's argument, both because it was factually more compelling and because there seemed to be evidence that selective incorporation of criminal procedure into delinquency adjudication hearings would not undermine the most important substantive differences between the two types of proceedings.

There are many reasons why *Gault* succeeded where other cases had failed. The scholarly literature had been dominated for two decades by studies and commentaries critical of the procedural informality that characterized juvenile courts. These demands for reform captured the attention of a Supreme Court deeply concerned with the rights of accused persons, a concern that Chief Justice Warren had articulated in the context of juvenile proceedings in 1964. *Gault* was an attractive case in which to voice this concern because it presented a sympathetic factual situation to the Court. The apparent injustice suffered by Gerald was so egregious that it provided a powerful justification for reforming juvenile court practices.[125] The ACLU, by maintaining complete control over the litigation, was also able to develop the legal issues presented by Gerald's commitment fully and unambiguously. Ultimately, the opponents of juvenile court procedural reform were more committed to traditional concepts of juvenile justice than the normative or empirical atmosphere would permit. The decision in *Gault* opened the door to further constitutional litigation concerning juvenile courts, and the cases that followed asked the Court to evaluate other aspects of juvenile court procedure on the basis of the analysis employed in *Gault*. That the ACLU really believed that juvenile proceedings ought to be bound by precisely the same procedural safeguards as ordinary criminal trials is implicit in the organization's leading role in litigating the cases that came after *Gault*.

6. Constitutional Challenges Beyond *Gault*

The impact of important constitutional decisions is felt in many different ways and in many different places. In the case of *Gault,* the Court intended and expected that the decision's principal point of impact would be the nation's juvenile courtrooms. In the view of Justice Fortas and his colleagues in the majority, the principles enunciated in *Gault* were destined to have a positive effect on those courts and the administrative apparatus surrounding them. Not surprisingly, the decision would also affect state legislatures and the juvenile court reform movement, although the majority did not expect any impact in these areas to be negative. Further, like many important decisions, *Gault* raised as many legal questions as it answered. Consequently, it served as a catalyst for additional constitutional demands on and challenges to juvenile courts.

Unanswered Questions

By establishing that the Bill of Rights applies to juvenile proceedings, *Gault* answered many of the constitutional questions about those procedures raised during the early 1960s. Yet the decision also left a number of specific questions about juvenile due process unanswered.[1] Among the more important of these were whether juveniles had a constitutional right to trial by jury in delinquency adjudication hearings and whether the state must prove allegations of delinquency beyond a reasonable doubt. The Court's silence on the jury trial issue in *Gault* was understandable, since the question had never been raised in the lower courts. The standard of proof issue, on the other hand, had been explicitly considered by the Arizona Supreme Court, which had ruled that delinquency petitions in that state must be proved by the intermediate probative standard of "clear and convincing evidence."[2] Dorsen and Rezneck had not challenged this standard in their submissions to the Supreme Court, and the Court chose not to venture outside the parameters set by the ACLU's brief to consider the issue.[3]

This silence did not mean, of course, that Dorsen and Rezneck were satisfied with the absence of these two particular elements of criminal due process from delinquency proceedings. Indeed, they later argued that the application of both jury trials and the reasonable doubt standard of proof to delinquency proceedings was consistent with, and perhaps even required by, the Court's analysis of juvenile proceedings in *Gault*.[4] At least with respect to the standard of proof issue, other legal commentators shared Dorsen and Rezneck's view.[5] One theme of the post-*Gault* commentaries was that the Court's criticism of the accomplishments of juvenile courts and its characterization of juvenile proceedings as similar in function to criminal proceedings provided sound constitutional and policy reasons for incorporating the criminal standard of proof into delinquency adjudication hearings.

Some state and lower federal court judges were also persuaded by Dorsen and Rezneck's view of the standard of proof issue. In terms of its symbolic importance, perhaps the most significant state decision came from the Illinois Supreme Court, which held in *In re Urbasek* (1967) that the state could no longer rely on the civil "preponderance of the evidence" standard to prove delinquency petitions brought under the state's Juvenile Court Act.[6] The court found in the language of *Gault* "a spirit that transcends the specific issues there involved," leading it to conclude "that . . . it would not be consonant with due process or equal protection to grant allegedly delinquent juveniles the same procedural rights that protect adults charged with crimes, while depriving these rights of their full efficacy by allowing a finding of delinquency upon a lesser standard of proof than that required to sustain a criminal conviction."[7] Consequently, the Illinois court ruled that delinquency adjudications based on criminal acts are "valid only when the acts of delinquency are proved beyond a reasonable doubt to have been committed by the juvenile charged."[8] That this decision would issue from the jurisdiction in which the procedurally informal, *parens patriae* juvenile court had been born is indicative of the legal revolution initiated by *Gault*.

The U.S. Court of Appeals for the Fourth Circuit adopted a similar rule in *United States v. Costanzo* (1968), where it held that federal delinquency proceedings that might result in institutional confinement must be considered criminal proceedings for the purposes of determining procedural standards.[9] Like the Illinois court, this federal court understood *Gault*'s main theme to be the similarity of delinquency proceedings to criminal trials. "We see a compelling similarity," the court explained, "between the enumerated safeguards due a juvenile in as full measure as an adult and the requirement of proof beyond a reasonable doubt." The court of appeals thus concluded that it would be a "patent violation of due process and equal protection" to provide allegedly delinquent juveniles with the protection of a lower standard of proof than the one available to adult criminal defendants.[10]

Daniel Rezneck had the first opportunity to present this view of the standard of proof issue (as well as other criminal due process requirements) to the Supreme Court in a case from Ohio, *In re Whittington* (1968).[11] Rezneck argued that Ohio's juvenile code improperly allowed the state's juvenile courts to find juveniles delinquent according to an unconstitutionally low standard of proof in the context of proceedings that also denied juveniles their constitutional rights to trial by jury, an impartial tribunal, bail, and the privilege against self-incrimination. The Court avoided a decision on these claims, however, by remanding the case for reconsideration by the Ohio Court of Appeals, which had not yet had the opportunity to assess the impact of *Gault* on juvenile proceedings in the state.[12]

In 1969, *DeBacker v. Brainard*,[13] on appeal from the Nebraska Supreme Court, presented the Court with a second opportunity to address both the jury trial and standard of proof issues. The Court again avoided the substantive issues of the case by deciding that it had improvidently granted certiorari in *DeBacker*. During oral argument, counsel for the juvenile (DeBacker) admitted that the evidence presented against his client at the delinquency hearing in question had indeed been sufficient to support an adjudication of delinquency under the reasonable doubt standard and under Nebraska's less rigorous preponderance of the evidence standard. In view of this "commendably forthright" admission, the Court decided that *DeBacker* was "not an appropriate vehicle for consideration of the standard of proof in juvenile proceedings."[14] The Court also declined to decide the jury trial issue on the grounds that this requirement had not yet been incorporated into criminal proceedings when DeBacker's juvenile hearing took place.

In re Winship (1970)[15] was thus the third occasion on which a case containing the standard of proof question reached the Supreme Court. Three characteristics distinguished *Winship* from both *Whittington* and *DeBacker*. First, it came to the Court from a state (New York) that had been one of the first to abandon various procedural elements of *parens patriae* juvenile proceedings. Second, reformers in that state had targeted for removal one of the few remaining *parens patriae* procedural components of the state's Family Court Act—reliance on the civil preponderance of the evidence standard to prove delinquency adjudications—and were actively seeking a suitable case to use as a vehicle for pursuing this objective. Third, the lower court record in *Winship* suggested that the family court's reliance on the preponderance standard had produced a delinquency adjudication that the court might not have reached under the reasonable doubt standard. These characteristics made *Winship* the obvious candidate to become the third decision in the trilogy of cases that constitutes the essence of the constitutional domestication of juvenile courts.

The *Winship* Case

LEGAL BACKGROUND AND LOWER COURT PROCEEDINGS

Unlike other states, New York provided its juvenile offenders with a relatively wide range of procedural safeguards similar to those enjoyed by adult defendants in regular criminal courts. The major reason for this difference was the state's 1962 Family Court Act, which guaranteed juveniles the statutory right to counsel, granted them a right to appellate review, provided for bifurcated adjudication and disposition proceedings, narrowed the definition of delinquency to include only criminal acts, and created a new jurisdictional category, Persons in Need of Supervision, to cover noncriminal misbehavior. Heightened procedural safeguards for New York's juveniles had also been imposed by several state court decisions.[16]

Although the Family Court Act clarified some of the procedural ambiguities of delinquency proceedings, it produced litigation of its own on two important issues: the privilege against self-incrimination and the appropriate standard of proof. Ironically, post–Family Court Act cases generally described delinquency and PINS proceedings as noncriminal.[17] Family Court judges in particular, however, were uncertain about the extent to which this designation made such proceedings exempt from criminal due process. In *In re Doe* (1964), for example, a family court judge ruled that, where the act was silent on procedural matters, the court should follow the rules of administrative hearings rather than of criminal trials.[18] Yet other judges were more willing to interpret the act as requiring various elements of criminal due process, despite its noncriminal character. In *In re Ronny* (1963), a New York City judge prohibited the use of uncorroborated confessions in both delinquency and PINS proceedings.[19] He characterized delinquency proceedings as "quasi-criminal" and declared that juveniles possessed the same constitutional rights as adults, with the exception of the right to trial by jury.[20] The family court judge in *In re Williams* (1966) followed a similar line of reasoning.[21] He concluded that the Family Court Act's provisions clearly indicated "that a child charged with being a juvenile delinquent is not to be shorn of all his constitutional rights by the simple expedient of calling his offense juvenile delinquency and not a crime."[22] Both due process and fair treatment, therefore, required that juveniles be protected against unreasonable searches and seizures.[23] The state court of appeals employed identical reasoning in a similar case decided in 1966.[24]

As the uncertainty of family court judges about the meaning of the Family Court Act indicates, by the mid-1960s a tension existed in New York between the elements of criminal due process imposed on delinquency proceedings by the Family Court Act and the act's attempt to retain a noncriminal posture toward delinquency. One consequence of this tension was the opportunity for reformers to challenge the act's remaining *parens patriae* procedural components. Indeed, during the middle part of the decade, the standard of proof used in delinquency hearings became of special concern to the appellate division of the Legal Aid Society's family court branch. The importance of this issue was such that it prompted the director of the appellate division, Rena Uviller, to circulate a memorandum to law guardians throughout New York City to request that they raise objections on the record to the Family Court Act's reliance on the preponderance standard in delinquency proceedings.[25] The memorandum was part of a general strategy by Uviller to build trial records on the remaining deficiencies in the act, which she believed could be removed more expeditiously through litigation than through legislative efforts.

Although the law guardians were not obliged to follow Uviller's instructions on the standard of proof issue, one who routinely did was Irene Rosenberg; her actions in turn produced a case whose record suited Uviller's broader objectives. The story of the case begins on March 28, 1967, when a furniture store saleswoman discovered that money was missing from the purse she had left in an unsecured locker near the store's washroom. Shortly after noticing that the money was missing, she saw a young boy emerge from the washroom and quickly run out of the store. One day later, the police took twelve-year-old Samuel Winship into custody on an unrelated matter and noticed a similarity between him and the description provided by the saleswoman of the boy who had run from the store. The officer contacted the woman, who identified Samuel as the boy whom she had seen. Three days after the alleged theft (March 30), the police filed a delinquency petition in the family court, alleging that Samuel had committed larceny.

Family court judge Millard Midonick held an adjudication hearing on the same day the petition was filed. Irene Rosenberg represented Samuel, who told the court that he had been home in bed when the alleged theft took place. Samuel's mother and uncle both testified that he had returned home from riding his bicycle almost an hour before the theft, eaten dinner, watched television, and gone directly to bed. They also testified that Samuel could not have left the house after dinner undetected. Unfortunately, Samuel's uncle proved to be a weak witness; he was confused about dates and offered conflicting testimony about when he had been at his sister's home. The saleswoman, on the other hand, impressed Judge Midonick with her knowledge of the boy, and the judge could see no reason why she would give false testimony. He perceived many motivations, however, for false testimony from Samuel's mother and uncle. Consequently, although Samuel did not have an unusual amount of money on his person or at home, Judge Midonick found the saleswoman's testimony more credible and declared the petition proved by a preponderance of the evidence.[26]

Consistent with the instructions contained in Uviller's memorandum, Rosenberg challenged the judge's reliance on the preponderance standard, and she moved to have the adjudication against her client dismissed for failing to meet the reasonable doubt standard. Her motion produced the following exchange with the judge:

> Mrs. Rosenberg: Well, I would like to make one more motion.
> The Court: What is that?
> Mrs. Rosenberg: That this finding by Your Honor violates the boy's equal protection rights because if he was 16, he would have to be found guilty beyond a reasonable doubt. Your Honor is making a finding by the preponderance of the evidence.
> The Court: Well, it convinces me.
> Mrs. Rosenberg: It's not beyond a reasonable doubt, Your Honor.
> The Court: That is true. I'm convinced of the facts alleged. Our statute says a preponderance and a preponderance it is. That is the only difference between children and grownups that I can see. I don't think its an unfair difference at all.[27]

Rosenberg persisted: "Although the State may lawfully make distinctions between adults and children," she argued, "the burden of proof and the quantum of the burden of proof has no relation to [the distinction] which the state is making between treatment of the children and adults."[28] Judge Midonick responded by referring to the noncriminal nature of delinquency proceedings; the different standard of proof was not inequitable, he argued, because juveniles were not subject to "adult imprisonment, adult records, adult punishments."[29]

This response produced another important exchange:

Mrs. Rosenberg: The distinctions between adults and the children may be valid themselves, but this particular distinction . . . [has] nothing to do with the State's distinction of treatment of these children as opposed to adults.

The Court: Well, this State can make distinctions and unequal laws depending upon reasonable differences.

Mrs. Rosenberg: Is there a valid distinction?

The Court: Yes. In this sense there is. Another factor here for the preponderance rule is that anybody who really wants to know knows that I can more easily make a mistake on preponderance than beyond a reasonable doubt basis and my finding isn't that certain.

Mrs. Rosenberg: No finding is certain.

The Court: No, not certain as a finding of an adult court because the rule is different. Somebody may not take my finding to be a solid basis as an adult finding because it's not made on the same basis.[30]

Judge Midonick's cryptic admission that his finding might not pass the reasonable doubt test weakened his earlier statements concerning the rationality of New York's reliance on the preponderance standard in delinquency proceedings. The possibility that errors might be made more frequently under the preponderance standard than under the reasonable doubt test seriously undermined any argument that the state's choice between the two standards was largely irrelevant, particularly given that fact-finding errors could lead to commitment to the state training school. Not surprisingly, these exchanges between Midonick and Rosenberg became an important component of the appellate attack against the Family Court Act's preponderance standard.

Indeed, despite finding that the evidence presented against Samuel Winship was much stronger than that in most delinquency hearings, Rena Uviller decided to appeal his commitment to the state training school after reading the exchange between Rosenberg and Midonick.[31] Armed with a lower court record indicating that a higher standard of proof might have produced a different outcome, Uviller asked the appellate division of the New York Supreme Court to reverse the family court's commitment order. On June 6, 1968, it summarily denied Uviller's appeal and affirmed the commitment order without issuing written reasons for its decision. Uviller's next step was an appeal to the New York Court of Appeals, where she attacked the Family Court Act's provision for the preponderance standard on both due process and equal protection grounds. None of her arguments, however, was sufficient to persuade a majority of the court of appeals to overturn the commitment order against Samuel. In a narrow four-to-three decision, the court upheld the act's reliance on the civil standard of proof.[32]

The principal rationale for the court's rejection of Uviller's appeal was the traditional *parens patriae* distinction between juvenile and criminal proceedings. The distinction, whose principle source in New York law was *People v. Lewis* (1932),[33] justified differential treatment of juveniles and adults and exempted juvenile proceedings from criminal due process. The majority opinion emphasized that the "main objective of the special system of law for treating young juvenile offenders is to hold them as children apart from the usual methods and ineradicable consequences of the criminal law." This objective, the opinion continued, made juvenile courts more concerned with "the totality of factors which cause a child to meet difficulty in his life" than with "the event which brings the child to the court." Because of the nature of this broader concern and the positive impact of its rise to prominence, the majority asserted that the "accoutrements of due process characteristic of criminal trials are often irrelevant" in juvenile courts.[34] Similarly, because the legislature had sufficiently distinguished delinquency matters from criminal proceedings, the majority did not find any violation of equal protection.[35]

Perhaps the most intriguing aspect of the opinion was the way in which it interpreted the relevance of *Kent* and *Gault* to the questions at issue in Winship's appeal. Although recognizing that these decisions had undermined "the concept of a juvenile court free from the technicalities of the criminal law," the majority lamented the apparent fact that the original ideal of nineteenth-century juvenile justice had suffered the "singular misfortune of being impaled on the sharp points of a few hard constitutional cases" that were unrepresentative of juvenile proceedings generally.[36] The majority therefore did not find any compelling reason why the principles underlying *Gault* should apply to procedural questions not explicitly considered in that case.

The three judges in the minority, however, were highly critical of this narrow view of the relevance of *Gault* to the case at bar. Led by the court's chief judge, they argued that *Gault* had explicitly rejected legislative declarations concerning the noncriminal nature of delinquency proceedings as a legitimate justification for lower procedural standards. What mattered were the actual consequences of such proceedings, which the Supreme Court had declared in *Gault* to be similar to the consequences of criminal proceedings. Although agreeing with the majority's view that juveniles benefited from the existence of separate judicial proceedings, the dissenting judges argued that this aspect was irrelevant for determining key procedural issues. The emphasis in *Gault* on the functional nature of juvenile proceedings thus led the dissenters to conclude "that due process of law is violated if a child may be found to have committed a crime and incarcerated for an appreciable length of time on evidence less than proof beyond a reasonable doubt."[37]

Rena Uviller pursued Samuel Winship's case to the New York Court of Appeals because of her conviction that litigation would be more successful than legislative reform in changing the standard of proof for delinquency adjudications. Although she failed to accomplish her objective by the slimmest of margins, the case she chose was a superb vehicle for bringing the issue before the Supreme Court. First, it involved a procedural provision that was potentially inconsistent with the spirit of the statute in which it was contained and with the major Supreme Court decision on juvenile law.[38] Second, there was a lower court record that highlighted possible deficiencies in the statutory provision. Finally, the highest state court was sharply divided on the provision's constitutionality. After two aborted attempts by the Supreme Court to examine *Gault*'s applicability to the standard of proof issue, *Winship* presented itself as an opportunity that could not be rejected.

ARGUMENTS IN THE SUPREME COURT

The jurisdictional statement Uviller filed early in summer 1969 asked the Supreme Court to decide whether the New York Family Court Act violated the Fourteenth Amendment's due process and equal protection clauses by permitting delinquency adjudications and institutional commitment on a preponderance of the evidence.[39] *Winship* became the first case, therefore, in which the procedural differences between criminal and juvenile proceedings were expressly challenged in the Supreme Court on equal protection grounds. Uviller argued in the jurisdictional statement that *Gault* should be interpreted as incorporating into delinquency adjudication hearings every procedural right essential to due process. The reasonable doubt standard of proof, which Uviller described as being "infused with the very essence of due process of law," was one such right because of its relationship to the presumption of innocence.[40] As the record from Samuel's delinquency hearing suggested, the use of the preponderance standard meant that the state could overcome that presumption with relatively weak evidence.

Uviller pursued both themes of the jurisdictional statement—equal protection and due process—in somewhat greater depth in the brief she filed on Samuel's behalf. In the equal protection component of her argument, Uviller took *Gault*'s implicit redefinition of childhood close to its logical conclusion. In her view, the fundamental principle established by *Gault* was that none of the differences between juvenile and adult criminal defendants was sufficiently important to justify denying juveniles the protection of basic elements of criminal due process when determining their guilt or innocence of various offenses. To put Uviller's argument another way, juvenile and adult defendants shared the same basic interest in liberty, and this interest was equally threatened in juvenile and criminal proceedings. Juvenile and adult defendants belonged to a single class of individuals whose liberty was at risk in judicial proceedings. Consequently, Uviller concluded, to withhold "a critical safeguard from some members of the class solely because of their youth is to deny them equal protection of the law."[41]

Uviller attempted to soften the implications of this argument by conceding that differences between juveniles and adults do matter at certain stages of case processing. Although she strongly asserted that these differences were "wholly unrelated to the standard of proof for determining guilt or innocence," she allowed that they could justify more flexible intake and dispositional procedures.[42] Her argument suggested that the differences between juveniles and adults permitted states to compartmentalize juvenile proceedings to a degree that would not be justified in the context of criminal proceedings. Although this position was certainly consistent with the Court's own view in *Gault*, the logic of the argument was not obvious. No reason was given why the generally similar liberty interests of juveniles and adults would be less threatened during juvenile intake or dispositional proceedings than during the pretrial and sentencing stages of criminal proceedings. The implicit conclusion of Uviller's equal protection argument was that no important differences really existed between juvenile and adult defendants that could justify separate judicial proceedings, except perhaps administrative convenience.

Perhaps because she recognized the incompatibility of this conclusion with the Court's general support for separate juvenile proceedings, Uviller emphasized the due process component of her argument. As in the equal protection component of the brief, Uviller focused the Court's attention on the fact that her client had been deprived of liberty as a result of the family court's reliance on a standard of proof less than proof beyond a reasonable doubt. "While comparatively low standards of proof may satisfy due process where interests less critical than liberty are in issue," she argued, "the very highest standard has always been employed where freedom is at stake."[43] This application was true, Uviller continued, despite the absence of any explicit requirement of proof beyond a reasonable doubt in either the Bill of Rights or in the Supreme Court's own jurisprudence on criminal procedure.[44] What made this standard of proof an implicit part of the "law of the land" in criminal proceedings was its relationship to the presumption of innocence. According to Uviller, the presumption of innocence and the reasonable doubt standard of proof functioned in tandem to provide the maximum level of protection to the most important right or interest at stake in criminal proceedings: liberty. As long as the Supreme Court held that the same interest was at stake in juvenile proceedings, she concluded, the Court was compelled to provide the same due process protection to juveniles.[45]

Uviller also argued that the reasonable doubt standard served to protect the right to exercise the privilege against self-incrimination that the *Gault* Court had found so important. She suggested that the lower standard of proof discouraged defendants from exercising the privilege because reliance on the preponderance standard made it necessary for defendants to testify once the state had made its prima facie case against them. Further, Uviller added the familiar claim that the worthwhile rehabilitative goals of juvenile proceedings would not be undermined by relying on a higher standard of proof. In support of this claim she cited studies by the Children's Bureau of the Department of Health, Education, and Welfare, the National Conference of Commissioners on Uniform State Laws, and the American Bar Association.[46]

Uviller's conclusion received the support of an amicus brief filed jointly by the Neighborhood Legal Services Program (NLSP) and the Legal Aid Agency (LAA) of Washington, D.C., both of which provided legal representation to juveniles. The NLSP was a part of the national network of legal services programs that received funding from the Office of Economic Opportunity to provide counsel to indigent defendants. Its reason for participating in *Winship* was consistent with the law reform objectives of this network, since NLSP had several cases pending before the U.S. Court of Appeals that involved the standard of proof issue. The LAA, which had a statutory responsibility to represent juveniles in delinquency proceedings, joined the appeal because, like New York's Legal Aid Society, it was actively pursuing litigation to raise the standard of proof necessary to support findings of delinquency.

The NLSP/LAA brief contained many of the major themes of Uviller's brief, including the importance of the reasonable doubt standard to criminal due process, the functional similarity of criminal proceedings and delinquency hearings, the relationship between a high standard of proof and effective exercise of the privilege against self-incrimination, and the compatibility of that standard of proof with the rehabilitative goals of juvenile courts.[47] "Both policy and the Constitution," the agencies asserted, "compel the adoption of the higher standard of proof in order to safeguard the fundamental rights of a youth charged with committing a delinquent act."[48] Although few of the arguments supporting this assertion were novel, the brief did make one contribution to Uviller's equal protection argument. Noting the ease with which juveniles could be transferred from juvenile courts to criminal courts, where they benefited from the entire range of due process safeguards, the agencies suggested that the lower standard of proof violated equal protection not because it represented differential treatment of juvenile and adult defendants on the basis of age but because it constituted differential treatment of juvenile defendants solely because of jurisdictional waiver.[49] Underlying this argument, of course, were two assumptions: juvenile and criminal proceedings are essentially similar, and waiver decisions are relatively arbitrary.

The NLSP/LAA brief provided some empirical evidence to support at least the first of these assumptions and a second argument that the reasonable doubt standard would enhance the rehabilitative capacity of the juvenile system. Citing a District of Columbia study concerning the adult consequences of delinquency adjudications, the brief showed that such adjudications carried essentially the same stigma as criminal conviction.[50] The agencies argued that this finding indicated even the long-term similarity between juvenile and criminal proceedings. Recidivism data from the same study also led the NLSP and the LAA to question the rehabilitative accomplishments of the juvenile system. In their view, these data confirmed Justice Fortas's speculation in *Kent* that juveniles derived few benefits from juvenile proceedings.[51] They concluded in their brief that a higher standard of proof would at least reduce the number of delinquency adjudications and institutional commitments, permitting scarce rehabilitative resources to be concentrated on the few juveniles who really needed them.[52]

The arguments advanced by Uviller and the NLSP/LAA coalition to support the imposition of the reasonable doubt standard on delinquency proceedings offered a somewhat radical interpretation of *Gault*. Instead of merely formalizing certain aspects of juvenile proceedings, Uviller interpreted the Court's landmark decision as a redefinition of the very nature of juvenile proceedings. In her view, *Gault* meant that delinquency adjudication proceedings were identical to felony trials, and she drew the conclusion that the sole issue in such proceedings should be a juvenile's guilt or innocence. This view was a sharp departure from the traditional one, which even the *Gault* Court was unwilling to abandon entirely, that adjudication proceedings are an integral part of a complex process to address the behavioral problems of children.[53] By emphasizing questions of guilt and innocence, Uviller implicitly shifted the focus of juvenile proceedings from delinquency as a broad behavioral problem to delinquency as criminal activity.

The task of defending the Family Court Act's preponderance standard against Uviller's attack fell to Stanley Buchsbaum, head of the appellate division of the Corporation Counsel's Office of New York City. Buchsbaum countered Uviller's reliance on the broad language of *Kent* and *Gault* by arguing that the Court's discussions of the similarities between delinquency proceedings and criminal trials were merely dicta and did not justify Uviller's broad interpretation of those decisions.[54] This strategy had first appeared in Buchsbaum's initial motion to dismiss the appeal, where he had argued that *Gault* should be interpreted narrowly to mean only that "those criminal law rights which are of constitutional dimension and part of due process of law are eligible for mandatory inclusion in juvenile proceedings."[55] Because the requirement of proof beyond a reasonable doubt did not have this status, nothing in the language of *Gault* explicitly required that it apply to juvenile proceedings. Nor, according to Buchsbaum, was this standard of proof required by concepts of "essential fairness" or considerations of sound policy.[56]

Although Buchsbaum's motion to dismiss failed, he pursued the same strategy in his brief on the merits.[57] He devoted most of his brief to the due process component of Uviller's argument. Responding to her equal protection argument, he stressed that there could be no denial of equal protection where reasonable classifications were involved and that the distinction between children and adults represented such a classification. This response, however, glossed over the fact that the Family Court Act, while retaining the distinction between juveniles and adults, had eliminated the distinction between delinquency and criminal activity. This point was key in Uviller's equal protection argument, and Buchsbaum did not really have an adequate response to it.

According to Buchsbaum, the *Gault* Court had meant to accomplish nothing more than to ensure that states balanced the legitimate objectives of juvenile justice against the requirements of due process and essential fairness. In other words, he stressed the need to approach juvenile due process from a contextual perspective that might allow for less rigorous application of the Bill of Rights. Not surprisingly, he disputed Uviller's claim that these less rigorous requirements included the reasonable doubt standard: "The fact that the reasonable doubt rule is related to what appellant calls the 'integrity of the fact-finding process' establishes neither its constitutional status nor its applicability to delinquency cases."[58] However, what *might* establish its applicability to delinquency proceedings, according to Buchsbaum, was the relationship of such proceedings to criminal trials. Indeed, Buchsbaum sought to raise the constitutional stakes of the case by focusing the Court's attention on the close relationship between the reasonable doubt standard and criminal proceedings.

Unlike the rights granted in *Gault*, Buchsbaum argued, the reasonable doubt standard belonged uniquely to criminal due process.[59] The issue in *Winship*, in his view, was not simply whether another element of criminal due process should be incorporated into delinquency hearings but whether those hearings were identical in every respect to criminal trials. The issue, in his words, was whether "the juvenile court in New York, its procedures and its operations are such that despite its label, it is in effect a criminal court."[60] Buchsbaum warned the Court that juvenile justice would suffer irreparable damage if the justices imposed the reasonable doubt standard on delinquency proceedings as a result of finding them to be equivalent to criminal trials.[61] The point Buchsbaum was pursuing in this line of argument, of course, was precisely that the Court could not agree with Uviller for any reason other than that delinquency proceedings are identical to criminal trials. He thus directly confronted Uviller's claim that a higher standard of proof would not harm the substantive benefits of juvenile proceedings.

Buchsbaum concluded his argument by speculating on the motivations for procedural complaints like those found in *Winship*. The reason for challenging the authority of state legislatures to determine such matters as the level of proof necessary in delinquency proceedings free from constitutional constraints, he argued, was not that juvenile court critics had suddenly discovered that juvenile courts were criminal courts in disguise but because those courts had not yet fulfilled the "dreams and hopes" of their founders.[62] Though Buchsbaum conceded that lack of success was an important consideration, he questioned Uviller's assertion that the performance of New York's juvenile court "fell so short of theoretical purpose as to require that it be treated as a criminal court so as to make applicable all of the constitutional guarantees available to adults."[63] According to Buchsbaum, there were still substantive reasons for maintaining procedural differences between juvenile and criminal proceedings.[64]

This view also permeated the arguments of the attorney general of New York, who filed an amicus brief to defend the constitutionality of the Family Court Act.[65] According to the attorney general, the essential difference between criminal law in New York and the state's delinquency provisions was that the former was "predicated upon the commission of certain acts and a prescribed punishment for those acts" and the latter provided for "supervision over a child . . . based upon a demonstrated need for psychological assistance."[66] The difficulty with the reasonable doubt standard, he claimed, was that it might prevent juvenile courts from intervening "while the child is still at a receptive age."[67] He also questioned the need for this standard in proceedings where decisions were made by expert judges rather than inexperienced juries. Finally, the attorney general saw few benefits to be gained from declaring "*any* particular measure of persuasion to be an indisposable element of due process," because to do so would "disturb and alter the historical development of the standards in juvenile courts."[68]

The essential disagreement between the litigants in *Winship* concerned the meaning of the *Gault* Court's finding that delinquency proceedings were "comparable in seriousness" to felony prosecutions.[69] Rena Uviller insisted that "comparable" meant "equivalent," or even "identical." In her view, this interpretation required the application of all procedural safeguards considered critical in criminal prosecutions to delinquency proceedings. Her opponents, on the other hand, argued that Uviller's position would transform delinquency proceedings into full adversarial criminal trials, which would violate both the spirit and letter of *Gault*. Buchsbaum conceded that *Gault* had placed limitations on the extent to which states could employ the rules of civil procedure in delinquency proceedings, but he disputed Uviller's claim that *Gault* had proscribed the use of civil procedure altogether. Although the Supreme Court ultimately sided with Uviller, the issue proved more divisive than *Gault*'s more sweeping questions.

THE COURT'S DECISION

By the Supreme Court's 1969 term, the Warren Court coalition, which had dominated the development of constitutional law in procedural matters during the 1960s, had begun to dissolve. Most important, Chief Justice Warren had retired, and Justice Fortas had been forced to resign as a result of the controversy surrounding his financial relationships and informal role as an adviser to the president. Nevertheless, when the Court delivered its decision in *Winship* on March 31, 1970, the result it communicated could not have been unexpected. The majority opinion, which defined the issue narrowly as "whether proof beyond a reasonable doubt is among the 'essentials of due process' " applicable to delinquency adjudication hearings in which "a juvenile is charged with an act which would constitute a crime if committed by an adult,"[70] came from Justice William Brennan Jr. Like Justice Fortas in *Gault*, Brennan relied on selective incorporation to reverse the judgment of the New York Court of Appeals and to announce the Court's finding that delinquency petitions must be proved beyond a reasonable doubt. Brennan also followed Fortas's example of caution by affirming that intake and disposition proceedings were immune from constitutional standards of due process and that New York's "in need of supervision" proceedings were exempt from the requirement of proof beyond reasonable doubt.[71] Finally, Brennan emphasized that *Winship* had no bearing on questions about the applicability of other "essentials of due process" to delinquency adjudication hearings, nor did the majority venture an opinion on whether different standards of proof for juveniles and adults constitute a violation of equal protection. Brennan did go further than Fortas in incorporating into juvenile proceedings a federal procedural right not explicitly found in the Bill of Rights.

Brennan's solution to the burden of proof problem presented by *Winship* proceeded in four steps. The first two steps were devoted to establishing that the requirement of proof beyond a reasonable doubt was part of the "scheme of ordered liberty" embodied in the Fifth and Fourteenth Amendments' due process clauses. Brennan began by arguing that there were three interests of "immense importance" at stake in criminal proceedings, which the reasonable doubt standard existed to protect: the defendant's dual interest in liberty and in avoiding unwarranted stigmatization, and the state's interest in maintaining public confidence in the criminal law.[72] In "a society that values the good name and freedom of every individual," Brennan asserted, criminal punishment should be imposed only in cases where there is reasonable certainty about an individual's guilt.[73] By protecting innocent individuals from unjust convictions, moreover, the reasonable doubt standard generates respect for, and confidence in, the law. Brennan thus agreed with Uviller that the reasonable doubt standard reduced "the risk of convictions resting on factual error" and provided "concrete substance for the presumption of innocence."[74]

The second step in Brennan's argument was to demonstrate that the interests protected by the reasonable doubt standard were sufficiently important to give it a constitutional dimension, despite the standard's absence from the Bill of Rights and the Court's own list of due process requirements. He approached this task both historically and comparatively, arguing that the importance of the reasonable doubt standard had long been recognized in the United States and in other countries with similar legal traditions. Citing McCormick's and Wigmore's treatises on evidence, Brennan traced the origins of the standard to the country's "early years as a Nation," or at least to 1798.[75] Similarly, Brennan asserted that "virtually unanimous adherence" to the reasonable doubt standard in other common law jurisdictions reflected a "profound judgment about the way in which law should be enforced and justice administered."[76] This tradition was sufficient, Brennan concluded, to warrant granting constitutional status to the standard.

Brennan's analysis of the reasonable doubt standard in the first two steps of his argument was not without difficulty.[77] First, contrary to Brennan's assertion, the standard had not developed in Anglo-American jurisprudence as a means of providing greater protection for criminal defendants but as a way of easing the burden of persuasion placed on prosecutors by an older "any doubt" test. The reasonable doubt test, in other words, was intended to limit the ability of juries to find reasons for acquittal. Second, although the reasonable doubt standard had first appeared in the United States even earlier than Brennan's authorities indicated (1770), it did not become the predominant standard of proof in criminal cases until well into the nineteenth century: Maryland courts, for example, did not start using the standard until 1870.[78] One conclusion suggested by this history is that the standard was not a settled component of American jurisprudence when either the Fifth or Fourteenth Amendments' due process clauses were written. Nevertheless, Brennan took advantage of *Winship* to declare explicitly for the first time in the Court's history "that the Due Process Clause protects the accused against conviction except upon proof beyond a reasonable doubt of every fact necessary to constitute the crime with which he is charged."[79]

After establishing the constitutional status of the reasonable doubt test, Brennan proceeded to the third and fourth steps of his argument, in which he undertook to show that this standard was an element of due process that also should be incorporated into juvenile proceedings. The third step, therefore, was to demonstrate that the same interests protected by the standard in criminal proceedings were also at stake in delinquency adjudication proceedings. This part of the argument did not require any innovation on Brennan's part; he simply relied on *Gault* to declare that "civil labels and good intentions" could not mask the true interests at stake in delinquency hearings. Consequently, he declared that "the same considerations that demand extreme caution in fact-finding to protect the innocent adult apply as well to the innocent child."[80]

The final step of the argument was to counter Buchsbaum's claim that the application of the reasonable doubt standard to delinquency adjudication proceedings would undermine other important interests at stake in juvenile proceedings, such as the interest in rehabilitation shared by juveniles and the state. Brennan argued that this interest was at stake primarily during intake and disposition proceedings, which were unaffected by both *Gault* and *Winship*. He thus rejected the view that the standard "would risk destruction of beneficial aspects of the juvenile process" or force states to abandon the "substantive benefits" of separate juvenile proceedings.[81] Although Brennan admitted that a higher standard of adjudicative proof might in some cases prevent judicial intervention intended to steer juveniles away from "a general course of conduct inimical to [their] welfare," he did not find this possibility sufficient to override the duty to protect juveniles from unwarranted institutional confinement and public reprobation.[82]

The final part of Brennan's opinion supplemented his abstract discussion of the relationship among the reasonable doubt standard, constitutional notions of due process, and the interests at stake in juvenile proceedings with specific reference to the concrete example of Samuel Winship's family court hearing. That hearing, according to Brennan, undermined any claim that the practical implications of the two standards of proof were insignificant.[83] The exchange between Irene Rosenberg and Judge Midonick during Winship's adjudication hearing took center stage at this point in the opinion. The exchange provided the Court with a clear example of an instance where the reliance on one standard of proof rather than another proved crucial to the defendant. The nature and outcome of Winship's hearing convinced Brennan that "the constitutional safeguard of proof beyond a reasonable doubt is as much required during the adjudicatory stage of a delinquency proceeding as are those constitutional safeguards applied in *Gault*."[84]

As Fortas had discovered in *Gault*, Brennan found it difficult to secure the unanimous agreement of his brethren with either his line of reasoning or his conclusion. Indeed, since *Winship* would signal how the Court intended to apply *Gault*, the construction of the majority opinion required a significant amount of compromise behind the scenes from Brennan.[85] On the one hand, Brennan had to satisfy Justice Douglas, who objected to any notion that criminal and juvenile due process could differ substantially when criminal offenses were involved. This necessity prevented Brennan from articulating a precise formula for determining the content of juvenile due process in future cases. On the other hand, although Justice Harlan agreed that proof beyond a reasonable doubt was required by the Constitution in delinquency proceedings, he did not want Brennan to imply that this requirement led either to additional procedural requirements (such as jury trials) or to the extension of criminal due process to proceedings involving noncriminal misbehavior. Brennan's opinion only partially satisfied Harlan, who concurred with his substantive conclusion but disagreed with the reasoning behind it. As he had argued in *Gault*, Harlan insisted that juvenile due process should not be based on the selective incorporation of rights derived from the similarity between juvenile and criminal proceedings but from a fundamental fairness standard that was more sensitive to the context and unique character of the former. According to Harlan, there was "no automatic congruence between the procedural requirements imposed by due process in a criminal case, and those imposed by due process in juvenile cases." [86] Juvenile due process, he argued, should be based on an independent determination of the value of each procedural safeguard in juvenile proceedings rather than on analogies with criminal proceedings. In terms of the question at issue in *Winship*, this difference meant assessing the "comparative social disutility" of each standard of proof in the context of juvenile proceedings themselves. [87]

According to Harlan's analysis, the reasonable doubt standard should apply to juvenile proceedings because the social and individual costs of declaring innocent juveniles delinquent were much higher than the costs of allowing some guilty juveniles to escape the rehabilitative interventions of the juvenile justice system. Thus, although Harlan disagreed with the majority's conclusion that juvenile proceedings are essentially "identical to those in a criminal case," he conceded that whatever differences exist would "not support a distinction in the standard of proof." [88] Since even rehabilitative intervention could be harmful where unnecessary, Harlan concurred that juvenile court judges "should be no less convinced of the factual conclusion that the accused committed the criminal act with which he is charged than would be required in a criminal trial." [89]

Like Harlan, Justice Black felt compelled by his own view of incorporation to write a separate opinion in *Winship*. In dissenting from the majority opinion, Black criticized Brennan's reasoning and substantive conclusion as well as Harlan's alternative rationale for the majority's decision. Black began by noting that, although the Constitution provided criminal defendants with the rights to counsel, indictment, notice, and jury trials, it was silent about the standard of proof required for conviction. "The Constitution," Black wrote, "goes into some detail to spell out what kind of trial a defendant charged with crime should have, and I believe the Court has no power to add to or subtract from the procedures set forth by the Founders."[90] Consistent with his total incorporation approach to due process, Black criticized the majority for interfering, without explicit constitutional authorization, with New York's decision to rely on a lower standard of proof in delinquency proceedings than that used in criminal proceedings. Indeed, in Black's view, the Fourteenth Amendment's due process clause would not even have prevented New York from relying on the preponderance standard in criminal proceedings themselves.[91]

Black saved his harshest criticism, however, for Harlan. He argued that the Constitution's due process clauses meant that "our governments are governments of law and constitutionally bound to act only according to law."[92] If the Court followed Harlan's suggestion and converted "due process" into "fundamental fairness," Black asserted, it would acquire the power to "declare invalid 'substantive' laws that sufficiently shock the consciences of at least five members of this Court."[93] The basic danger in this, he continued, was that the United States would become a nation governed by judges instead of by law. Black found it infinitely preferable to put his faith "in the words of the written Constitution itself rather than to rely on the shifting, day-to-day standards of fairness of individual judges."[94]

Black concentrated on the broader issues of constitutional interpretation implicated in *Winship*, but Chief Justice Burger shared Harlan's concern about the message the Court was communicating through its interpretation of due process in the juvenile context. In a dissent joined by Justice Stewart, Burger wondered whether Harlan's approach could indeed avoid "eroding the differences between juvenile courts and traditional criminal courts."[95] In Burger's view, *Kent, Gault,* and *Winship* were products of professional dissatisfaction with "inadequate juvenile court staffs and facilities."[96] Juvenile courts were performing poorly, Burger suggested, not because of procedural weaknesses but because states were unwilling to commit sufficient resources to guarantee their success. In responding to this situation by imposing criminal due process on juvenile courts, he argued, the Court risked discouraging states from making necessary improvements, thereby ensuring the demise of juvenile courts.[97] Burger worried, therefore, that *Winship* would "spell the end of a generously conceived program of compassionate treatment intended to mitigate the rigors and trauma of exposing youthful offenders to a traditional criminal court."[98]

Winship demanded that the Court choose between two different conceptions of the presumption of innocence in juvenile proceedings. The traditional conception, which formed the basis of New York's defense of its Fam-

ily Court Act, was rather complex. In one sense, traditional juvenile jurisprudence viewed this presumption as absolute; it held that because of environmental and psychological factors, children (except in rare cases) could
not be held criminally responsible for their actions and should be shielded
from criminal prosecution. In this sense, children were legally innocent, although they might violate the law. In another sense, however, the traditional
view reversed the presumption by assuming that mere referral to a juvenile
court indicated the necessity of state intervention; the only question was the
type and duration of this intervention. This second aspect of the traditional
conception of the presumption of innocence followed logically from the
first; because questions of guilt or innocence were not at issue in juvenile
proceedings, it was unnecessary to justify intervention according to rigorous
procedural standards.

The alternative to the traditional view was the one embodied in Rena
Uviller's brief. Uviller, like Dorsen, Rezneck, and Fortas before her, viewed
juvenile proceedings in functional terms. To Uviller, New York's objective in
delinquency adjudication proceedings was similar to its objective in criminal proceedings—to prove that an individual committed a criminal offense
for which the state can impose sanctions. The possibility that those sanctions might be rehabilitative rather than punitive was irrelevant. Both types
of sanctions established a similar obligation to protect the individual from
unwarranted intervention through the presumption of innocence, which
could be given practical effect only by the reasonable doubt test. By choosing
this view over the traditional one, the *Winship* majority implicitly rejected
an important component of the nineteenth-century understanding of childhood that formed the basis of *parens patriae* juvenile justice. Seemingly
without realizing it, the *Winship* majority dealt a blow to the notion that
juvenile courts are concerned with "who the child is" rather than with "what
a child does." Perhaps because of this effect, commentators have suggested
that, despite the majority's caution and the apparent predictions of members of the Court,[99] *Winship*'s impact on traditional juvenile jurisprudence
was even greater than *Gault*'s.[100]

The Renaissance of Contextual Due Process and
Fundamental Fairness

Winship was the final case in which selective incorporation guided the
Court's review of juvenile due process. Beginning with *McKeiver v. Pennsyl-*

vania,[101] decided in 1971, the Court began to shift toward the context-driven standard of fundamental fairness as the framework for its analysis of juvenile due process. At issue in *McKeiver* was whether the due process clause of the Fourteenth Amendment "assures the right to trial by jury in the adjudicative phase of a state juvenile court delinquency proceeding." Before addressing this issue directly, the author of the Court's plurality opinion— Justice Harry Blackmun—reviewed the Court's earlier decisions on juvenile procedure and highlighted four aspects of those decisions. Blackmun declared that the two most important features of the earlier decisions were that, although "some of the constitutional requirements attendant upon the state criminal trial have equal application to that part of the state juvenile proceeding that is adjudicative in nature," not "*all* rights constitutionally assured to an adult accused of crime also are to be enforced or made available to the juvenile in his delinquency proceeding."[102]

According to Blackmun, although the previous decisions had established that juvenile proceedings are not "devoid of criminal aspects" simply because states label them civil proceedings, neither had the Court found juvenile proceedings to be criminal prosecutions.[103] Moreover, Blackmun asserted that the "applicable due process standard in juvenile proceedings" developed in *Gault* and *Winship* was "fundamental fairness."[104] Thus Blackmun argued that the appropriate method for resolving the question at issue in *McKeiver* was to balance the importance of jury trials for accurate fact-finding against their impact on desirable features of juvenile proceedings. Relying on *Duncan v. Louisiana* (1965)[105] and *Williams v. Florida* (1970),[106] Blackmun denied that jury trials are necessary to ensure reliable fact-finding. At the same time, he noted that jury trials would probably burden juvenile courts with the "traditional delay, the formality, and the clamor of the adversary system and, possibly, the public trial."[107] On balance, therefore, jury trials would do more harm than good in juvenile proceedings. Blackmun thus concluded that they were not a constitutionally required element of juvenile due process.

As should be evident from the discussions of *Gault* and *Winship,* Justice Blackmun's analysis in *McKeiver* of the rationale underlying those previous decisions is puzzling. His conclusion that neither *Gault* nor *Winship* had described juvenile proceedings as criminal prosecutions, for example, was, at the very least, questionable. Though this precise language did not appear in either decision, the Court's acceptance of the functional similarity argument and its constant reference to specific examples of that similarity throughout its decisions created a strong impression that it viewed delinquency proceedings as far more criminal than civil. More significantly, Blackmun's assertion that the Court had described "fundamental fairness" as the reason for imposing the privilege against self-incrimination and the requirements of notice, counsel, confrontation, and cross-examination, as well as proof beyond a reasonable doubt, on juvenile courts was simply mistaken. Justices Stewart, Harlan, White, and Black and Norman Dorsen and Daniel Rezneck[108] were certainly under the impression that selective incorporation was at the core of the majority decision in *Gault;* and Harlan had the same impression of *Winship.* What Blackmun accomplished through this reinterpretation of prior decisions, however, was to provide a theoretical rationale for abandoning the Court's functional similarity approach in order once again to emphasize the contextual differences between juvenile and criminal proceedings.

The Court affirmed its new emphasis on the distinctive nature of juvenile proceedings as a guide to procedural review under the fundamental fairness standard in *Breed v. Jones* (1975).[109] At issue in *Jones* was whether the Fifth Amendment's double jeopardy clause prohibits juvenile courts from holding waiver hearings after delinquency adjudication hearings. In approaching this question, a unanimous Court distanced itself significantly from the largely negative image of juvenile courts evident in *Kent, Gault,* and *Winship.* Although acknowledging that the earlier decisions had uncovered "a gap between the originally benign conception of the [juvenile] system and its realities," the *Jones* Court argued that the failure of juvenile courts to meet the high expectations of their supporters "in no way detracts from the broad social benefits sought or from those benefits that can survive constitutional scrutiny."[110] Following *McKeiver,* the Court averred that elements of procedural flexibility and informality that "relate uniquely to the goals of the juvenile-court system" would survive such scrutiny.[111]

In applying this standard to the question at issue in *Jones,* the Court reached two important conclusions: that prohibiting jurisdictional waiver after adjudication would not impose unacceptable burdens on the juvenile justice system and that holding waiver hearings prior to adjudication would promote the aims of that system.[112] One of the Court's principal concerns was that the possibility of postadjudication waiver might force juveniles and their attorneys to adopt a "posture of adversary wariness" that would not be conducive to "establishing innocence or seeking a disposition best suited to individual correctional needs."[113] This result, the Court argued, would be "at odds with the goal that, to the extent fundamental fairness permits, adjudicatory hearings be informal and nonadversary."[114] Consequently, the Court held that waiver hearings must be conducted prior to adjudication hearings.

Although *Jones* incorporated another element of criminal due process into juvenile proceedings, the Court has subsequently employed the fundamental fairness doctrine to remove itself from further participation in the constitutional domestication of juvenile courts that it so boldly announced in *Gault*.[115] In *Fare v. Michael C.* (1975),[116] for example, the Court refused to hold elements of *Miranda v. Arizona* (1966)[117] applicable to juvenile proceedings. The specific issue in *Michael C.* was whether a juvenile's request during a police interrogation to speak to a probation officer constituted a per se invocation of Fifth Amendment rights under *Miranda,* requiring the police to cease questioning a juvenile. A majority of the Court again approached the issue by measuring the benefits of this additional due process safeguard against its cost to the informality, speed, and flexibility of juvenile proceedings. According to five justices, neither probation officers nor any other "trusted guardian figures" could adequately serve the protective function envisioned for attorneys in *Miranda*.[118] In ruling against the respondent, the majority held that extending *Miranda* rights in this direction "would impose the burdens associated with the rule of *Miranda* on the juvenile justice system and the police without serving the interests that rule was designed simultaneously to protect."[119] This holding echoed the Court's decision in *Goss v. Lopez* (1975), in which a bare majority determined that hearings were not required prior to the temporary suspension of students from school.[120] In words strikingly similar to those later used in *Michael C.,* the Court held that a formal hearing requirement would impose administrative burdens far out of proportion both to the interests at stake and any increase in the accuracy of the suspension process. According to the majority, effective notice and an informal hearing would sufficiently protect students' interests. The due process revolution that had had such an impact on juvenile jurisprudence was clearly coming to an end.

Strikingly absent from *Jones* and *Michael C.* was the cynicism toward juvenile proceedings that permeated *Kent, Gault,* and *Winship*. Indeed, the decisions in the two former cases appear to have relied on a revival of interest in traditional juvenile jurisprudence among the justices of the Supreme Court. Nowhere was this revival more apparent than in *Schall v. Martin* (1984).[121] At issue in *Martin* was the constitutionality of a section of the New York Family Court Act that authorized pretrial preventive detention of accused juvenile delinquents based on a finding of a "serious risk" that the juvenile "may before the return date commit an act which if committed by an adult would constitute a crime." In a majority opinion authored by William Rehnquist, the Court rejected a class action suit seeking a declaratory judgment that pretrial detention of juveniles violated their rights under the Fourteenth Amendment's due process clause. Rehnquist found that states could employ preadjudication preventive detention on the grounds that it promoted the legitimate state interest in community protection by temporarily removing potentially dangerous offenders from the community. He held, moreover, that pretrial detention also advanced the equally important state interest in protecting juveniles "from the hazards of pretrial crime." [122]

Although Rehnquist recognized that juveniles had a "countervailing interest in freedom from institutional restraints," he stressed that this interest is qualified by the fact that "juveniles, unlike adults, are always in some form of custody." [123] "Children," Rehnquist argued, "are not assumed to have the capacity to take care of themselves . . . [and] . . . are assumed to be subject to the control of their parents, and if parental control falters, the State must play its role as *parens patriae*." [124] In making these statements, Rehnquist gave new life to traditional views of juvenile justice that appeared to have been discredited in *Gault*. [125] He concluded that the limited liberty interests of juveniles could be subordinated to this "*parens patriae* interest in preserving and promoting the welfare of the child" without violating due process. [126] This conclusion, Rehnquist asserted, was consistent with the Court's general objective of striking a delicate balance between "the 'informality' and 'flexibility' that characterize juvenile proceedings and [the requirement] that such proceedings comport with the 'fundamental fairness' demanded by the Due Process Clause." [127]

Rehnquist's rehabilitation of the *parens patriae* concept from its status in *Gault* as a "murky" doctrine whose application to juvenile proceedings produced intolerable procedural arbitrariness underscores the importance of the Court's shift from selective incorporation to fundamental fairness. As the majority of cases decided since *Gault* indicate, Dorsen and Reznick's suspicion in 1966 that fundamental fairness would not be a productive theory on which to develop juvenile due process was well founded. Although the Court sustained five of seven juvenile due process claims under selective incorporation, only one of four claims succeeded under the fundamental fairness standard. [128] The fate of these failed claims raises two key questions: Why did the Court choose selective incorporation in 1967, and why did it abandon that approach four years later?

The answer to both questions has something to do with the nature of the cases in which the Court has considered juvenile due process. The most important similarity found in *Kent, Gault,* and *Winship* is that each involved a significant loss of liberty by the juvenile involved. The importance of this similarity is that in only one case—*Kent*—did the state attempt to confine the juvenile for committing a serious offense; in both *Gault* and *Winship* the offenses were relatively minor. Indeed, the disproportionality between Gerald Gault's punishment and the seriousness of his offense, along with the apparent absence of any element of procedural fairness in his delinquency proceedings, tended to confirm the worst criticisms of *parens patriae* juvenile proceedings. Moreover, the particularly egregious facts of *Gault* exaggerated the potential benefits of procedural reform and depreciated the problems caused by Arizona's vague definition of delinquency and its code's provision for wide judicial discretion to set indeterminate dispositions. Because these problems could not be solved by procedural reform of the adjudicative process alone, the Court's initial estimate of the benefits of criminal due process was more generous than the realities of juvenile justice might have suggested.

The Court's enthusiasm for adjudicative procedural reform waned only after it began to hear cases in which the procedural violations were less egregious and the sanctions more proportionate and justifiable. These cases presented the Court with more subtle constitutional questions, thereby forcing the justices to confront more directly the potential cost of applying criminal due process to juvenile proceedings. More precisely, these cases forced the Court to take the context in which they arose more seriously than did the prior cases. Its earlier response to the facts of *Gault* and *Winship* posed a dilemma, however. The Court's emphasis in those cases on the liberty interests of juveniles and on selective incorporation of the Bill of Rights to safeguard those interests did not provide any obvious justification for refusing to uphold procedural claims whose impact on the distinctive character of juvenile proceedings might be more damaging. The easiest way to resolve this dilemma was for the Court to engage in historical revisionism and to articulate the fiction that its previous decisions had rested on what it called fundamental fairness. The danger in relying on this fiction, however, was that it could produce decisions like *Martin,* which might be inconsistent with developments in juvenile justice that the *Gault* decision had precipitated but which the Court could not control.[129] It is therefore important to understand how juvenile court officials, state legislatures, and the juvenile court reform movement reacted to *Gault.*

7. Constitutional Domestication and the New Juvenile Court

In 1967, after almost seventy years of silence on the matter, the Supreme Court found it necessary to begin imposing constitutionally derived procedural standards on juvenile proceedings in order to prevent perceived abuses of power by juvenile courts.[1] At the national level, the reaction to this decision among juvenile justice professionals, some judges, and other members of the legal profession was generally positive.[2] Although recognizing that the Supreme Court's "constitutional domestication" of juvenile proceedings would have a profound impact on the administration of juvenile justice, most commentators shared the view of Justices Fortas and Brennan that the decisions would not drastically alter the basic nature of juvenile courts.[3] Fortas expected *Gault* to provide juveniles with constitutional protection against the procedural arbitrariness he had criticized in *Kent,* but he did not believe that it would "compel the States to abandon or displace any of the substantive benefits of the juvenile process," a view that Brennan reiterated in *Winship.*[4] Judge Orman Ketcham, whose waiver decision the Court had overturned in *Kent,* argued that *Gault* would produce a "new, fairer and more effective form of juvenile court proceeding" without threatening "the foremost goals of the juvenile court system."[5]

The advocates of procedural reform on the Court and among juvenile justice professionals were confident that the decisions would provide juveniles with immediate constitutional protection against arbitrary proceedings without inflicting long-term damage on beneficial elements of juvenile justice policy. Indeed, some commentators interpreted the Court's silence on various procedural matters in *Gault* as evidence of its desire not to restrict the juvenile court's rehabilitative efforts with the "strait-jacket" of procedural inflexibility.[6] One of the most intriguing aspects of the juvenile justice decisions, therefore, is that their actual legacy was almost precisely the opposite of the effect that the Court and its supporters predicted. I shall explore this legacy by focusing on the impact of constitutional domestication in three areas: juvenile courtrooms, the juvenile court reform movement, and state legislation.

The Impact on Juvenile Courtrooms

One of the principal assumptions underlying the Supreme Court's decisions was that, whatever their long-term consequences, those decisions would at least confer important procedural benefits on juveniles in the short term. The naïveté of this assumption quickly became apparent, however, as studies conducted within a few years of the Court's judgment in *Gault* indicated poor compliance with many of its procedural requirements.[7] In one study of three urban juvenile courts, researchers found that the highest rate of compliance with *Gault*'s requirement that juveniles be informed of their right to counsel was only 56 percent in one court, with the next best rate reaching barely 3 percent in the second one.[8] The third juvenile court in this study did not inform juveniles of their right to counsel at all. The study focused on *Gault*'s notification requirements because of its authors' assumption that successful implementation of the Court's procedural reforms depended on the effective communication of these rights to juveniles, and the authors attributed the lack of compliance to ambiguities in the decision itself. Juvenile court judges largely believed that they were not bound by *Gault*'s requirements if there was little likelihood that a delinquency adjudication would result in incarceration. The same study found limited compliance with *Gault*'s confrontation and privilege against self-incrimination requirements; the highest compliance rates were 38 percent for the right to confrontation and 33 percent for the privilege against self-incrimination. Other researchers also reported that very few juveniles received "complete and unprejudiced advice of their right to counsel" and that compliance with *Gault* in rural areas was sporadic even two years after the decision.[9] A basic lack of familiarity among rural judges with the Court's decision in *Gault*, combined with their personal influence on procedures in their own courtrooms, apparently led to these results. Although compliance with at least the counsel requirement improved over time, studies conducted as late as the mid-1980s revealed that many juveniles were not adequately informed of their right to counsel and appeared at delinquency hearings without legal representation.[10]

The emphasis placed on the participation of counsel in juvenile hearings by these studies reflects the importance that the Court itself placed on it and the widespread view that counsel was necessary to ensure that juveniles would benefit from other due process rights.[11] Mere participation, however, was itself considered insufficient. The impact of the decisions was also thought to depend on counsel's performing the same advocacy function in juvenile courts that it performed in criminal courts; and contrary to expectations, the extent to which this practice occurred varied widely across jurisdictions.[12] The factors contributing to these variations included markedly different opinions among lawyers about the rights of children from those articulated by the Court and a different conception of the relationship between due process and rehabilitation.[13] Uncertainty and ambivalence among attorneys about their role in juvenile courts led some to perpetuate the traditional view that "non-criminal sanctions and paternal guidance" were positive benefits for their clients and to cooperate with juvenile court authorities against the objective interests of their clients.[14] Moreover, in many cases where attorneys did act as forceful advocates in juvenile courts, they did so on behalf of the parents who retained their services rather than on behalf of juvenile defendants.[15]

As these studies indicate, the Court's prediction that its decisions would revolutionize juvenile proceedings did not materialize, at least not in the short term. Resistance to the reforms by some legislators, appellate courts, police, probation and juvenile corrections personnel, and juvenile court judges meant that key participants in the juvenile court system simply failed to implement *Gault* as expected.[16] As Gerald Rosenberg has pointed out, the Court lacked the capacity to change the philosophy and beliefs driving the practices of juvenile court judges and other personnel.[17] The only possible way of enforcing the rules would have been through appellate review of juvenile court decisions, since judges who found their decisions constantly overturned on procedural grounds might eventually have begun to comply with *Gault* and its progeny. By refusing to grant juveniles a constitutional right to appellate review, however, the Court ensured that even this weak enforcement tool would be unevenly available.

To be sure, many states recognized the lack of compliance with *Gault* and attempted to manage the problem by increasing the familiarity of juvenile justice administrators with the requirements of due process, by removing some of the qualifications the Court attached to the rights granted in *Gault* and *Winship*,[18] and by granting juveniles additional rights by statute, such as verbatim transcripts,[19] jury trials,[20] and bail.[21] Nevertheless, critics argued that significant gaps remained in the procedural protections available to minors in juvenile proceedings. Indeed, they suggested that the "administrative assumptions and operations" of juvenile courts had been criminalized more quickly than juvenile procedure and that it was simply bad public policy "to maintain a separate juvenile criminal court whose sole distinguishing characteristic is its persisting procedural deficiencies."[22] Consequently, serious arguments were made that juvenile courts be abolished.[23] Abolitionists argued that procedural reform was inadequate because it failed to acknowledge "the incalculable damage done to the institution of law through the juvenile justice process." Moreover, the efforts of reformers "to reformulate the notion of delinquency as a legal concept only provide[s] evidence of our inability to restore vitality to a diseased organ."[24]

The abolitionist argument had little practical impact on juvenile justice policy. Nevertheless, the long-term legacy of the juvenile justice trilogy was the creation of an institution whose substantive goals continue to move closer to those of criminal courts but whose procedures lag behind. Both parts of this legacy—substantive changes in the character of juvenile justice and uneven procedural development—represent one set of consequences of the Supreme Court's legal analysis of the policy questions surrounding juvenile justice in the 1960s. The appellants in *Kent, Gault,* and *Winship* convinced the Court that it should "constitutionalize" juvenile proceedings because children possess liberty interests similar to those of adults. In accepting this proposition, the Court articulated a new conception of childhood that embodied a broader understanding of children's capacity for independent judgment and action. This new perspective encouraged both reform advocates and state legislatures to shift the focus of juvenile court proceedings from identifying and eliminating the behavioral causes of delinquency to holding juveniles more directly accountable for the harm caused by their offenses.

The Impact on the Juvenile Court Reform Movement

Despite the Court's confidence that partial adoption of criminal due process would not alter the most important institutional characteristics of juvenile courts, there has been a significant departure from the framework established by the Illinois Juvenile Court Act. In short, the juvenile justice decisions unintentionally set in motion a substantive convergence between juvenile and criminal courts. Its extent was readily apparent in the differences between the founding principles of juvenile justice and policy developments during the 1970s and 1980s. During those two decades, the original vision of juvenile courts was challenged by reform proposals seeking to eliminate bias, inequality, and disproportionality from juvenile justice decisionmaking.

IJA-ABA STANDARDS

Perhaps the most important set of reform proposals to appear in the aftermath of the juvenile justice decisions resulted from a joint effort by the

Institute of Judicial Administration (IJA) and the American Bar Association (ABA). Working together, these organizations produced twenty-three volumes of juvenile justice standards and commentary that reexamined the premises on which juvenile justice was based.[25] In designing the standards, the IJA-ABA Joint Commission sought to unify juvenile court laws by combining the diverse components of the juvenile justice system and by codifying relevant case law, administrative decisions, statutory innovations, and fundamental principles. Underlying this goal was a desire to increase the fairness of juvenile law by eliminating "inconsistencies in a juvenile's rights and liabilities that are caused by the accident of geography." The commission advocated uniformity both among and within states, with the first step in that direction to be the replacement of juvenile courts by family courts whose jurisdiction would include divorce, adoption, separation, and youthful criminal behavior.[26]

In addition to uniformity, another important theme of the project was to reduce the discretionary authority of decisionmakers, particularly court officials. This objective was evident in the commission's rejection of the assumption that coercive treatment is necessarily beneficial for juveniles or that delinquency adjudications automatically justify therapeutic care.[27] Indeed, one of the most important aspects of the IJA-ABA proposals was the commission's willingness to emphasize dispositions and corrections—subjects about which earlier reports were largely silent and on which the Supreme Court had endorsed the traditional view. By contrast, the IJA-ABA project concluded that "the greatest weakness in the juvenile system lies in the final stages of dispositions and corrections." The joint commission concluded that dispositional practices were both the most significant aspect of juvenile justice and the element that required the most improvement. Consequently, the commission set out ten principles to guide dispositional decisionmaking, deriving each one from theories of fairness, justifiable intervention, proportionality, determinacy, and objectivity in decisionmaking.[28]

In articulating these principles, the commission unequivocally rejected the traditional rehabilitative model of juvenile justice and the *parens patriae* doctrine that supplied its legal justification.[29] The principles also endorsed a novel view of the capacity of children to make decisions on their own behalf by assuming that juveniles were capable of making decisions about their own lives and freedom unless proof to the contrary was offered. This assumption was evident in the commission's view of the purpose of juvenile corrections. It argued that dispositions should aim at reducing "juvenile crime by maintaining the integrity of the substantive law proscribing certain behavior and by developing individual responsibility for lawful behavior."[30]

The commission proposed to replace the vague dispositional criteria of the nineteenth-century treatment model with a set of standards designed to make the duration and severity of sanctions proportionate to the seriousness of a juvenile's offense. The standards thus divided juvenile offenses into five classes according to the maximum sentence authorized for adults convicted of the same offense:

Class One: crimes punishable by death, life imprisonment, or a prison term of more than twenty years;
　Class Two: crimes punishable by a prison term of five to twenty years;
　Class Three: crimes punishable by a prison term of between one and five years;
　Class Four: crimes punishable by a prison term of between six months and one year;
　Class Five: crimes punishable by less than six months in prison, or those actions for which no adult sentence exists.[31]

The standards also established three types of sanctions: conditional freedom, nonsecure placement, and secure confinement.[32] Proportionality among the offense classes was achieved by matching them to the available sanctions on a dispositional grid that specified the maximum duration of the sanction for each class. The maximum sanction for juveniles adjudicated delinquent for committing a Class One offense, for example, would be thirty-six months of conditional freedom, twenty-four months placement in a nonsecure facility, or twenty-four months confinement in a secure facility. The maxima for Class Three offenses would be eighteen months of conditional freedom, six months of nonsecure placement, or six months of secure confinement. Proportionality within offense classes was less clearly established, since similarly situated juveniles in the same class could still receive dispositions of both a different type and length. Still, the stipulation of maximum dispositions was consistent with the commission's rejection of indeterminate sentencing. It attempted to narrow dispositional discretion even further by establishing stringent standards governing disposition procedures and by reducing the authority of the agencies who administered correctional facilities and programs. The commission was especially critical of what it described as the erratic performance of probation agencies.[33]

Consistent with these changes in dispositional practices, the commission's standards called for even greater procedural formality than that required by the Supreme Court. Because the commission saw extensive involvement of counsel as key in juvenile proceedings characterized by a reliance on formal rules, the standards required that all parties be represented by counsel to safeguard their interests at every stage of proceedings.[34] In addition to representation by counsel and the other rights required by the Court in *Gault* and *Winship*, the standards recommended that states adopt a wide variety of other elements of due process, including verbatim transcripts, jury trials, public trials, and appellate review.[35] The standards also required that the rules of evidence in contested juvenile proceedings be identical to those employed in criminal trials. The standards stopped short, however, of recommending that juveniles be given a right to bail as an alternative to detention or unconditional release.[36]

In view of this nontraditional approach to adjudication and disposition procedures, it is noteworthy that the standards for waiver and transfer for trial in criminal courts were conventional.[37] The commission rejected a lower minimum age for waiver and legislative waiver of juveniles charged with violent offenses. The standards stipulated that waiver should be used as a last resort for juveniles above the age of sixteen charged with Class One offenses but only after a hearing in which the prosecution proves (1) "that the juvenile is not a proper person for handling by the juvenile court"; (2) "the inefficacy of the available dispositions as demonstrated by previous dispositions"; and (3) "the appropriateness of the dispositional alternatives" offered by the criminal justice system. The criteria for determining whether a juvenile was not an appropriate individual for handling in the juvenile court included the seriousness of the alleged offense and a prior record of having been adjudicated delinquent for conduct "involving infliction or threat of significant bodily harm."

THE TWENTIETH CENTURY FUND

The most striking feature of the IJA-ABA's proposal was its emphasis on offenses rather than on offenders, and it was this feature that subsequent reform proposals developed more fully. One year after the IJA-ABA group completed its work, the Twentieth Century Fund's Juvenile Justice Task Force issued a report on sentencing policy toward young offenders. The fund's effort was simultaneously broader and narrower than the IJA-ABA project: broader because it dealt with sentencing practices toward youth in both juvenile and criminal courts, narrower because it dealt exclusively with sentencing. In *Confronting Youth Crime*, the task force adopted a sentencing system for young offenders in which the legislature specified maximum sentences but in which judges retained some discretion to determine the length of sentences and the necessity of confinement in individual cases.[38] The system also included a centralized correctional authority that could authorize early release from judicially mandated sentences. These recommendations reflected both the fund's rejection of indeterminate sentencing and its refusal to endorse presumptive sentences.[39] It advocated the use of this system in both juvenile and criminal courts in order to guarantee consistent and coherent sentencing and because of the difficulty it had in fixing a precise age during adolescence as the dividing line between juvenile and adult sentencing.[40]

Underlying these recommendations was the fund's rejection of the "omnibus" theory of delinquency, "which invokes the coercive power of the state in proportion to what a child needs rather than to what he has done." The task force included among its goals narrowing the delinquency jurisdiction of juvenile courts, reducing the number of youths placed under formal social control, and linking maximum sentences to offense severity. Consistent with these goals, four principles guided the task force's specific recommendations: culpability, diminished responsibility resulting from immaturity, the importance of providing room to reform, and proportionality.[41]

The task force's emphasis on culpability and offense severity paralleled traditional common-law age distinctions in its argument that "at age thirteen or fourteen, an individual may appropriately be considered responsible, at least to a degree, for the criminal harms that he or she causes." These individuals could be held responsible, the task force claimed, because they were generally aware of the harm caused by their criminal acts. Consequently, they should be held morally and legally responsible for "intentionally destructive behavior." The task force also concluded, however, that adolescents mature at differing rates and are "more vulnerable, more impulsive, and less self-disciplined than adults."[42] Thus, it argued that adolescents should be held less responsible than adults who commit similar acts. The task force did not wish to return to the common law distinctions, yet it rejected the absolute distinction between juveniles and adults with respect to culpability that was advocated by the nineteenth-century juvenile court movement.

The task force's qualification of its view that adolescents must be held responsible for their acts stemmed from its desire to provide young offenders with room to reform. It distinguished this concept from rehabilitation, which it described as the use of "coercive state power to socialize and mature young offenders."[43] "Room to reform" meant "providing young offenders with the opportunity to pass through this crime-prone stage of development with their life chances intact."[44] This goal required that young offenders be protected from the social stigma and disapprobation attached to criminal conviction and custodial confinement. Unfortunately, the task force offered few concrete suggestions as to how young offenders could be held responsible for their actions without exposing them to the risks of stigmatization, confinement, and social reprobation.

One subject to which the task force paid particular attention was that of serious and violent young offenders. Its approach produced a truncated form of the sentencing table adopted by the IJA-ABA project. The fund proposed the establishment of three classes of violent offenses. Class One would include assaults without serious threat of harm and robbery committed without weapons or bodily harm; Class Two offenses would be those that threatened the victim's life or person more directly; and Class Three would include murder and attempted murder, forcible rape, and arson with intent to commit bodily harm. The maximum juvenile court sentence for these offenses would range from eighteen months (Class One offenses) to thirty months (Class Three offenses), with no mandatory minimum sentence.[45]

In contrast to the IJA-ABA standards, which viewed transfer to criminal courts as a last resort, the task force argued that it was the least harmful method of dealing with extremely serious cases.[46] It set fifteen years as the minimum transfer age and established two criteria to guide the transfer decision: (1) probable cause that the youth committed a serious or violent crime or both; and (2) the necessity of punishment substantially more severe than that available to the juvenile court. Transferred juveniles, however, were to be treated as a special class of defendants in criminal courts, and the maximum sentencing options would be significantly lower for violent young offenders than for adults convicted of similar offenses.[47] One member of the task force dissented vigorously from this recommendation, arguing that "serious crime should be treated seriously regardless of the offender's age."[48]

As a whole, the authors of *Confronting Youth Crime* presented a curious mixture of recommendations. They supported sentencing policies toward youthful offenders that recognized their culpability for criminal harm and held them responsible for it, thus rejecting the basic premises and several essential elements of the *parens patriae* approach, including indeterminate sentences keyed to the offender's needs. The task force's emphasis on culpability also created an expanded role for criminal courts with respect to violent young offenders. At the same time, however, their concept of "room to reform" softened somewhat the concern with culpability, as was reflected in continued reliance on judicial and correctional discretion, the rejection of presumptive sentences, and support for special treatment of violent young offenders in criminal courts. The task force sought a middle ground between the rigidity of the common law approach and the unlimited flexibility of *parens patriae*. It reinstituted the common law's concern with culpability and responsibility but retained the juvenile court movement's desire to protect "young offenders from the full force of the criminal law."[49]

THE NATIONAL ADVISORY COMMITTEE

The National Advisory Committee for Juvenile Justice and Delinquency Prevention (NAC), which was the creation of the 1974 Juvenile Justice and Delinquency Prevention Act, offered a third set of post-1970 reform proposals.[50] The JJDP Act had two objectives: to separate juveniles from adult offenders and to remove status offenders from institutional confinement. The act provided for the distribution of federal funds to aid states in reducing the number of juveniles held in adult jails and the number of status offenders confined to juvenile institutions; failure to meet federally mandated reductions by specified target dates made states ineligible for continued funding. The act also created juvenile justice advisory groups in each state to advise governors on the allocation of the funds. At the national level, the act created the Office of Juvenile Justice and Delinquency Prevention (OJJDP) to develop regulations for implementing the act's mandates. It also established the NAC, whose responsibilities included recommending standards for the administration of juvenile justice and methods to facilitate their adoption.[51] After some initial confusion over the NAC's authority, the committee published a full set of standards in 1980.

The standards represented both continuity and change in juvenile justice policy; they continued the protective aims of the original juvenile court movement but abandoned certain features of it that the NAC thought were inconsistent with the movement's protective goals. Of the five themes underlying the NAC's recommendations, four shared the 1960s' concern with limiting government intervention into juveniles' lives; the fifth accepted rehabilitation as a legitimate justification for such intervention.[52] This was a step back from the IJA-ABA recommendations and reflected the dual character of the JJDP Act itself. The act's rejection of adult jails as appropriate holding facilities for juveniles was consistent with the aim of avoiding criminal stigmatization of children; deinstitutionalization of status offenders, on the other hand, was part of the modern attempt to limit juvenile court intervention. Both provisions had the protection of juveniles as their ultimate goal.

The standards covered a wide range of topics over more than 500 pages. Because of their potential impact on the traditional practices of juvenile courts, the most significant standards were those involving the court's adjudicative function. In considering adjudication, the NAC sought to address the jurisdiction and organization of juvenile courts; the rights of the parties in delinquency, noncriminal misbehavior, and neglect and abuse proceedings; and the criteria and procedures applicable to intake, detention, and disposition decisions. The overall intent was to "provide for greater equity, consistency and fairness in proceedings affecting juveniles, a more efficient and respected court, and a stronger, more effective system of justice for juveniles, their families, and the public."[53]

The first set of adjudication standards recommended establishing a single family court whose delinquency jurisdiction applied only to conduct that would be a criminal offense if committed by an adult.[54] This jurisdiction extended to crimes committed by individuals between the ages of ten and eighteen, with the court retaining jurisdiction over such individuals until their twenty-first birthday.[55] The court's jurisdiction would also include noncriminal misbehavior, defined as habitual truancy, repeated absences from home, repeated disregard of lawful parental authority, and acts of delinquency committed by juveniles under the age of ten.[56] In addition, the standards identified nine situations in which the family court could invoke its jurisdiction over neglect and abuse.[57]

Although the standards prohibited the court from exercising its delinquency jurisdiction over juveniles below the age of ten, they permitted the court to waive jurisdiction over juveniles and transfer them to a court of general criminal jurisdiction. The standards stipulated that, in order to waive jurisdiction, the court had to find that the juvenile was at least sixteen; that there was probable cause to believe that the individual committed the offense in question; that there was probable cause to believe that the act was heinous, aggravated, or part of a serious offense pattern; and that there was clear and convincing evidence that the juvenile was not amenable to treatment or would not benefit from the dispositions available in the juvenile court.[58] In the NAC's view, the purpose of transferring juveniles for whom the juvenile court's specialized services and programs were inappropriate was twofold: It relieved the political pressure to lower the maximum jurisdictional age for delinquency, and it allowed the court to expend its resources on those juveniles most likely to respond to rehabilitative efforts.[59]

The NAC's approach to jurisdiction and waiver covered familiar territory and proposed few innovations in those areas; the same could be said about its approach to due process. Despite noting the importance of procedural formality,[60] the standards did not expand juvenile due process much beyond where the Supreme Court had taken it. Although the standards provided for the rights to appeal, public trial, and a verbatim record,[61] they excluded the rights to grand jury indictment, trial by jury, and bail.[62] There were two important exceptions to this generalization, however. First, the standards extended due process to proceedings involving noncriminal misbehavior and to neglect and abuse proceedings. Second, the standards regarded attorneys as zealous defenders of the interests of all parties, including juveniles.[63] Thus, they explicitly endorsed an adversarial approach to family court matters, rejecting a model of advocacy in which attorneys would cooperate with the juvenile court in determining the best interests of juveniles without consulting their clients.[64]

The least traditional recommendations from the NAC involved dispositional criteria. Following the model established in some states, the standards proposed separate adjudication and disposition hearings;[65] and like the Twentieth Century Fund, the NAC recommended classifying delinquent acts by seriousness and specifying the maximum term for each offense class.[66] The objective of disposition hearings under the standards was to select the least restrictive dispositional alternative consistent with the seriousness of the offense, the juvenile's role in committing the offense, the age of the juvenile, and his or her prior record.[67] The purpose of these criteria was "to promote dispositional consistency and provide a basis for explanation, comparison, and review of dispositional decisions."[68] Under the NAC's standards, offense criteria would govern the length of dispositions and degree of restraint involved.[69] Within this broad constraint, however, the standards relied on the juvenile's needs and interests (offender criteria) to determine the type of program or services accompanying the disposition.[70] This dual set of criteria conformed to the committee's desire both to limit government intervention and to retain rehabilitation as an important objective of dispositions, clear evidence of the protective thrust of the NAC standards. The committee sought to protect juveniles from the abuses of the traditional juvenile court and the consequences of criminal prosecution. Borrowing, in slightly modified form, the most famous phrase in Justice Fortas's opinion in *Kent,* the NAC argued in the preface to its report that juveniles deserved the "best of both worlds," in which they receive the "protections accorded to adults" and the "solicitous care and regenerative treatment postulated for children."[71] Thus, the dispositional recommendations employed offense criteria to limit the amount of government intervention while relying on rehabilitation to determine the type of intervention.

In 1984, under the impetus of a new administration, the NAC abruptly abandoned its protective stance toward juvenile offenders. Arguing that federal policies had been misdirected during the previous decade, the NAC recommended that federal efforts shift toward policies designed to reduce serious, violent, and chronic delinquent behavior.[72] The committee based this recommendation on its finding that the JJDP Act had failed to address the essential fact that "a very small number of youth account for a very large proportion of serious juvenile crime."[73] The 1984 report, in advocating a new, more limited role for the federal government, rejected the view that it could impose effective solutions on states and local governments and recommended ending the practice of tying federal funding to compliance with OJJDP regulations.[74] The committee argued instead that the federal role should be limited to research, demonstration projects, information dissemination, and training and technical assistance.[75] The NAC envisioned an expansion of the federal role only in programs involving juveniles prosecuted in adult criminal courts.[76]

The 1984 committee had in mind projects like the one conducted by the National Council of Juvenile and Family Court Judges (NCJFCJ) under a grant from the OJJDP. This project produced thirty-eight recommendations on the juvenile court and serious offenders, covering disposition policies and guidelines, cause and prevention, transfer, confidentiality, treatment programs, the juvenile court's status within the legal system, and resources.[77] The NCJFCJ recommendations, however, merely grafted a concern with serious offenders onto the existing juvenile court and its delinquency programs. Although conceding that "youth must be held accountable for their behavior," the NCJFCJ declared that "proposals which would materially and adversely alter traditional individualized rehabilitative models and treatment philosophies of the juvenile justice system are unacceptable. Juvenile justice resources should accordingly primarily continue to be directed toward individualized treatment."[78] Thus, the NCJFCJ recommended that dispositions for serious offenses be established by systemwide state commissions but that there be adequate judicial discretion to pursue individualized treatment.[79]

Indeed, the recommendations did not depart from the nineteenth-century notion that individualized treatment should be considered for every juvenile or that rehabilitation should be the primary goal of the juvenile court.[80] The NCJFCJ embraced the view that dispositions must be individualized, since "no two children have the same personalities, strengths and weaknesses, nor the same family supports and pressures." Similarly, it retained the principle that "the public is best protected and the children best helped by focusing on the future and preventing new offenses by rehabilitating the individual delinquent, rather than focusing on the past by punishing an offense which is over and done." These views were evident in the specific programs the NCJFCJ supported, such as the establishment of substance abuse programs and separate mental health treatment facilities.[81]

In examining these various national reform proposals, one sees four principal themes emerge: the reorganization of jurisdiction over juveniles and the gradual narrowing of its delinquency component; the need for formal adjudication procedures and the expansion of due process in juvenile courts; a somewhat greater emphasis on offenses than on offenders; and the need to limit dispositional discretion. Each of these themes departed significantly from the nineteenth-century vision of juvenile courts and from important aspects of the Supreme Court's juvenile justice decisions.

The Impact on State Legislation

These four themes became evident at the state legislative level during the late 1970s and throughout the 1980s in juvenile court statutes that were more explicitly punitive and that established juvenile courts that functioned more like criminal courts than social welfare agencies. This "criminalization" of juvenile courts was characterized by the removal of noncriminal misbehavior ("status offenses") from the court's jurisdiction, more frequent transfer of serious offenders to criminal courts, and the imposition of increasingly punitive sanctions by juvenile court judges.[82] It was also evident in the fact that public safety, punishment, and juvenile accountability became important components of the purpose clauses of juvenile court statutes in some states. The objectives of California's Welfare and Institutions Code, for example, included "protect[ing] the public from criminal conduct by minors . . . [and] impos[ing] on the minor a sense of responsibility for his or her own acts." Minnesota's statute sought to "promote the public safety and reduce juvenile delinquency by maintaining the integrity of the substantive law prohibiting certain behavior and by developing individual responsibility for lawful behavior." The purpose clauses of Delaware, Florida, Maine, Nebraska, and West Virginia were only slightly less explicit.[83] Given the origins of juvenile court statutes, the establishment of punishment-oriented statutory preambles was truly noteworthy. The willingness of state legislators to include criminal law purposes in juvenile court statutes expressed a new, or at least a more candid, understanding of the role of juvenile courts. This perception was particularly evident in other substantive changes, which moved juvenile courts further from the nineteenth-century Illinois ideal.

One set of such changes concerned the jurisdiction of juvenile courts. Significantly, most states narrowed the definition of delinquency to include only those acts that would be criminal offenses if committed by an adult. One of the consequences of *Gault* was the widespread adoption of a distinction between delinquents and "persons in need of supervision,"[84] because of the Court's narrow application of the *Gault* requirements to delinquency proceedings only. Thus, by creating a separate category for misbehavior like truancy and running away, states could circumvent constitutional standards of due process in those cases. Later, the movement to divert status offenders from formal court processing encouraged further developments in this direction.

A second set of substantive changes occurred in the area of dispositional proceedings. The bifurcation of the adjudication and dispositional phases of juvenile proceedings was a significant change whose intent was to circumscribe dispositional discretion. With a similar objective in mind, states formalized dispositional hearings. Thus, although in many states the usual rules of evidence were not applicable to dispositional hearings,[85] thirty-four states eventually permitted juveniles (or their counsel) to examine the social report on which dispositional decisions are based and to cross-examine the writer of the report.[86] In addition, representation by counsel at the disposition hearing was expressly provided for in those states that guaranteed the right to counsel "at all stages of the proceedings," and it was held to be a requirement of due process by some state courts.[87] There remained questions, however, about the effectiveness of counsel in representing their clients' interests during the dispositional phase of juvenile proceedings.[88]

Another change in dispositional practices was to link the substance of dispositions more directly to specific acts. The impetus for this development was twofold: the desire to control discretionary decisionmaking and dispositional discrepancies and the realization that the failure to establish a relationship between acts and their consequences undermined the deterrent value of juvenile court intervention.[89] These factors were evident in the movement of some states away from indeterminate dispositions[90] and in the development of restitution as either a sole disposition or as a condition of probation.[91] The two most important new strategies for linking dispositions more directly to specific acts, however, involved jurisdictional waiver and special provisions to deal with serious, chronic, or violent juvenile offenders.

Waiver proceedings, in which the juvenile court relinquishes its jurisdiction to a criminal court, continued the tradition (which began with the House of Refuge movement) of separating minor and serious juvenile offenders. The proceedings were incorporated into comprehensive juvenile court laws as a "safety valve" to protect the rehabilitative ideal from any "public hostility and frustration" that might be associated with the juvenile court's limited capacity to deal with particularly heinous crimes.[92] Consistent with the juvenile court's rehabilitative objectives, waiver was traditionally based on a judicial determination of a juvenile's "amenability to treatment" and "dangerousness."[93] In the 1980s this traditional approach came under increasing criticism, with Barry Feld emerging as the most outspoken opponent of judicial waiver.[94] At the heart of Feld's criticism was his conclusion that juvenile court judges, even when their discretion is circumscribed, are poorly equipped to make the predictive clinical diagnoses necessary to determine amenability to treatment and dangerousness. This incapacity, according to Feld, resulted in the inconsistent application of waiver criteria, regardless of how specific those criteria might be.[95]

Feld offered two alternatives to judicial waiver. In his view, the best approach was for waiver to be based on objective offense and offense history characteristics incorporated into legislatively mandated waiver criteria that excluded certain juveniles from the court's jurisdiction altogether (i.e., legislative waiver).[96] A less desirable option was to give juvenile and criminal courts concurrent jurisdiction over some offenses, permitting prosecutors to choose the forum in which they wished to proceed (prosecutorial waiver). Legislators in twenty-three states and the District of Columbia reached conclusions similar to Feld's, adopting one or both of these alternatives to judicial waiver.[97] The offenses excluded under legislative waiver provisions generally included capital offenses; various degrees of murder, rape, and other sex crimes; robbery; and kidnapping. In all but three of the eight states that adopted some form of prosecutorial waiver, its use was restricted to certain serious felonies.[98] As Feld pointed out, however, in states where prosecutorial waiver was unrestricted, it suffered from the same deficiencies as judicial waiver.[99]

Legislators adopted legislative waiver, prosecutorial waiver, and tighter judicial waiver standards as one strategy for implementing a more punitive approach to juvenile crime. Their assumption was that certain juveniles could be held more accountable by subjecting them to the harsher sentences of the adult system. The evidence suggests, however, that waiver did not accomplish this objective. In New York, for example, one study indicated that only 4 percent of all serious juvenile offenders tried in criminal courts received more severe sanctions than those that could have been imposed by the family court.[100] In Massachusetts, the transfer rate decreased steadily between 1980 and 1985, and those juveniles transferred to criminal courts were unlikely to be incarcerated more often or for longer periods than minors retained in the juvenile system. Moreover, transferred juveniles exhibited the same recidivism rates as nontransfers.[101] There are two possible explanations for these findings: First, criminal courts generally treat defendants transferred from juvenile courts as first offenders;[102] second, most prosecutors had not yet developed a coherent system for using juvenile court records in criminal prosecutions.[103]

As waiver demonstrated itself to be a relatively ineffective method of satisfying the desire to hold juveniles more accountable for their criminal behavior, legislators turned to another dispositional reform. Serious offender statutes attempted to subject a particular type of juvenile offender to distinctively more punitive treatment within the juvenile court's own jurisdiction. The rationale for serious offender statutes was that juvenile courts should respond more harshly to certain classes of offenders without altering their response to the minor offenders who constitute the bulk of their caseload. In general, these statutes required that juveniles who meet the definition of "serious offender" be committed to state juvenile institutions for a specified period of time.[104] One mid-1980s survey of state dispositional practices found serious offender statutes in California, Colorado, Delaware, Georgia, Illinois, Kentucky, New York, and North Carolina.[105] Perhaps the harshest of these statutes was the Illinois Habitual Juvenile Offender Act, which mandated that habitual juvenile offenders be incarcerated in a correctional facility until the age of twenty-one.[106] Enacted in 1979 to limit prosecutorial discretion and to protect the public,[107] the act defined a "habitual juvenile offender" as one who had twice been adjudicated delinquent for a felony and was subsequently adjudicated delinquent for murder, manslaughter, sexual assault, aggravated battery, burglary, home invasion, robbery, or aggravated arson. In 1984 the Illinois Appellate Court liberally interpreted this statute to permit the eight-year commitment of a thirteen-year-old juvenile offender with two delinquency adjudications.[108]

Serious offender statutes, legislative and prosecutorial waiver, offense-specific judicial waiver, and more direct links between dispositions and specific criminal acts reflected an evolution away from offender-oriented to offense-oriented juvenile courts. Perhaps the most striking example of this new wave of juvenile codes was the 1977 Washington State Juvenile Justice Act. Its objectives were to "protect the citizenry from criminal behavior," "make the juvenile offender accountable for his or her criminal behavior," "provide for punishment commensurate with the age, crime, and criminal history of the juvenile offender," and create a juvenile justice system "capable of having primary responsibility for, being accountable for, and responding to the needs of youthful offenders."[109] To achieve these purposes, the act removed juvenile court jurisdiction over noncriminal misbehavior, shifted responsibility for intake decisions from probation officers to prosecutors, and implemented accountability-oriented programs for juveniles diverted from formal court processing.

The most distinctive feature of the act was its provision for the establishment of juvenile sentencing standards, which were to be developed by a nine-member commission and approved by the state legislature. The commission adopted three objectives in developing the standards: justice and accountability, community safety, and youth development and treatment.[110] The third one was given the least emphasis, since treatment needs were not to be used as a variable in determining the length of sentences. Instead, the system encouraged juveniles who might benefit from additional rehabilitative services to continue in treatment programs voluntarily after completing their dispositions.

Each set of standards mandates presumptive and determinate sentences proportionate to the seriousness of the offense, the offender's age, and the juvenile's prior offense history. All offenses are ranked by severity, creating three statutorily defined classes into which a juvenile may fall.[111] Serious offenders are juveniles fifteen years or older found guilty of a Class A felony or of a Class B+ felony in which bodily harm or a weapon was involved. Minor/first offenders are juveniles sixteen years or younger who have committed three or fewer offenses with no felonies or who have committed a Class B felony without any prior offenses. All other offenders are referred to simply as juvenile offenders.

The second component of the standards is a system in which points are calculated on the basis of age, offense severity, and the recency and severity of prior offenses. The presumptive disposition is then determined by the number of points accumulated by the juvenile offender. The standards contain several dispositional alternatives, including determinate commitment to state juvenile institutions or local facilities, community supervision, community service, and fines. For serious offenders, the only option is commitment to a state juvenile institution for a determinate period. Minor/first offenders are generally subject only to community supervision, community service, or fines. The greatest opportunity for judicial discretion is with the middle class of ordinary juvenile offenders, for whom judges have available three sets of options composed of combinations of four dispositional alternatives. For any class, judges may depart from the presumptive disposition only upon a written finding that the disposition would constitute a "manifest injustice" to the juvenile or to the public.

According to one study, the implementation of the act produced significant changes in decisionmaking throughout Washington's juvenile justice system.[112] The new decisionmaking rules eliminated informal adjustment of cases at intake and produced sentences that were far more uniform and proportionate than those imposed under the previous legislation. The act produced these results without increasing the overall severity of juvenile sentences; indeed, aggregate sentence severity actually decreased during the act's first two years of operation. The new legislation also accomplished its objective of removing noncriminal misbehavior from the court's jurisdiction without producing unintended negative consequences. Moreover, a higher proportion of juvenile offenders was held accountable by some form of sanction under the new statute. Unfortunately, the evaluators found it impossible to determine the act's impact on recidivism since it was difficult to distinguish actual changes in juveniles' behavior from changes in official decisionmaking that might affect recidivism rates.

The Washington act was the most consistently offense-oriented statute developed in any state in the aftermath of constitutional domestication. The aspect that made it especially unique is that it implicitly replaced traditional juvenile jurisprudence with the revived concept of "just deserts." The principle of just deserts, or proportionate punishments, underlies what is undoubtedly the oldest approach to criminal sanctions. According to this principle, sanctions should be imposed primarily to express society's moral condemnation of the criminal act. Consequently, proportionate sanctions are retrospective in that they seek to reflect the moral quality of the act already committed rather than to prevent future criminal acts; future-oriented goals, such as rehabilitation, deterrence, and incapacitation, are considered insufficient justifications for coercive intervention into offenders' lives.[113] The basic component of the just deserts approach is culpability, understood as responsibility for the actual or potential harm caused by an act. The introduction of a just deserts sentencing policy into a juvenile statute represented a strong rejection of the rationale underlying individualized, discretionary decisionmaking in the juvenile justice system.

Even the 1977 Washington act, however, did not completely abandon traditional elements of juvenile justice. For example, it retained the traditional *parens patriae* approach to waiver proceedings.[114] Moreover, the act did not grant juveniles the right to jury trials, despite its obviously punitive orientation. The persistence of traditional theories of juvenile justice was particularly evident in *State v. Lawley* (1979), in which the Washington Supreme Court refused to require jury trials in juvenile proceedings conducted under the new legislation.[115] The court concluded that, since punishment and treatment are often interchangeable, delinquency proceedings were exempt from certain elements of criminal due process even when punishment became the principal goal of juvenile justice.

The principal legacy of constitutional domestication was a further revolution in juvenile justice policy, although perhaps not exactly the revolution the Supreme Court intended. Indeed, neither Justice Fortas nor Justice Brennan (the majority opinion writers in *Kent, Gault,* and *Winship*) perceived their decisions as being particularly revolutionary. Their only expectation was that juvenile court delinquency procedures would improve and that the philosophical core and broader objectives of juvenile justice would remain undisturbed. Yet in none of the key decisions did the Court speak with a single, unified voice. Throughout the constitutional domestication process two dissenting themes constantly emerged. On the one hand, there was the view, forcefully articulated by Justice Stewart in *Gault,* that the Court was gravely mistaken in its characterization of juvenile proceedings as adversarial in nature, which led to the obvious conclusion that the Court was wrong to impose any element of criminal due process on juvenile courts. On the other hand, Justice Black constantly sounded the second theme, that the Court was wrong to stop short in its criminalization of delinquency proceedings once it had erased the line demarcating juvenile hearings from criminal trials. Ultimately, both themes found receptive audiences among the individuals charged with implementing constitutional domestication.

The first theme was enthusiastically embraced, of course, by juvenile court judges, many of whom simply refused to follow the rules laid down by the Court. As a result, the majority's first expectation—improved delinquency adjudication procedures—foundered on the intransigence of officials who possessed a radically different understanding of their role from that articulated by Justice Fortas. The Court could lay down rules, but it could not transform attitudes and philosophies. The second theme caught the attention of both liberal and conservative critics of the unreconstructed juvenile court of the 1960s and 1970s. For liberal reform groups like the IJA-

ABA and the Twentieth Century Fund, Hugo Black's admonition to take constitutional domestication to its logical conclusion provided a means to address legislatively the procedural deficiencies that persisted even after the Supreme Court's intervention. For conservative reformers, like those who dominated the NAC after 1980, the same admonition presented an opportunity to inject punitive objectives into juvenile justice policy. The irony of this confluence of forces is that the Court majority's procedural expectations could be met only by developments that contradicted its substantive expectations.

It would be incorrect to posit a direct link between the Court's constitutional domestication of juvenile justice and the "criminalization of juvenile courts" in the 1980s and 1990s. It is correct, however, to stress the catalytic impact of the Court's decisions. By questioning, and even undercutting to some degree, the traditional assumptions of juvenile justice policy, the Court facilitated future legislative reform by unclogging the channels of political change. This opening provided an opportunity for critics of juvenile courts and their surrounding philosophy to engage in a project of institutional redesign. That this project took a different direction from the one the reformers of the 1960s and their allies on the Court expected is quite clear. The due process worldview of the Warren Court that one finds in *Gault*—in which discretion is circumscribed by the procedural safeguards of formal adversarial proceedings—is quite different from the "just deserts" approach—in which discretion is circumscribed by a philosophy of individual responsibility and retribution. The gravamen of this difference is that the worldview underlying constitutional domestication focused on the means by which discretion is exercised, and the more contemporary approach emphasizes the ends toward which its exercise is directed. Rehabilitation and individual treatment no longer constitute the defining goals of juvenile justice policy.

In the 1960s, the Supreme Court was at the cutting edge of juvenile court reform, and it transformed academic policy critiques into new constitutional rules designed to change the manner in which juvenile justice would be administered. Though juvenile courts were slow to adopt these changes, juvenile court reformers and state legislatures embraced the principles underlying them and pushed the "criminalization" of juvenile justice further than the *Gault* majority could have anticipated or probably would have supported. As legislatures pushed forward, the Court's development of constitutional law for juvenile courts stagnated, and thus a disjunction developed between the new juvenile court and the constitutional law under which it operates. There is in the history of the Court's participation in juvenile procedural reform an echo of Alexander Bickel's warning about the policymaking capacity of the judicial process: "It has difficulty controlling the stages by which it approaches a problem. It rushes forward too fast, or it lags; its pace hardly ever seems just right."[116]

8. Litigation and Juvenile Court Reform

When the Supreme Court first directed its attention toward juvenile justice policy in 1966, the meaning of constitutional domestication was relatively clear and straightforward: to graft modern adjudicative procedures onto the nineteenth-century juvenile court ideal. According to most commentators of the period, this simple operation would go a long way toward solving the administrative deficiencies of juvenile courts that placed the liberty of youthful offenders at risk and undermined the effectiveness of rehabilitation efforts. In this purely legal understanding of the term, constitutional domestication was largely successful. In *Kent, Gault, Winship,* and *Breed v. Jones,* reform-oriented litigants were able to persuade the Supreme Court to interpret statutes and the Constitution in a manner that significantly altered the procedural rules of juvenile courts. These litigants and the Court failed to foresee, however, that changes to the rules would not necessarily translate into changes in administrative or adjudicative practice. Consequently, in operational terms constitutional domestication was far less successful, since local officials resisted new rules articulated by a Court that had little enforcement power over them. Moreover, by formulating the problem of juvenile justice in procedural terms, the reform movement of the 1960s departed from the idea of the juvenile court as the institutional centerpiece of a complex and integrated system for dealing with a phenomenon that the juvenile court's founders had considered to be social rather than legal. Although this shift made juvenile justice reform more judicially manageable, it meant that the language of criminal justice policy began to overtake the language of social welfare policy as the dominant feature of juvenile justice discourse. As this new discourse gathered momentum, it facilitated the legislative reconstruction of juvenile justice policy.

Clearly, the question of analytical importance is whether this history of constitutional domestication represents a unique phenomenon driven by idiosyncratic forces or whether it reflects a more systematic activity in the nature of institutional reform litigation. Drawing on the important contributions of other commentators to our understanding of institutional reform litigation, I have suggested that the answer to this question might be found by examining the political environment in which the cases arose and were decided, the efforts of organized interest groups who lobbied and litigated for reform both before and after *Gault,* and the composition of the Court and its institutional attributes. I now provide an analysis of how each of these factors contributed to the legal success of constitutional domestication, to its operational failure, and to longer-term developments, including the Court's decision to disengage from juvenile justice reform.

Political Environment

Institutional reform litigation is triggered by two factors connected to the political environment. First, growing dissatisfaction with the policy orientation and performance of a particular institution generates a general demand for reform. Second, specific events create legal disputes that provide reformers with the minimum threshold necessary to pursue their agenda through litigation. The success or failure of litigation is further influenced by general developments in constitutional theory, which make courts more or less amenable to reform efforts. These environmental factors undoubtedly played an important role in the initial success of constitutional domestication. At a general level, legal criticism of discretionary justice and arbitrary decision-making combined with mounting public criticism of rising juvenile crime rates to produce a loss of faith in the rehabilitative ideal and its corresponding procedural framework, which generated significant demands for juvenile justice reform by the early 1960s. Specifically, the circumstances surrounding Morris Kent Jr.'s and Gerald Gault's cases provided the legal disputes necessary to push those demands into the adjudicative arena, where reformers benefited from a theoretical climate generally favorable to the expansion of due process and its extension to state proceedings.

Indeed, each of the three key cases in the process of constitutional domestication was set apart by unique characteristics, which reasonably could be viewed as constituting an egregious injustice to the youths involved. In *Kent,* the extremely severe sentence that Morris received from the district court buttressed the argument that waiver was a critically important determination of the sort that requires a hearing. In *Gault,* the discrepancy between the disposition of Gerald's case and the statutory penalty for his offense, along with the absence of any procedural formality during his two delinquency hearings, made the case for procedural reform easier to argue. Finally, Rena Uviller's selection of *Winship* as the case with which to challenge New York's use of the preponderance standard in delinquency hearings resulted from rather extraordinary judicial remarks concerning the unreliability of that standard relative to the reasonable doubt test. Indeed, these remarks encouraged Uviller to proceed with the case despite her belief that the proof against Samuel Winship was stronger than the evidence that she usually saw in delinquency hearings.

Ironically, the same political environment that facilitated legal success contributed to operational failure. The values of the national juvenile court reform movement were not shared by the local officials charged with implementing and administering the new rules. They maintained their faith in the rehabilitative ideal and, understandably, disputed the assertion that their decisions were rendered arbitrarily. They also saw *Gault*, in particular, as the atypical product of poorly trained juvenile court officials. If not prohibited from doing so by statute, juvenile court judges used the connection drawn in the Court's decisions between the prospect of confinement and the need for due process to avoid the new rules.[1] The fact that vindication of the rights granted in *Gault* and the other cases required the cooperation of widely scattered juvenile court judges whose philosophy, legal education, and skills varied significantly from jurisdiction to jurisdiction weakened compliance with the decisions. Moreover, there was little or no political pressure on these judges to comply from either the public or politicians, who were concerned about juvenile crime and suspicious of the Supreme Court's procedural decisions in ordinary criminal cases. Indeed, there was probably significant support for judges who refused to allow juveniles to use procedural maneuvers to escape the consequences of their actions.

In general, the political environment allowed the advocates of a procedurally strong, rehabilitatively oriented juvenile court to win the important legal battles while losing the overall operational and philosophical struggle over juvenile justice policy. As Gerald Rosenberg has pointed out, "Courts may serve an ideological function of luring movements for social reform to an institution that is structurally constrained from serving their needs, providing only an illusion of change."[2] In the case of juvenile justice reform, the relatively easy procedural victories led reform advocates to focus on juvenile courts rather than on other institutions responsible for implementing juvenile justice policy. For example, since most expert observers conceded that juveniles were not receiving proper access to treatment and rehabilitative services, one option for reforming litigants might have been to seek a significant augmentation of the resources allocated to juvenile justice and to attempt sweeping substantive improvements in the rehabilitative programs available to juvenile courts and their associated institutions. This option could have been pursued constitutionally by drawing an analogy between commitment to juvenile institutions by juvenile courts and civil commitment to mental health institutions by ordinary courts. This entirely plausible analogy would have provided access to the "right to treatment" doctrine that was gaining momentum in the mental health field at precisely the same time that reformers were conducting their program of constitutional domestication of juvenile courts.[3] Given the knowledge about conditions in the institutions to which juvenile courts sent young offenders, it is not difficult to imagine a scenario in which those institutions, rather than juvenile courts, might have become the central focus of reform litigation in the same way that prisons became the target of public interest litigation. The reform movement of the 1960s and 1970s remained trapped within the parameters of its initial procedural definition of the problem, however.

Such boundaries did not apply for the new reformers who emerged in the wake of the decision. Still influenced by a political environment characterized by skepticism toward rehabilitation and public concern about juvenile crime, they developed a different philosophical orientation that focused on more extensive criminalization of juvenile justice policy. Both liberal and conservative critics of traditional juvenile justice policy found common ground in the promotion of the philosophy of "just deserts" as a way of achieving the (predominantly liberal) goal of system accountability and the (predominantly conservative) goal of individual responsibility for criminal conduct. Nowhere was this new alliance more evident than in the development of the 1977 Washington State Juvenile Justice Act. Developed over ten years of discussion, the act garnered support from a diverse coalition, including prosecutors, public defenders, and law enforcement officials. Prosecutors and law enforcement agencies applauded the law's emphasis on personal responsibility for wrongdoing, and public defenders were satisfied by increased procedural formality and reduced judicial discretion at the intake and disposition stages of proceedings. Not surprisingly, judges, probation officers, court administrators, and social service case workers—all of whom had their roles and responsibilities redefined by the act—exhibited the lowest level of support for the law.[4] Nevertheless, an ideologically diverse coalition of critics of traditionalism was able to overcome this opposition from influential defenders of the status quo.

Interest Groups

One of the distinctive features of institutional reform litigation is that courts are relatively passive institutions in that they have little control over the cases litigated before them and thus depend on other people to frame the issues and to gather a significant proportion of the information necessary for their decisionmaking.[5] This passivity also means that the constraints and incentives that reformers face in designing litigation strategies are important factors in determining the effectiveness of judicial policymaking. Interest groups must ensure centralized control over litigation and devise strategies that do not require unusual departures from established legal doctrine to reach the desired result.[6] One way of achieving this objective is to generate favorable litigation through the use of specially selected test cases. Neither *Kent* nor *Gault*, however, was a pure test case or the product of a systematic strategy to challenge juvenile court traditionalism through litigation. *Gault*'s national importance as a challenge to the doctrine of *parens patriae* and its associated procedural framework emerged only when it reached the New York offices of the ACLU. Only *Winship* might be characterized as the result of a conscious decision to pursue juvenile justice reform through litigation, albeit at the state rather than the national level. Despite reformers' dissatisfaction with juvenile court practices in the mid-1960s, a full-fledged "children's rights" movement organized to achieve its objectives in the courts had not yet evolved.

Although the cases emerged on the national scene relatively unsystematically, they nevertheless exhibited some or all of the qualities that Bruce Hafen has described as the classic elements of successful public interest litigation involving children: cooperation between local plaintiffs' counsel and national resource offices, the involvement of young lawyers committed to helping disadvantaged groups, a specific procedural issue linked to underlying symbolic needs, a unity of interest between parents and children, and the proposal of a theoretically unambiguous judicial response to the perceived problem.[7] In addition to these positive characteristics, none of the three cases decided between 1966 and 1970 suffered from the internal conflicts among its participants about goals, strategies, and tactics that can plague children's rights litigation.[8] These conflicts generally arise because of the relative inability of children to articulate or represent their own interests and from the tension that frequently exists between the interests of children and those of their parents. None of the participants in *Kent, Gault,* or *Winship* disagreed about the fact that they were seeking the best interests of their immediate clients, their clients' parents, or children generally. Only their opponents challenged the premise that children would be well served if procedural restrictions were imposed on the juvenile court's pursuit of its rehabilitative goals.

The lack of conflict in these three cases resulted in large measure from the high degree of control and centralized development of litigation strategies exercised by the principal litigants in each case. In *Kent,* Richard Arens's direction of the *Durham* project allowed him to redefine the appeal as a juvenile procedure challenge. Although this approach weakened *Kent*'s value as an insanity-defense test case, it proved instrumental in ensuring the appeal's eventual success. More typical of such control was the ACLU's involvement in *Gault.* Once the appeal left Arizona, participation by the local counsel virtually ended. By gaining complete control over the litigation, the ACLU ensured that there would be no conflict between its objectives and strategy and those of Gerald Gault's Arizona attorney; Norman Dorsen and Daniel Rezneck were thus able to hone their arguments without outside interference. Similarly, not only did the Legal Aid Society exercise complete control over *Winship,* but Rena Uviller was able to develop her case without close supervision by her superiors at the LAS.[9] Moreover, in neither *Gault* nor *Winship* was there any significant conflict between the litigants and amicus participants.[10] In the three cases, centralized control reduced the number of conflicting signals that might have introduced confusion and ambiguity into the Court's deliberations.

The strategy selected by each of the litigants, who framed their requests for relief in the form of specific procedural claims while generally avoiding more problematic equal protection issues, also reduced the potential for confusion and ambiguity.[11] The appellants were able to soften the novelty of their claims and avoid putting the Court in the position of having to rule on the constitutionality of juvenile courts per se. The ACLU went so far as to argue in *Gault* that the right to counsel would be consistent with the *parens patriae* doctrine since it would protect juveniles from potential abuses associated with the informality and judicial discretion permitted within that concept. Indeed, Dorsen and Rezneck contrasted data about the modern rehabilitative deficiencies of juvenile courts with historical material concerning the trade-off between informality and rehabilitation.[12] They invited the Court to draw the conclusion that informality actually hampered rehabilitation efforts. The Court could thus reach the desired result without breaking entirely from years of lower court decisions.

Although the actions taken by interest groups in bringing the juvenile justice cases and in developing appropriate litigation strategies and tactics increased the likelihood of legal victory, those same actions possibly contributed to the subsequent confusion at the level of policy. For example, conflict among litigants, though making development of a litigation strategy more difficult, is perhaps also a more accurate reflection of the complex interests and choices involved in the types of cases with which public interest litigants generally concern themselves. Moreover, the selection and use of facts and supporting data further reduced the apparent complexity of the cases. Further, the strategic decision to formulate concerns about unsuccessful rehabilitation in procedural terms, along with tactical decisions about the selection and use of facts, glossed over some important policy-relevant aspects of *Gault* and *Winship*.

In *Gault*, for example, the problem with Arizona's juvenile court law was not simply, or even primarily, procedural informality during adjudication proceedings. Equally responsible for the discrepancy between the juvenile court's disposition of Gerald's case and the adult penalty for his offense was the fact that juvenile court judges enjoyed almost unlimited discretion to impose indeterminate dispositions. Dorsen and Rezneck overlooked this problem because it struck too deeply at the juvenile court ideal that the Court had refused to abandon in *Kent*. Similarly, Rena Uviller downplayed the possibility that replacing the preponderance test by the reasonable doubt standard might require the establishment of a direct link between dispositions and offenses. The effect of such a link would have been to reduce significantly the dispositional flexibility that even the Supreme Court considered necessary for effective rehabilitation. Ultimately, the process of mounting a successful litigation strategy in these cases helped to obscure the policy questions embedded in the issues the Court was deciding. There existed a tension, in other words, between the requirements of that strategy and the conditions required for providing the information necessary for identifying, evaluating, and selecting among the policy alternatives that were hidden just below the surface of the legal issues raised in the cases. Given the constraints of institutional reform litigation, the ACLU or other groups could do little to alleviate this tension without reducing their probability of victory.

Nor could these groups monopolize the course of juvenile justice reform outside the adjudicative arena. Clearly, once the Court's decisions loosened the rehabilitative ideal's hold on juvenile justice policy, other interest groups were free to occupy the field. Groups such as the IJA–ABA Commission, the Twentieth Century Fund, and the federal government's National Advisory Committee put forward proposals that eventually were reflected in state legislative reforms that embraced to some degree a just deserts philosophy alien to the original values of the nineteenth-century founders of the juvenile court, to the litigating groups such as the ACLU, NLADA, and legal aid societies, and to the Warren Court that precipitated the third juvenile justice "revolution." Indeed, the procedural rules articulated by the Court made the adoption of an explicitly punitive juvenile justice philosophy more defensible.

Judicial Personnel and Institutional Attributes

Despite the important role played by interest groups in developing and controlling the litigation in these cases, their history suggests that, if one fails to distinguish between the Supreme Court and lower appellate and trial courts, it is possible to exaggerate the passivity of adjudication. The Supreme Court has greater control over its docket than other courts, especially for the purposes of setting "norms of general applicability."[13] Indeed, the Court selects cases precisely "because of the general importance of the issues" implicated in them.[14] Moreover, as occurred in the instance of Chief Justice Warren's 1964 speech, the Court can send powerful signals about the reform agenda it is willing to entertain. The circumstances surrounding *Gault*'s selection provide some evidence of such signals, but the clearest example is the substitution of *Winship* for *DeBacker* as the vehicle for deciding the standard of proof issue. In these instances it is vitally important that the selected case present as many sides of the issue and represent as many of the interests implicated in that issue as possible. The Court, however, tends to select cases not because they reflect the complexity of difficult policy issues but because they facilitate relatively easy choices. Individual cases, in other words, are often "outliers" that do not reflect the general nature of the policies in question. The problem is that individual cases

> do not give any idea of how the system in general operates. Just as hard cases make bad law (sometimes), egregious examples lead to bad policy (sometimes). They can lead one to believe that the problems identified are common rather than isolated. Consequently, they can result in policies that prevent the worst case, but make things worse in most situations.[15]

Since judicial discretion begins with case selection and continues to the final decision, individual judicial values and institutional decisionmaking attributes clearly will play a crucial role in institutional reform litigation.

The juvenile court reform cases bear out this observation exceptionally well. In the seven cases decided between 1966 and 1985, sixteen justices ruled on one statutory and nine constitutional claims (see Table 8.1).[16] Leaving aside the single case in which the Court's decision was unanimous,[17] there

Table 8.1. Judicial Acceptance of Juvenile Procedure Rights

	Waiver	Notice	Counsel	Cross-ex.	Self-incrimination	Transcript	Appeal	Proof	Jury	Jeopardy	Miranda	Detain
Black	N	Y	Y	Y	Y			N	Y			
Blackmun									N	Y	N	N
Brennan	Y	Y	Y	Y	Y			Y	N	Y	Y	Y
Burger								N	N	Y	N	N
Clark	Y	Y	Y	Y	Y			Y	Y			
Douglas	Y	Y	Y	Y	Y				Y	Y		
Fortas	Y	Y	Y	Y	Y			Y				
Harlan	N	Y	Y	N	N	Y		Y	N			
Marshall								Y	Y	Y	Y	Y
O'Connor												N
Powell										Y	Y	N
Rehnquist										Y	N	N
Stevens											Y	Y
Stewart	N	N	N	N	N			N	N	Y	N	
Warren	Y	Y	Y	Y	Y				N	Y	N	
White	N	Y	Y	N	N			Y	N	Y	N	N

were nine claims about which the justices disagreed. Two justices—Brennan and White—heard every claim, with Brennan accepting eight of nine claims and White only three of nine. At the other end of the participation spectrum, three justices—Clark, Warren, and Fortas—only participated in the two cases involving the first five claims; however, they were in complete agreement with one another in accepting the five claims. Three other justices—Douglas (seven of seven), Marshall (four of four), and Stevens (two of two)—also accepted all the claims made in the cases in which they participated. Of the remaining eight justices, only Hugo Black was a consistent supporter of juvenile rights claims, accepting five of the seven that he heard. Two justices—Harlan (four of eight) and Powell (one of two)—divided their votes equally between acceptance and rejection. Justices Stewart, Burger, Blackmun, Rehnquist, and O'Connor rejected every claim they heard in the disputed cases.

Additional insights into the impact of judicial attitudes on the resolution of these cases are possible by examining inter-agreement patterns among the justices on the various issues presented in the seven cases and by comparing those patterns to the general pattern of inter-agreement during the relevant period (see Table 8.2). In general, there was not a large difference between overall inter-agreement rates during the relevant terms and the inter-agreement pattern evident in the subset of juvenile justice issues decided by the Court. Overall, the mean inter-agreement rate between pairs of justices was 62.7 percent; the mean inter-agreement rate between justices on juvenile rights issues was 60.1 percent. This finding supports the generally predictable nature of judicial behavior, which suggests the presence of relatively stable attitudes and value orientations.

At the same time, five justices (Douglas, Marshall, Rehnquist, Stevens, and Stewart) did exhibit somewhat atypical behavior on juvenile justice issues. Marshall, Stevens, and Stewart found themselves more isolated in the juvenile justice cases than usual. In the case of Marshall and Stevens, their support for juvenile rights claims on a Court increasingly unreceptive to such claims pushed their inter-agreement rates well below normal. For Marshall, this stance produced a mean inter-agreement rate of 49.2 percent in the juvenile justice cases versus an overall rate of 58.6 percent. The difference for Stevens was even more striking: 27.8 percent (juvenile justice) versus 58.7 percent (overall). Similarly, Stewart's role as the principal opponent of constitutional domestication from the outset had the same effect, producing a juvenile justice inter-agreement mean of 39.3 percent versus an overall mean of 62.4 percent. By contrast, Rehnquist displayed a leadership role in later

Table 8.2. Agreement Rates in Juvenile Justice Cases and the Court's Docket, 1965–1984 (in percentages)

	White	Warren	Stewart	Stevens	Rehnquist	Powell	O'Connor	Marshall	Harlan	Fortas	Douglas	Clark	Burger	Brennan	Blackmun
Black	42.9 / 57.5	80.0 / 63.4	28.6 / 51.1	—	—	—	—	50.0 / 54.9	42.9 / 47.1	80.0 / 60.1	71.4 / 60.9	80.0 / 67.8	50.0 / 58.5	57.1 / 57.8	0.0 / 55.8
Blackmun	100.0 / 69.9	—	100.0 / 63.9	0.0 / 61.0	100.0 / 65.0	66.7 / 70.0	100.0 / 66.5	25.0 / 61.3	100.0 / 57.1	—	50.0 / 37.0	—	100.0 / 72.1	50.0 / 62.5	
Brennan	50.0 / 63.2	100.0 / 92.7	22.2 / 60.3	100.0 / 64.5	33.3 / 42.5	66.7 / 53.9	0.0 / 55.5	80.0 / 88.6	57.1 / 54.0	100.0 / 81.7	85.7 / 69.3	100.0 / 78.5	40.0 / 48.4		
Burger	80.0 / 73.9	—	100.0 / 67.0	0.0 / 53.8	100.0 / 83.8	66.7 / 80.8	100.0 / 84.1	20.0 / 47.4	50.0 / 64.5	—	33.3 / 35.6	—			
Clark	40.0 / 72.9	100.0 / 74.4	0.0 / 65.2	—	—	—	—	—	40.0 / 60.2	100.0 / 69.7	100.0 / 62.3				
Douglas	42.9 / 51.1	100.0 / 74.7	0.0 / 46.3	—	100.0 / 29.4	100.0 / 39.6	—	100.0 / 66.7	42.9 / 42.7	100.0 / 71.2					
Fortas	40.0 / 68.0	100.0 / 85.7	0.0 / 60.4	—	—	—	—	—	40.0 / 52.3						
Harlan	100.0 / 59.3	40.0 / 52.2	57.1 / 70.1	—	—	—	—	50.0 / 58.2							
Marshall	40.0 / 59.5	50.0 / 52.2	25.0 / 61.2	100.0 / 60.9	33.3 / 40.9	66.7 / 53.0	0.0 / 50.2								
O'Connor	100.0 / 76.1	—	—	0.0 / 58.2	100.0 / 86.8	100.0 / 81.6									
Powell	66.7 / 72.4	—	50.0 / 74.8	0.0 / 57.9	100.0 / 78.0										
Rehnquist	100.0 / 71.9	—	100.0 / 67.7	50.0 / 52.3											
Stevens	0.0 / 59.2	—	0.0 / 60.8												
Stewart	66.7 / 65.0	0.0 / 60.3													
Warren	40.0 / 74.0														

Source: Harvard Law Review, 1966–1985.

Note: Lower figures represent the overall rate of inter-agreement, 1965–1984.

cases by opposing juvenile rights claims and persuading his colleagues to agree with him 81.7 percent of the time in the three cases in which he participated (versus an overall rate of 61.8 percent). Douglas found himself agreeing completely with Rehnquist and Powell, two justices with whom his overall inter-agreement rate was only 29.4 and 39.6 percent. This finding is explained by the fact that the only issue these three justices considered together was double jeopardy, an issue on which the Court was unanimous. This example serves as a reminder that judicial behavior does not explain everything; on some occasions the correct result in a case is so obvious that it transcends attitudinal differences.

The overview of the voting behavior of individual justices in these cases suggests two important reasons why claims made in earlier cases fared much better than those made in later cases. First, by the later cases, the Court was dominated by justices unfavorably disposed toward juvenile rights claims. Second, there was nothing ambivalent in these justices' rejection of additional procedural safeguards in juvenile proceedings; it applied across the spectrum of issues. Given this shift in composition from a court that contained four members who almost always accepted juvenile rights claims to one that contained four members who always rejected such claims, it is hardly surprising that three of the four claims made after 1970 failed.

Perhaps the most important personnel change that occurred during this period was the failed elevation of Abe Fortas to the chief justiceship and the eventual replacement of Earl Warren in that position by Warren Burger in 1969. In addition to his known support for defendants' rights and the expansion of due process, Fortas's early exposure to legal realism had made him receptive to the functional similarity argument advanced by the ACLU and to the use of law review articles and other material to buttress that argument. In sharp contrast to Fortas, with his often theoretical approach to the law and generally prodefendant attitude, Burger had been appointed as chief justice in 1969 by Richard Nixon as part of the new president's attack on crime and Warren Court liberalism. Known more for judicial pragmatism than for constitutional theorizing, Burger had practiced law in Minnesota before joining the federal court of appeals for the District of Columbia. As a federal judge, Burger was a frequent critic of both the Warren Court's expansive understanding of due process and the aggressive behavior it encouraged among criminal defense attorneys.[18] He dissented frequently from his more liberal colleagues on the court of appeals, arguing that additional procedural safeguards were impractical, impeded effective law enforcement, and failed in their principal objective of protecting suspects placed in custody. As Fred Graham has said, Burger was "appointed as a law-and-order judge, and nobody who approved of those qualities later complained of his performance." [19] Not only did Burger reject every contested juvenile rights claim he heard, but his position as chief justice gave extra weight to those judgments. Had Lyndon Johnson succeeded in promoting Abe Fortas, it is possible that the juvenile justice cases decided after 1969 might have been resolved differently.

Led by Justice Fortas's functional analysis, the justices composing the late Warren Court responded enthusiastically to the litigants' strategy of asking the Court to recognize the punitive nature of juvenile detention and to implement procedural safeguards against arbitrary confinement. The legal grounds for the Court's decisions rested on a novel view of the status of juvenile courts and the extent to which children are autonomous citizens capable of independently claiming the protections of the Constitution and the Bill of Rights. The Court decided that although states had labeled juvenile proceedings civil instead of criminal, they resembled criminal prosecutions in most vital respects. In particular, much of the behavior that juvenile courts dealt with was clearly criminal in nature; and some of the consequences of delinquency adjudications—especially confinement in state institutions—resembled the consequences of criminal conviction. According to the Court, these similarities were sufficient to limit the juvenile court's immunity from the requirements of criminal due process. From the perspective of constitutional doctrines of due process, the Court had to choose between selective incorporation—which gave priority and greater constitutional weight to the liberty interests of children—and fundamental fairness—which gave priority to the integrity of traditional juvenile proceedings.

Although the Court chose selective incorporation, it did not completely ignore the claim that rehabilitation, despite skepticism about it, should remain a principal policy objective of juvenile justice. In crafting its remedy, the Court rejected the argument that rehabilitation would be impossible to achieve within the adversary atmosphere that would most likely be created by incorporating the Bill of Rights into juvenile proceedings. Instead, the justices adopted the opposite view that procedural formality would actually contribute to the rehabilitative objectives of juvenile justice. In the final analysis, the Court based its decisions on the following calculation: Limited procedural formality would preserve the noncriminal nature of juvenile courts while promoting effective rehabilitation through more accurate fact-finding and a sense of fair treatment among juveniles.

It should be apparent that, contrary to Donald Horowitz's idealized adjudicative model, the Court did not entirely disregard policy considerations or the potential costs of its remedy on juvenile proceedings. The justices were concerned about the possibility of overburdening juvenile justice officials with procedural requirements, which was evident in the Court's choice of selective incorporation as the appropriate standard for altering juvenile court procedures. By its very nature, selective incorporation allows the Court to take into account policy considerations—such as the impact of a procedural requirement on the administration of justice—when engaging in due process review. Although not so flexible as the purely contextual doctrine of fundamental fairness, selective incorporation is certainly more flexible than total incorporation. Policy considerations were particularly evident in *Gault* and *Winship* in the narrow application of the Court's due process remedy to delinquency adjudication proceedings. The Court clearly wanted to impose its remedy in a way that would not undermine the traditional "informality, flexibility, or speed" of juvenile proceedings; nor did it wish to undermine the "substantive benefits" of those proceedings. Indeed, the potential contribution of the Court's legal remedy to achieving the policy goals of juvenile justice was an important consideration in *Gault*.

Nevertheless, the Court's policy analysis was somewhat clumsy in these cases, largely because of the adjudicative affinity for historical facts and retrospective decisionmaking. A number of studies have suggested that this attribute of adjudication hampers the communication and processing of policy-relevant information in both trial and appellate courts. In trial courts the principal problem is a decisionmaking format that reduces the comprehensiveness, quality, and integrity of information; promotes unrealistic simplification; and hinders the "logical order needed for a systematic consideration of findings on a specific topic."[20] The most important weakness of appellate court litigation is that it exaggerates the authoritativeness of information and encourages courts to treat hypotheses as axioms.[21] Moreover, even when adequate information about legislative facts is available, judges appear to have a difficult time evaluating and analyzing that information.[22] As Eleanor Wolf has put it, "The courtroom is the best place to decide whether X committed a murder; it is a poor place to consider the causes of homicide."[23]

Many of these difficulties were evident in *Kent, Gault,* and *Winship.* For example, in each case the appellants relied on law review articles and standards promulgated by national organizations to lend added authority to their arguments.[24] The utility and reliability of such material as a source of policy-relevant information is questionable, however. Arthur Selwyn Miller and Jerome Barron have argued that, although law review articles often appear to be "dispassionate disquisitions of a topic," they are usually written from a particular point of view and should be treated not as independent sources of information but as briefs advocating a particular policy position.[25] Indeed, interest groups may stimulate the production of law review articles to advance novel legal theories and to provide the sociological evidence necessary to achieve law reform.[26] The use of professional standards and guidelines has also been criticized because they frequently reveal more about the aspirations and self-interests of professional associations than they do about the minimum standards states must meet in order to conform to the Constitution.[27] These problems are exacerbated by the limited opportunity for adversaries to challenge such information, particularly in appellate courts. Only in *Winship*, for example, was there an explicit attempt to challenge the appellants' interpretation of law review articles or statements of professional standards.[28]

Such extrinsic evidence often goes unchallenged because of the relative strength of adversaries.[29] In the three key juvenile court reform cases, the appellants' counsel had more litigation experience and greater specialized expertise in the matters under consideration than opposing counsel. The most striking example of this phenomenon was *Gault*. Not only did the ACLU's attorneys have extensive experience in litigation concerning criminal procedure generally, but they were also able to assemble a team of constitutional lawyers with a special expertise in social welfare law. Arizona, on the other hand, assigned *Gault* to a generalist attorney who had only recently graduated from law school. The appellees in *Kent* and *Winship* were similarly represented by generalists, but their opponents were more specialized. Rena Uviller, for example, had focused exclusively on juvenile court law for over three years before taking *Winship* to the Supreme Court.

Another explanation for unchallenged extrinsic evidence is the practice of "judicial notice," through which courts incorporate "well-known facts" into their decisions that are not found in the record. For example, in *Gault* the majority cited forty-two items in its opinion (other than cases or statutes) to support its conclusions about the theory, practice, and accomplishments of juvenile courts and the measures necessary to improve those institutions. Three of these items were carried over from *Kent*, and sixteen had been cited in one or more of the briefs. Twenty-three items were thus the product of the independent research efforts of the justices or their clerks. Although the majority of these items dealt with legal issues, they also included national juvenile court standards, a study of the quality and competence of juvenile court judges, data on juvenile recidivism rates, and reflections on the role of counsel in New York delinquency hearings before and after implementation of the 1962 Family Court Act. Most important, these items included the President's Commission Report on Law Enforcement and Administration of Justice, which dealt with the relationship between procedural informality and the juvenile court's rehabilitative objectives. Although this report at least addressed a critical policy issue raised by *Gault,* its use by the Court was somewhat questionable; speculation among professionals about the possible relationship between the juvenile court's procedural and substantive elements became hard empirical evidence in the minds of the majority.

To some degree, the relative inadequacy of the lower court records in the juvenile justice cases made it necessary for the Court to look elsewhere for information. For example, *Kent*'s initial development as an insanity-defense test case did not lend itself to the development of the information necessary to consider some of the broader issues raised by the case, such as Justice Fortas's concern with the "adequacy of custodial treatment facilities and policies." [30] More specifically, the legislative facts necessary to determine the "critical importance" of waiver were never really developed in either the lower court record or in the briefs presented to the Court. The Court's reliance on this characteristic of waiver, however, should have required that it have some information about the frequency with which juveniles transferred to criminal courts received harsher sentences than those imposed by juvenile courts. The majority simply assumed, without sufficient data one way or the other, that juveniles fare worse in criminal courts. Ironically, the Court provided its own counterexample to this assumption one year later; in *Gault* the juvenile penalty was far more severe than the adult criminal penalty.

The deficiencies in the lower court record were even more marked in *Gault,* where the record consisted entirely of the juvenile referral report, the delinquency petition, a note from the deputy probation officer to Gerald's mother, the commitment order, and testimony elicited during the habeas corpus hearing. This material was singularly unhelpful in unraveling what really occurred during Gerald's delinquency hearings, and it constituted a dubious source of information about juvenile court practices in either Arizona or the nation generally. Moreover, by refusing to grant juveniles a right to a transcript of juvenile court proceedings, the *Gault* Court failed to address the one issue about which the lower court record was revealing.

Part of the problem in *Gault* was that, because very few states required significant elements of criminal due process in juvenile court proceedings, empirical data was lacking on the relationship between adversary proceedings and rehabilitation in 1967. By the time the Court heard oral argument in *Winship*, however, the absence of empirical data was less of a problem since some formalization of juvenile court proceedings had taken place after *Gault*. More significantly, New York had had nearly seven years of experience with elements of criminal due process in its juvenile proceedings on which the Court could have drawn for information. In addition, the lower court record in *Winship* spoke directly to the question of whether juveniles were harmed by the state's reliance on a lower standard of proof to support delinquency adjudications. The Court, however, did not take advantage of the empirical opportunities offered by *Winship* and instead relied uncritically on *Gault's* conclusions about the impact of procedural formality on juvenile courts. The most glaring omission from the information considered by the Court was the assessment of *Gault's* impact that Norman Lefstein, Vaughan Stapleton, and Lee Teitelbaum had published in *Law & Society Review* five months before the Court noted jurisdiction in *Winship*.[31] Whether it would have affected the Court's legal conclusions is uncertain, but it would have raised a number of interesting and difficult questions for the Court's consideration.

One means by which courts attempt to deal with their limited legislative fact-finding capacity is to engage in what Rachel Moran has termed "avoidance." "By restating issues in narrow, legal terms," Moran notes, "courts can not only minimize the significance and visibility of broad, indeterminate social issues but also restructure their decisionmaking responsibility."[32] As Bruce Hafen explains, "Lawyers are most comfortable with procedure. . . . By focusing on procedure, counsel can minimize or even avoid complex evidentiary or policy questions. Finally, judges can be persuaded with relative ease that one more formality can only increase fairness."[33] Courts, moreover, are thought to possess special expertise in procedural matters.[34] In many instances, however, this confidence may be misplaced. The procedural complexion of such cases often deflects attention from substantive issues about which courts may make unwarranted assumptions, a tendency that is especially true where the anticipated behavior of nonjudicial participants in the criminal justice system (for example, police, defense lawyers, prosecutors, and corrections agencies) is at issue.[35]

Avoidance may have contributed to the gradual transformation of *Kent* from an insanity-defense test case to a juvenile procedure matter. As Kent's trial suggested, using that case to expand the productivity rule articulated in *Durham* would have forced the Court to reopen a complex set of policy issues surrounding the definition of criminal responsibility and the protection of defendants who could not be held responsible. The *Kent* Court also avoided important policy questions concerning the meaning, relevance, and application of the concepts of "amenability to treatment" and "dangerousness" by focusing on the procedures by which juvenile courts waive jurisdiction. As legislative developments in this area indicate, determining the juvenile court's response to serious, violent, and chronic young offenders is much more difficult and complex than judicial waiver suggests. Similarly, avoidance may have contributed to the *Gault* majority's unwillingness to accept the somewhat pessimistic conclusions of the president's commission regarding the rehabilitative capacity of juvenile courts. More important, the Court simplified a number of complicated policy issues, such as the criminal capacity of children and the relationship between dispositions and offenses, by simply dismissing various *parens patriae* assumptions as constituting nothing more than "labels of convenience" used to justify procedural arbitrariness.

The *Winship* majority's uncritical adherence to *Gault's* conclusion with respect to the impact of procedural formality on juvenile courts also illustrates the tension between the adjudicative process and the effective use of policy-relevant information. "The continuity of law and the citation of precedent," Eleanor Wolf has argued, "are at odds with the use of scientific knowledge as evidence."[36] Social science evidence is the tentative product of a continuous process of reevaluation and revision, which is inherently incompatible with the authority implicit in judicial adherence to past decisions. Moreover, when a single precedent is cited in a sequence of related cases, the evidence on which it is based acquires authoritative momentum, narrowing policy choices and precluding certain decisions. In each successive juvenile court reform decision, the Court's view of the choices it faced was limited by the narrow facts of the immediate case and by the general conclusions of prior decisions. It escaped these facts and conclusions in *McKeiver* only by arguably misstating the basis for its prior decisions.

A final attribute of adjudication speaks to the difficulties of implementation evident in these cases. Since the adjudicative process focuses on remedying past wrongs rather than on shaping future relationships, courts have little need or incentive to test systematically their assumptions about how individuals and institutions will react to their decisions. The problem is not that judicial decisions have unexpected or unintended consequences or both, but that the reliance on litigants to initiate adjudication can make the process of discovering and responding to unintended consequences unusually cumbersome.[37] Management and control of the decisions' outcome was therefore difficult. Subsequent litigation, including *Winship,* did not address *Gault's* implementation or the accuracy of the Court's predicted consequences. As a result, the Court had little opportunity to monitor or to review its decisions in a systematic fashion. Moreover, by failing to grant juveniles a constitutional right to appellate review, the Court did nothing to ensure that it would have such an opportunity.

Ironically, this weakness may stem from the very characteristics of adjudication that make it an attractive decisionmaking process to groups interested in social and legal reform. Adjudication reduces the number of participants in decisionmaking, allowing courts to reach decisions on controversial issues more quickly and authoritatively than legislatures. There is evidence, however, that groups excluded at the adjudication phase of decisionmaking reappear later to block implementation.[38] The experience with *Roe v. Wade* (1973)[39] is a case in point. Although antiabortion groups found themselves unable to recriminalize abortion throughout the 1970s and 1980s, they did find it possible to limit *Roe's* impact through legislation prohibiting public funding of abortions.[40] Ultimately, poor compliance with and the weak impact of judicially formulated policies can be traced to the difficulty of the judicial process in gathering and processing the type of information necessary for policymaking. These difficulties hinder the communication of expected consequences to individuals and institutions affected by the decisions, leading to frustration and inhibiting compliance.[41] Indeed, as Phillip Cooper found, the attempt by courts to frame remedies in ways that reduce the degree of judicial intrusion and soften the impact of the remedy often creates ambiguity that can adversely affect implementation. This practice was certainly one difficulty hindering the implementation of the juvenile justice reform decisions.

Changes in judicial personnel, along with the inherent decisionmaking attributes of the Supreme Court, had an impact on the various outcomes in the juvenile justice cases. Initially dominated by justices who possessed a liberal view of due process and their own responsibility to supervise state judicial proceedings, the Court in *Kent, Gault,* and even *Winship* was receptive to the procedural claims advanced by the juvenile court reform movement. The nature of the adjudicative process also made it easier for the Court to focus on the legal questions at issue and to relegate the policy questions to secondary status. This pattern promoted a somewhat optimistic view of the operational consequences that would follow changes in procedural rules. By contrast, the post-1970 Court increasingly included justices who were less than enthusiastic about the impact of the Warren Court's due process revolution on both criminal and juvenile proceedings. To Chief Justice Burger, in *Winship* and subsequent cases, that revolution had threatened the vitality of the juvenile court system. Later, to Justice Rehnquist in *Schall v. Martin*, the negative reaction to the earlier cases seemed to be driven by the public danger posed by juvenile offenders. The problem that remained constant from one era to the next, however, was the difficulty of controlling and managing the direction and speed of juvenile justice reform through litigation.

Epilogue

Kent, Gault, and *Winship* were landmark developments in the evolution of American juvenile justice policy because they rejected the nineteenth-century idea that procedural informality and unlimited judicial discretion are indispensable for rehabilitating young offenders. Noting high recidivism rates among juveniles generally and harsh treatment of individual juveniles in three specific cases, the Court accepted the critical view of juvenile courts that had blossomed early in the 1960s. It concluded that juvenile courts were failing in their mission to rehabilitate children and to protect them from the punitive consequences of coercive state intervention against actions that were essentially criminal behavior. The Court's solution was to erect a procedural barrier to prevent the transfer of juveniles to criminal courts and to reconstitute the adjudicative element of juvenile court delinquency proceedings along the lines of criminal trials. The Court was confident that these changes would eliminate the most egregious abuses of discretionary justice in juvenile courts while leaving intact the most essential elements of informality and flexibility. Neither the Court nor the interest groups who promoted constitutional domestication, however, anticipated the criminalization of juvenile courts.

I have suggested in my analysis that one explanation for this lack of foresight is that the political environment, interest groups, and the composition of the Court combined to make the problems underlying the deficiencies of juvenile courts in the mid-1960s appear more straightforward than they actually were. In addition to procedural matters, the cases raised a number of theoretical questions concerning the appropriate state response to criminal behavior by young offenders and several empirical questions about the consequences of waiver, the frequency with which juveniles received the unjust treatment evident in *Gault*, and the substantive impact of criminal due process on juvenile proceedings. None of these questions received adequate consideration in the process of institutional reform litigation that produced constitutional domestication. Consequently, the Court reached unrealistic conclusions about both the short- and long-term impact of the decisions.

How did this lack of consideration occur? To simplify the choices with which the Court was faced, the more experienced interest group litigants, with legal resources superior to their opponents, used strategies that obscured the complexity of the issues underlying the cases. The adjudication process did not provide a way of correcting for this initial simplification; by viewing these issues through the narrow lens of relatively easy, single case studies, the Court avoided the necessity of gathering or processing the type of information that could have revealed the complexity of the problems for which it was seeking a solution. Just as the original juvenile court movement was more than a procedural innovation, the juvenile justice cases raised substantive issues about the nature of childhood and the proper role of the state in regulating children's behavior, criminal or otherwise. Further, the Court's performance in juvenile justice reform supports the assertion that the attempt to solve complex and multifaceted policy problems through decision-making techniques designed to resolve concrete disputes strains the information-gathering, processing, and evaluating capacity of adjudication. In order to ease this strain, both litigants and courts tend to choose "easy" cases, to emphasize their familiar and highly visible procedural elements, and to avoid complex underlying issues. This practice increases the possibility of inadequate implementation and compliance and the potential for unintended consequences. Although legislatures and administrative agencies also face these problems, the limited policy-review capacity of courts imposes on the judicial process a greater vulnerability to these deficiencies.

The juvenile justice decisions rendered by the U.S. Supreme Court between 1966 and 1970, and *Gault* in particular, are often cited as paradigmatic examples of the generous approach to due process characteristic of the Warren Court era. It is thus tempting to dismiss subsequent Court decisions, such as *Schall v. Martin* (1984), as simply the unfortunate consequence of changes in judicial personnel. Although these changes certainly played a role, a close examination of the juvenile justice trilogy and the cases that followed it reveals that important elements must be added to this conventional explanation. On the one hand, the contrasting approaches to juvenile justice reform taken by the Court before and after 1970 were products of their time in a broad sense. Before 1970, despite criticism of the procedural consequences of the rehabilitative ideal, there was still considerable support for the theory of rehabilitation. Indeed, procedural control of arbitrary decisionmaking was intended to enhance the rehabilitative accomplishments of juvenile courts. After 1970, with the criminalization of juvenile justice fully under way, the punitive philosophy embedded in such measures as the preventive detention provision challenged in *Schall v. Martin* was fully acceptable to the Court. Moreover, regardless of personnel, the review of juvenile justice policy that occurred in the judicial arena was constrained by the institutional decisionmaking attributes of the adjudicative process. The final lesson of the constitutional domestication of juvenile courts is not that litigation will necessarily fail to produce social reform—rules did change, as did the orienting philosophy of juvenile justice—but that litigation unleashes legal, political, and social forces over which the initiators of institutional reform litigation have little control.

Notes

1. *Kent v. United States*, 383 U.S. 541, 556, 555 (1966). The District of Columbia Juvenile Court Act allowed waiver after the completion of a "full investigation." The Court held that this requirement could be satisfied only by a hearing.

2. *In re Gault*, 387 U.S. 1 (1967).

3. Ibid., 13.

4. *In re Winship*, 397 U.S. 358 (1970). The phrase "constitutional domestication" is from *Gault*, 387 U.S., 22.

5. Indeed, in a major history of the American Civil Liberties Union, which argued *Gault* before the Supreme Court, the author devotes only three paragraphs to the case. See Samuel Walker, *In Defense of American Liberties: A History of the ACLU* (New York and Oxford: Oxford University Press, 1990), 253–54. The most extensive analysis of *Gault* in the context of institutional reform litigation can be found in Donald L. Horowitz, *The Courts and Social Policy* (Washington, DC: Brookings Institution, 1977), 171–219. Another analysis along these lines is found in Gerald Rosenberg, *The Hollow Hope: Can Courts Bring About Social Change?* (Chicago: University of Chicago Press, 1991), 314–16.

6. Susan Gluck Mezey, *Children in Court: Public Policymaking and Federal Court Decisions* (Albany: State University of New York Press, 1996), 2.

7. See, e.g., Colin S. Diver, "The Judge as Political Powerbroker: Superintending Structural Change in Public Institutions," *Virginia Law Review* 65 (1979): 43–106; Arthur Selwyn Miller and Jerome A. Barron, "The Supreme Court, the Adversary System, and the Flow of Information to the Justices: A Preliminary Inquiry," *Virginia Law Review* 61 (1975): 1187–1245; Donald L. Horowitz, "Decreeing Organizational Change: Judicial Supervision of Public Institutions," *Duke Law Journal* (1983): 1265–1307; Eleanor Wolf, *Trial and Error: The Detroit School Segregation Case* (Detroit: Wayne State University Press, 1981); Rogers Elliott, *Litigating Intelligence: IQ Tests, Special Education, and Social Science in the Courtroom* (Dover, MA: Auburn House, 1987); and Rosenberg, *Hollow Hope*. More positive assessments can be found, however. See Leif H. Carter, "When Courts Should Make Policy: An Institutional Approach," in *Public Law and Public Policy*, ed. John Gardner (New York: Praeger, 1977), 141–57; Ralph Cavanagh and Austin Sarat, "Thinking About Courts: Toward and Beyond a Jurisprudence of Judicial Competence," *Law and Society Review* 14 (1980): 371–420; and Susan E. Lawrence, *The Poor in Court: The Legal Services Program and Supreme Court Decision-making* (Princeton, NJ: Princeton University Press, 1990).

8. John Hart Ely, *Democracy and Distrust: A Theory of Judicial Review* (Cambridge: Harvard University Press, 1980), 21, 88. This is the assumption that Donald Horowitz started with in his own analysis of the *Gault* case.

9. See, e.g., Clement E. Vose, *Caucasians Only: The Supreme Court, the NAACP, and the Restrictive Covenant Cases* (Berkeley: University of California Press, 1959); Anthony Lewis, *Gideon's Trumpet* (New York: Vintage Books, 1966); Richard Kluger, *Simple Justice* (New York: Vintage Books, 1975); Liva Baker, *Miranda: Crime, Law and Politics* (New York: Atheneum, 1983); and Charles Lofgren, *The Plessy Case: A Legal-Historical Interpretation* (New York: Oxford University Press, 1987).

10. This literature is summarized in Tracey E. George and Lee Epstein, "On the Nature of Supreme Court Decision Making," *American Political Science Review* 86 (1992): 323–37. On impact, see Stephen L. Wasby, *The Impact of the United States Supreme Court* (Homewood, IL: Dorsey Press, 1970), and Rosenberg, *Hollow Hope.*

11. 397 U.S. 358 (1970). In this case, a majority of the Court, led by Justice William Brennan, went beyond the explicit provisions of the Bill of Rights to impose the criminal standard of proof beyond a reasonable doubt on state delinquency proceedings.

1. LITIGATION AND THE DYNAMICS OF SOCIAL REFORM

1. *Dred Scott v. Sandford,* 60 U.S. 393 (1857).

2. *Civil Rights Cases,* 109 U.S. 3 (1883); *Plessy v. Ferguson,* 163 U.S. 537 (1896).

3. *Lochner v. New York,* 198 U.S. 45 (1905); *Adkins v. Children's Hospital,* 261 U.S. 525 (1923); *Schecter Poultry Corp. v. United States,* 295 U.S. 495 (1935); *United States v. Butler,* 297 U.S. 1 (1936); *Carter v. Carter Coal Co.,* 298 U.S. 238 (1936).

4. *Brown v. Board of Education,* 347 U.S. 483 (1954).

5. Robert M. Cover, "The Origins of Judicial Activism in the Protection of Minorities," *Yale Law Journal* 91 (1982): 1287–1316.

6. Tinsley E. Yarborough, "The Political World of Federal Judges as Managers," *Public Administration Review* 45 (1985): 660.

7. In the 163 years prior to *Brown,* the Court overturned an average of slightly more than four state laws, acts of Congress, and its own decisions each year. After *Brown,* this annual average increased to about fifteen. See David M. O'Brien, *Constitutional Law and Politics,* vol. 2, *Civil Rights and Civil Liberties* (New York: W. W. Norton, 1991), 38.

8. George Tsebelis, *Nested Games: Rational Choice in Comparative Politics* (Berkeley: University of California Press, 1990), 92–118.

9. Lee Epstein and Joseph F. Kobylka, *The Supreme Court and Legal Change: Abortion and the Death Penalty* (Chapel Hill: University of North Carolina Press, 1992), 5.

10. Susan Lawrence, *The Poor in Court: The Legal Services Program and Supreme Court Decision-making* (Princeton, NJ: Princeton University Press, 1990), 40.

11. Robert C. Wood, ed., *Remedial Law: When Courts Become Administrators* (Amherst: University of Massachusetts Press, 1990), 36.

12. Philip J. Cooper, *Hard Judicial Choices: Federal District Court Judges and State and Local Officials* (New York: Oxford University Press, 1988), 16–24.

13. Wood, ed., *Remedial Law,* 89–91.

14. For a discussion of when U.S. federal courts may disengage from monitoring desegregation orders, see *Freeman v. Pitts,* 118 L.Ed. 2d 108 (1992).

15. Epstein and Kobylka, *Supreme Court and Legal Change,* 9.

16. Donald L. Horowitz, *The Courts and Social Policy* (Washington, DC: Brookings Institution, 1977).

17. Oliver Wendell Holmes, *The Common Law* (Boston: Little, Brown, 1940), 1.

18. Laura Kalman, *Legal Realism at Yale, 1927–1960* (Chapel Hill: University of North Carolina Press, 1986), 14–16.

19. C. Herman Pritchett, *The Roosevelt Court: A Study in Judicial Politics and Values, 1937–1947* (New York: Macmillan, 1948).

20. Glendon Schubert, *The Judicial Mind: The Attitudes and Ideologies of Supreme Court Justices* (Chicago: Northwestern University Press, 1965), and *The Judicial Mind Revisited: Psychometric Analysis of Supreme Court Ideology* (New York: Oxford University Press, 1974).

21. See, e.g., S. Sidney Ulmer, "Dissent Behavior and the Social Background of Supreme Court Justices," *Journal of Politics* 32 (1970): 580–98, and Ulmer, "Social Background as an Indicator to the Votes of Supreme Court Justices in Criminal Cases, 1947–1956 Terms," *American Journal of Political Science* 17 (1973): 622–30; James L. Gibson, "Judges' Role Orientations, Attitudes, and Decisions: An Interactive Model," *American Political Science Review* 72 (1978): 911–24.

22. Gibson, "Judges' Role Orientations," 918.

23. I have omitted three additional cases from my list: *In re Wittington,* 391 U.S. 341 (1968); *DeBacker v. Brainard,* 396 U.S. 28 (1969); and *New Jersey v. T.L.O.,* 469 U.S. 325 (1985). Although these three cases raised constitutional questions about juvenile proceedings, the Court avoided making a substantive decision on those questions in each of them.

24. Kalman, *Legal Realism at Yale,* 111–13.

25. The nature of the early Douglas-Fortas relationship is explored in Bruce Allen Murphy, *Fortas: The Rise and Ruin of a Supreme Court Justice* (New York: William Morrow and Company, 1988), 3–32.

26. *Gideon v. Wainwright,* 372 U.S. 335 (1963). In this case, Fortas successfully persuaded the Supreme Court to rule that states must provide all indigent defendants with legal counsel.

27. *Miranda v. Arizona,* 384 U.S. 436 (1966).

28. Jeffrey A. Segal, "Supreme Court Justices as Human Decision Makers: An Individual-Level Analysis of the Search and Seizure Cases," *Journal of Politics* 48 (1986): 938–55.

29. Lee Epstein, Thomas G. Walker, and William J. Dixon, "The Supreme Court and Criminal Justice Disputes: A Neo-institutional Perspective," *American Journal of Political Science* 33 (1989): 825–41.

30. Horowitz, *Courts and Social Policy*, 34–56.

31. See T. Alexander Smith, *The Comparative Policy Process* (Santa Barbara, CA: Clio Books, 1975); Randall B. Ripley and Grace A. Franklin, *Congress, the Bureaucracy, and Public Policy* (Homewood, IL: Dorsey Press, 1980); Arnold J. Heidenheimer and Michael Parkinson, "Equalizing Educational Opportunity in Britain and the United States: The Politics of Implementation," in *Perspectives on Public Policy-making*, ed. William B. Gwynn and George C. Edwards III (New Orleans: Tulane University Press, 1975), 141–65; Robert Putnam, "Bureaucrats and Politicians: Contending Elites in the Policy Process," in Gwynn and Edwards, eds., *Perspectives on Public Policy-making*, 199–202; Richard L. Siegel and Leonard B. Weinberg, *Comparing Public Policies: United States, Soviet Union and Europe* (Homewood, IL: Dorsey Press, 1977).

32. Abram Chayes, "The Role of the Judge in Public Law Litigation," *Harvard Law Review* 89 (1976): 1282–83.

33. Colin S. Diver, "The Judge as Political Powerbroker: Superintending Structural Change in Public Institutions," *Virginia Law Review* 65 (1979): 77–88, 90–103.

34. Ibid., 46–48.

35. Horowitz, *Courts and Social Policy*, 33.

36. Ibid., 51.

37. Gerald Rosenberg, *The Hollow Hope: Can Courts Bring About Social Change?* (Chicago: University of Chicago Press, 1991), 10.

38. Ibid., 33–35.

39. Ibid., 10.

40. See, e.g., Reginald S. Sheehan, William Mishler, and Donald R. Songer, "Ideology, Status, and the Differential Success of Direct Parties Before the Supreme Court," *American Political Science Review* 86 (1992): 464–71.

41. Clement Vose, "Litigation as a Form of Pressure Group Activity," *Annals of the American Academy of Political and Social Science* 319 (1958): 20–31.

42. Karen O'Connor and Lee Epstein, "Rebalancing the Scales of Justice: Assessment of Public Interest Law," *Harvard Journal of Law and Public Policy* 7 (1984): 483.

43. William C. Louthan, *The Politics of Justice* (Port Washington, NY: Kennikat Press, 1979), 120.

44. Robert Mnookin, *In the Interests of Children: Advocacy, Law Reform, and Public Policy* (New York: W. H. Freeman, 1985), 4.

45. Robert L. Rabin, "Perspectives on Public Interest Law," *Stanford Law Review* 28 (1976): 216.

46. Ibid., 222. Environmental groups also concentrate their efforts on cases with national applicability and the possibility of wide impact rather than on suits against individual polluters for noncompliance with regulations. See R. Shep Melnick, *Regulation and the Courts: The Case of the Clean Air Act* (Washington, DC: Brookings Institution, 1983), 362.

47. Rabin, "Perspectives on Public Interest Law," 221.

48. This phrase is taken from *United States v. Carolene Products,* 304 U.S. 144, 152–53 n.4 (1938). A discrete and insular minority is any group that is identifiably different from the majority of citizens and is denied the power to defend or advance its interests through ordinary political action.

49. Clement E. Vose, *Caucasians Only: The Supreme Court, the NAACP, and the Restrictive Covenant Cases* (Berkeley: University of California Press, 1959), 39, 44.

50. Restrictive covenants were held unconstitutional by the U.S. Supreme Court in *Shelley v. Kraemer,* 334 U.S. 1 (1948). Segregation in public schooling was declared unconstitutional in *Brown v. Board of Education,* 347 U.S. 483 (1954). The voting rights story is slightly more complicated. Jim Crow voting restrictions were struck down in *Smith v. Allwright,* 321 U.S. 659 (1944); and in *Reynolds v. Sims,* 377 U.S. 533 (1964), the Court declared its "one man, one vote" apportionment principle. Though not exclusively an "African American rights" case, *Reynolds* benefited African Americans living in urban centers.

51. Marc Galanter, "Why the 'Haves' Come Out Ahead: Speculations on the Limits of Legal Change," *Law and Society Review* 9 (1974): 95–160.

52. Ibid., 98.

53. Lawrence, *The Poor in Court,* 14.

54. Susan Olson, "Interest Group Litigation in Federal District Courts: Beyond the Political Disadvantage Theory," *Journal of Politics* 52 (1990): 854–82.

55. Ibid., 858.

56. Mark V. Tushnet, *The NAACP's Legal Strategy Against Segregated Education, 1925–1950* (Chapel Hill: University of North Carolina Press, 1987), 2; Richard Kluger, *Simple Justice* (New York: Vintage Books, 1975), 388–90.

57. Kim Lane Scheppele and Jack L. Walker, "The Litigation Strategies of Interest Groups," in *Mobilizing Interest Groups in America: Patrons, Professions and Social Movements,* Jack L. Walker Jr. (Ann Arbor: University of Michigan Press, 1991), 161–68.

58. Two additional elements of the model presented by Scheppele and Walker are the substance of policy and the organizational character of interest groups. On the first point, they argue that groups concerned with domestic and welfare policies will more frequently litigate because foreign policy is largely immune from judicial review in the United States. On the second point, Scheppele and Walker argue that profit and nonprofit sector groups will use litigation differently.

59. There is an extensive literature on these choices and their impact. See Karen O'Connor, *Women's Organizations' Use of the Courts* (Lexington, MA: D. C. Heath, 1980); Joel F. Handler, *Social Movements and the Legal System: A Theory of Law Reform and Social Change* (New York: Academic Press, 1978); Karen O'Connor and Lee Epstein, "The Rise of Conservative Interest Group Litigation," *Journal of Politics* 45 (1983): 479–89; and Stephen L. Wasby, "Civil Rights Litigation by Organizations: Constraints and Choices," *Judicature* 68 (1985): 337–52.

60. See Ronald Manzer, "Public Policy-making as Practical Reasoning," *Canadian Journal of Political Science* 17 (1984): 588.

61. Tushnet, *NAACP's Legal Strategy*, 50.

62. Ibid., 34.

63. Although no formally organized groups participated in *Kent*, there was an amicus brief filed by fourteen individuals, led by a law professor from American University in Washington, DC.

64. Lawrence, *The Poor in Court*, 25–26, 36–37, 166, 116.

65. Finley Peter Dunne, "The Supreme Court's Decisions," in *Mr. Dooley's Opinions* (New York: R. H. Russell, 1901), 26. Robert Dahl's more sober version of this point is that the Court cannot remain out of step with national political trends for long periods. See Robert Dahl, "Decision-making in a Democracy: The Supreme Court as a National Policy Maker," *Journal of Public Law* 6 (1957): 279–95.

66. Lawrence, *The Poor in Court*, 3.

67. Rosenberg, *Hollow Hope*, 304.

68. Herbert L. Packer, *The Limits of the Criminal Sanction* (Palo Alto, CA: Stanford University Press, 1968), 158, 157.

69. Ibid., 163–64.

70. *Weeks v. United States*, 232 U.S. 383 (1914); *Wolf v. Colorado*, 338 U.S. 25 (1949).

71. Ralph A. Rossum and G. Alan Tarr, *American Constitutional Law: Cases and Interpretation*, 2d ed. (New York: St. Martin's Press, 1987), 434.

72. *Elkins v. United States*, 364 U.S. 206 (1960). See O'Brien, *Constitutional Law and Politics*, 2: 890.

73. *Mapp v. Ohio*, 367 U.S. 643 (1961).

74. *Miranda v. Arizona*, 384 U.S. 436 (1966).

75. Ibid., 448, 445, 455, 467, 460.

76. Laurence H. Tribe, *American Constitutional Law* (Mineola, MN: Foundation Press, 1978), 502.

77. Christopher P. Manfredi, "Human Dignity and the Psychology of Interrogation in *Miranda v. Arizona*," *Canadian Journal of Law and Society* 1 (1986): 110–12; Packer, *Limits of Criminal Sanction*, 165–66.

78. Welsh S. White, "Police Trickery in Inducing Confessions," *University of Pennsylvania Law Review* 127 (1979): 628; Mark Berger, *Taking the Fifth: The Supreme Court and the Privilege Against Self-incrimination* (Lexington, MA: Lexington Books, 1980), 32.

79. *Gitlow v. New York*, 268 U.S. 652 (1925). The Court, however, had applied certain elements of the Fifth Amendment to the states in 1896 and 1897. See O'Brien, *Constitutional Law and Politics*, 2: 280.

80. For a summary of these differences, see Ralph A. Rossum, *The Politics of the Criminal Justice System: An Organizational Analysis* (New York: Marcel Dekker, 1978), 118–25.

81. *Cohen v. Hurley*, 366 U.S. 117, 158 (1961), Brennan, J., dissenting and citing *Palko v. Connecticut*, 302 U.S. 319, 325 (1937).

82. *Lisenba v. California*, 314 U.S. 219, 236 (1941), Roberts, J., majority opinion.

83. Lawrence, *The Poor in Court*, 11, 156.

84. Epstein and Kobylka, *Supreme Court and Legal Change*, 8 (emphasis in original).

2. DISCRETIONARY JUSTICE

1. Charles N. Glaab and A. Theodore Brown, *A History of Urban America* (New York: Macmillan, 1967), 107–32; Blake McKelvey, *The Urbanization of America, 1860–1915* (New Brunswick, NJ: Rutgers University Press, 1963), 86–98.

2. Illinois Juvenile Court Act, 1899 *Ill. Laws* 131.

3. Ellen Ryerson, *The Best-Laid Plans: America's Juvenile Court Experiment* (New York: Hill and Wang, 1978), 25.

4. David Rothman, *The Discovery of the Asylum: Social Order and Disorder in the New Republic* (Boston: Little, Brown, 1971), 78.

5. Rothman, *Discovery of the Asylum*, 210, 213; Robert M. Mennell, *Thorns and Thistles: Juvenile Delinquents in the United States, 1825–1940* (Hanover, NH: University Press of New England, 1973), 3–31; Alexander W. Pisciotta, "Treatment on Trial: The Rhetoric and Reality of the New York House of Refuge, 1857–1935," *American Journal of Legal History* 29 (1985), 151–81.

6. Mennel, *Thorns and Thistles*, 124.

7. David Matza, *Delinquency and Drift* (New York: John Wiley and Sons, 1964), 3–12.

8. Ryerson, *Best-Laid Plans*, 22; Edwin M. Schur, *Radical Nonintervention: Rethinking the Delinquency Problem* (Englewood Cliffs, NJ: Prentice-Hall, 1973), 29–31.

9. Daniel Levine, *Jane Addams and the Liberal Tradition* (Westport, CT: Greenwood Press, 1971), 119.

10. Allen F. Davis, *American Heroine: The Life and Legend of Jane Addams* (New York: Oxford University Press, 1973), 49, 57, 59, 63.

11. Levine, *Jane Addams and the Liberal Tradition*, 119; Davis, *American Heroine*, 151.

12. Davis, *American Heroine*, 150. Hull House also established a kindergarten, a playground, and a variety of clubs and recreational activities.

13. Sophonisba P. Breckenridge and Edith Abbott, *The Delinquent Child and the Home* (New York: Russell Sage Foundation, 1912), 4.

14. Davis, *American Heroine*, 150; Levine, *Jane Addams and the Liberal Tradition*, 119.

15. According to Joseph Hawes, the creation of an umbrella jurisdiction covering both criminal and noncriminal misbehavior was the most important innovation of the Illinois Juvenile Court Act. *See* Joseph Hawes, *Children in Urban Society: Juvenile Delinquency in Nineteenth-Century America* (New York: Oxford University Press, 1971), 171–73.

16. Julian Mack, "The Juvenile Court," *Harvard Law Review* 23 (1909): 104, 119–20.

17. See *Children's Courts in the United States: Their Origin, Development and Results*, U.S. Congress, H. Doc. 701, 58th Cong., 2d sess. (1904). The founding father of the Denver Juvenile Court, Judge Ben Lindsey, expressed this principle: "The criminal court for child-offenders is based on the doctrine of fear, degradation and punishment. It was, and is, absurd. The Juvenile Court was founded on the principle of love. We assumed that the child had committed not a crime, but a mistake, and that he deserved correction, not punishment. Of course, there is firmness and justice, for without these there would be danger in leniency. But there is no justice without love." Lindsey's remarks are quoted in Lincoln Steffens, *Upbuilders* (1909; rpt., Seattle: University of Washington Press, 1968), 113–14.

18. David Rothman, *Conscience and Convenience: The Asylum and Its Alternatives in Progressive America* (Boston: Little, Brown, 1980), 215.

19. Jeffrey L. Bleich, "Legislative Trends," in *From Children to Citizens*, vol. 2, *The Role of the Juvenile Court*, ed. Francis X. Hartmann (New York: Springer-Verlag, 1987), 31–32.

20. Hastings M. Hart, *Juvenile Court Laws in the United States Summarized* (New York: Russell Sage Foundation, 1910), 138.

21. Bernard Flexner and Roger N. Baldwin, *Juvenile Courts and Probation* (New York: Century Company, 1916), 256, 261, 262.

22. Herbert H. Lou, *Juvenile Courts in the United States* (Chapel Hill: University of North Carolina Press, 1927), 232, 238.

23. Samuel M. Davis, *The Rights of Juveniles: The Juvenile Justice System*, 2d ed. (New York: Clark Boardman, 1987), appendix A, 1–53.

24. Hart, *Juvenile Court Laws in the United States Summarized*, 123–24.

25. Ibid., 126.

26. Flexner and Baldwin, *Juvenile Courts and Probation*, 256–57.

27. Lou, *Juvenile Courts in the United States*, 233.

28. Hart, *Juvenile Court Laws in the United States Summarized*, 129.

29. Ibid., 130–31.

30. Ibid., 129–30. The principal reason for this provision appears to have been the protection of parental property rights (rather than children's liberty interests),

which might be affected by dispositions imposing fines or requiring payment of damages.

31. Ibid., 132.

32. Flexner and Baldwin, *Juvenile Courts and Probation*, 260, 261–62.

33. Lou, *Juvenile Courts in the United States*, 238.

34. The relevant state authorities are set out in *Pee v. United States*, 274 F.2d 556, 561–63 (D.C. Cir. 1959).

35. Hart, *Juvenile Court Laws in the United States Summarized*, 134–35.

36. Flexner and Baldwin, *Juvenile Courts and Probation*, 260–61.

37. Lou, *Juvenile Courts in the United States*, 238.

38. Davis, *Rights of Juveniles*, 28–29.

39. Francis A. Allen, *The Decline of the Rehabilitative Ideal: Penal Policy and Social Purpose* (New Haven: Yale University Press, 1981), 2.

40. Ibid., 3, 12, 28. For a less detailed overview of the developments covered in this chapter, see Arnold Binder, Gilbert Geiss, Dickson Bruce, *Juvenile Delinquency: Historical, Cultural, Legal Perspectives* (New York: Macmillan, 1988), 240–49.

41. Rothman, *Conscience and Convenience*, 268, 248. See also Hawes, *Children in Urban Society*, 190 (noting the poor development of American social and behavioral science at the turn of the century).

42. Edward Lindsey, "The Juvenile Court Movement from a Lawyer's Standpoint," *Annals of the American Academy of Political and Social Science* 52 (1914): 140, 141.

43. Rothman, *Discovery of the Asylum*, 238.

44. Lindsey, "Juvenile Court Movement from a Lawyer's Standpoint," 147.

45. Solon L. Perrin, "The Future of the Children's Court," *American Bar Association Journal* 8 (1922): 767, 768.

46. Ibid., 768.

47. David Bogen, " 'Justice' Versus 'Individualized Treatment' in Juvenile Court," *Journal of Criminal Law, Criminology and Police Science* 35 (1944): 252.

48. See James Gilbert, *A Cycle of Outrage: America's Reaction to the Juvenile Delinquent in the 1950s* (New York: Oxford University Press, 1986), 63–78.

49. Federal Bureau of Investigation, *Uniform Crime Reports* (Washington, DC: Government Printing Office, 1950–1965).

50. During this period, serious crimes against persons included criminal homicide, forcible rape, robbery, and aggravated assault. Serious property crimes included burglary, larceny, and auto theft.

51. Juvenile arrests as a proportion of all serious property-crime arrests actually declined, however, from 54 to 51.6 percent between 1956 and 1960.

52. See U.S. Bureau of Census, Statistical Research Division, *Historical Statistics of the United States*, Series A, 119–34, *Population, by Age, Sex, Race, and Nativity: 1790 to 1970* (Washington, DC: GPO, 1971). Data for the three-column list also comes from this source (Series H, 1119–24, p. 419).

53. Marvin E. Wolfgang, Robert M. Figlio, and Thorsten Sellin, *Delinquency in a Birth Cohort* (Chicago: University of Chicago Press, 1972).

54. Gilbert, *A Cycle of Outrage*, 143–61.

55. Arnold Binder, "The Juvenile Justice System: Where Pretence and Reality Clash," *American Behavioral Scientist* 22 (1979): 621, 639.

56. Ryerson, *Best Laid Plans*, 158.

57. Paul Tappan, *Juvenile Delinquency* (New York: McGraw Hill, 1949), 208.

58. Ibid., 204.

59. Ibid., 213.

60. Ibid., 219–23.

61. Fred E. Ellrod and Don H. Melaney, "Juvenile Justice: Treatment or Travesty?" *University of Pittsburgh Law Review* 11 (1950): 277, 287.

62. Lewis Diana, "The Rights of Juvenile Delinquents: An Appraisal of Juvenile Court Procedures," *Journal of Criminal Law, Criminology and Police Science* 47 (1957): 561, 562, 567.

63. Sol Rubin, "Protecting the Child in the Juvenile Court," *Journal of Criminal Law, Criminology and Police Science* 43 (1952): 425, 426.

64. Ibid., 432.

65. Monrad Paulsen, "Fairness to the Juvenile Offender," *Minnesota Law Review* 41 (1957): 547, 569.

66. Ibid., 567.

67. Jack J. Rappeport, "Some Legal Aspects of Juvenile Court Proceedings," *Virginia Law Review* 46 (1960): 908, 909, 923 (emphasis in original).

68. Mathew J. Beemsterboer, "The Juvenile Court—Benevolence in the Star Chamber," *Journal of Criminal Law, Criminology and Police Science* 50 (1960): 464, 472, 467, 474.

69. Chester James Antieau, "Constitutional Rights in Juvenile Courts," *Cornell Law Quarterly* 46 (1961): 387, 415.

70. William B. McKesson, "Right to Counsel in Juvenile Proceedings," *Minnesota Law Review* 45 (1961): 843, 846, 851–52.

71. Francis A. Allen, "Criminal Justice, Legal Values and the Rehabilitative Ideal," *Journal of Criminal Law, Criminology and Police Science* 50 (1959): 226, 229, 231.

72. Matza, *Delinquency and Drift*, 112, 115. The concept of individualized justice assumes that every case is unique and therefore that there are no like cases to be treated similarly.

73. Note, "Juvenile Delinquents: The Police, State Courts, and Individualized Justice," *Harvard Law Review* 79 (1966): 775–810.

74. Ibid., 808, 810.

75. *O'Malley v. Woodrough*, 307 U.S. 277, 281 (1938); Charles Evans Hughes, "Forward," *Yale Law Journal* 50 (1941): 727; *West Virginia State Board of Education v. Barnette*, 319 U.S. 624, 634–35 (1943).

76. Clement Vose, *Caucasians Only: The Supreme Court, the NAACP, and the Restrictive Covenant Cases* (Berkeley: University of California Press, 1959), 68–71, 161; Richard Kluger, *Simple Justice* (New York: Vintage Books, 1975), 315–21.

77. Nochem Winnet, "Fifty Years of the Juvenile Court: An Evaluation," *American Bar Association Journal* 36 (1950): 363–66.

78. Anthony M. Platt, *The Child Savers: The Invention of Delinquency* (Chicago: University of Chicago Press, 1969); Sanford J. Fox, "Juvenile Justice Reform: An Historical Perspective," *Stanford Law Review* 22 (1970): 1187–1239.

79. Platt, *Child Savers*, 67, 139.

80. Fox, "Juvenile Justice Reform," 1229.

81. J. Lawrence Schultz, "The Cycle of Juvenile Court History," *Crime and Delinquency* 19 (1973): 457–76.

82. Allen, "Criminal Justice, Legal Values, and the Rehabilitative Ideal," 33–34, 45.

83. Kenneth Culp Davis, *Discretionary Justice: A Preliminary Inquiry* (Baton Rouge: Louisiana State University Press, 1969), 4.

84. In addition to state legislative initiatives, the federal Juvenile Delinquency and Youth Offenses Control Act was enacted in September 1961 (Public Law 87–274). The purpose of the act was to provide federal financial assistance for projects aimed at developing delinquency prevention and control techniques. The act also provided for personnel training and technical assistance services.

85. See Edwin Lemert, *Social Action and Legal Change: Revolution Within the Juvenile Court* (Chicago: Aldine, 1970), 92–155. Lemert's book is the most authoritative account of the events surrounding the 1961 amendments to the Welfare and Institutions Code and is the source for the summary of events that follows.

86. Ibid., 101.

87. Ibid., 102.

88. Quoted in Ibid., 119.

89. Ibid., 153–55.

90. Calif. Welf. and Inst. Code ss. 600–602, s.626 (1961).

91. Ibid., ss. 627, 633, 634, 679, 700.

92. Ibid., ss. 800, 677.

93. Ibid., s. 680.

94. Thomas Murphy, "History of the Juvenile Court of Buffalo," in *Children's Courts in the United States*, H. Doc. 701, 12.

95. Ibid., 191.

96. Robert H. Twichell, "Current Legislation: New York State's Family Court Act," *Syracuse Law Review* 14 (1963): 481–96.

97. Nanette Dembitz, "Ferment and Experiment in New York: Juvenile Cases in the New Family Court," *Cornell Law Quarterly* 48 (1963): 499, 509.

98. Twichell, "Current Legislation," 484.

99. Ibid., 495. See also Michael Fabricant, *Juveniles in the Family Court* (Lexington, MA: D. C. Heath, 1983), 19; Dembitz, "Ferment and Experiment in New York," 512.

100. Comment, "The *Gault* Decision and the New York Family Court Act," *Syracuse Law Review* 19 (1968): 755.

101. See *Practice Commentary*, N.Y. Fam. Ct. Act s. 711 (McKinney Supp. 1983).

102. Dembitz, "Ferment and Experiment in New York," 501.

103. N.Y. Fam. Ct. Act s. 712 (1962).

104. Ibid., ss. 711, 742–45.

105. Dembitz, "Ferment and Experiment in New York," 505; Fabricant, *Juveniles in the Family Court*, 25.

106. President's Commission on Law Enforcement and Administration of Justice, *The Challenge of Crime in a Free Society* (Washington, DC: Government Printing Office, 1967), 311.

107. President's Commission on Law Enforcement and Administration of Justice, *Task Force Report: Juvenile Delinquency and Youth Crime* (Washington, DC: Government Printing Office, 1967), 7.

108. Ibid., 8.

109. President's Commission, *Challenge of Crime in a Free Society, 80*.

110. President's Commission, *Task Force Report*, 2.

111. Ibid., 9. This theme was especially apparent in the report's criticism of traditional rehabilitation-oriented criteria for jurisdictional waiver like "dangerousness" and "amenability to treatment." The task force's discussion of this subject included legislative and prosecutorial waiver, two ideas that would not become prominent until the late 1970s (see 24–25).

112. Ibid., 20.

113. Ibid., 31–40.

114. Ibid., 40.

115. Ibid., 31.

116. Ibid. (emphasis added). For a discussion of this conclusion, see Donald Horowitz, *The Courts and Social Policy* (Washington DC: Brookings Institution, 1977), 177–83.

117. President's Commission, *Challenge of Crime in a Free Society*, 85 (emphasis added). See Horowitz, *Courts and Social Policy*, 176.

118. President's Commission, *Task Force Report*, 35.

119. Herbert L. Packer, *The Limits of the Criminal Sanction* (Palo Alto: Stanford University Press, 1968), 149–73.

120. Jack L. Walker Jr., "The Diffusion of Innovations Among the States," *American Political Science Review* 63 (1969): 880–99; Virginia Gray, "Innovation in the States: A Diffusion Study," *American Political Science Review* 67 (1973): 1174–93.

121. Beemsterboer, "Juvenile Court," 474.

122. Earl Warren, "Equal Justice for Juveniles," *Juvenile Court Judges Journal* 15 (1964): 14.

123. This metaphor is taken from Marc Miller, "Changing Legal Paradigms in Juvenile Justice," in *The Juvenile Rehabilitation Reader*, ed. Peter Greenwood (Santa Monica, CA: Rand Corporation, 1985).

3. AN UNEXPECTED OPPORTUNITY

1. *Kent v. United States*, 383 U.S. 541 (1966).

2. 34 *Stat.* 73 (1906), chap. 960. The history of the District of Columbia juvenile court is summarized in the Brief for the United States, *Kent v. United States*, 383 U.S. 541 (1966), 15–16, 22–25. See also *A Report Covering the Work of the Juvenile Court During the Period from July 1, 1906, to June 30, 1926*. U.S. Congress, S. Doc. 236, 69th Cong., 2d sess., 1927, 35–73.

3. 34 *Stat.* 73 (1906), chap. 309, s. 1. The delinquency jurisdictions of the other courts were established in 1885 (police court), 1892 (Board of Children's Guardians), and 1901 (other courts).

4. Ibid.

5. See Herbert Lou, *Juvenile Courts in the United States* (Chapel Hill: University of North Carolina Press, 1927), 232–46.

6. These comments are found in the *Congressional Record* 81, 1937, 1004.

7. 52 *Stat.* 596 (1938), chap. 309, s.1.

8. Ibid., s. 6(1).

9. Ibid., s.13. The relevant section of the act stated that "if a child sixteen years of age or older is charged with an offense which would amount to a felony in the case of an adult, the judge, after full investigation, may waive jurisdiction and order such child held for trial under the regular procedure of the court which would have jurisdiction of such offense if committed by an adult."

10. 52 *Stat.* 596 (1938), chap. 309, s.14.

11. This deviation from the NPA's model law was motivated by constitutional concerns about the possible applicability of the Bill of Rights to juvenile proceedings in the District. See *Congressional Record* 81, 1937, 1004.

12. *Pee v. United States*, 274 F.2d 556 (D.C. Cir. 1959).

13. 236 F.2d 666, 669 (D.C. Cir. 1956).

14. 247 F.2d 595 (D.C. Cir. 1957).

15. *Harling v. United States*, 295 F.2d 161, 163–64 (D.C. Cir. 1961).

16. 61 *Stat.* 92 (1947), chap. 56. See also *Congressional Record* 93, 1947, 3354, 4566.

17. This memorandum is reproduced in *Kent*, 383 U.S., 565–68 (1966). In establishing these rules, the chief judge was exercising his statutory responsibility "to frame and publish rules and regulate the procedure for cases arising within the provisions of this Act." See 52 *Stat.* 596 (1938), chap. 309, s. 29.

18. *United States v. Dickerson*, 271 F.2d 487 (D.C. Cir. 1959). In an earlier case, *Briggs v. United States* (226 F.2d 350 [D.C. Cir. 1955]), the court of appeals had

denied that the Juvenile Court Act's waiver provision should be found constitutionally "void for lack of standards."

19. 271 F.2d, 491.

20. *Wilhite v. United States,* 281 F.2d 642 (D.C. Cir. 1960).

21. 308 F.2d 303, 304 (D.C. Cir. 1962).

22. 343 F.2d 278 (D.C. Cir. 1964).

23. 355 F.2d 104 (D.C. Cir. 1965).

24. 343 F.2d, 281–82.

25. 355 F.2d, 105.

26. 214 F.2d 862 (D.C. Cir. 1954).

27. Ibid., 866.

28. Ibid., 871. Bazelon discusses *Durham,* as well as *Kent* and general issues of juvenile justice, in David Bazelon, *Questioning Authority: Justice and Criminal Law* (New York: Knopf, 1988), 39–70, 118–36.

29. 214 F.2d, 874–75.

30. Richard Arens, *Make Mad the Guilty* (Springfield, IL: Charles C. Thomas, 1969), 3.

31. Ibid., 17.

32. Ibid., 17, 19.

33. Ibid., 20.

34. Ibid., 21.

35. Ibid., 22–24.

36. 52 *Stat.* 596 (1938), chap. 309, s.14.

37. See, e.g., *Corpus Juris Secondum* 43 (1978), 234, and Samuel M. Davis, *The Rights of Juveniles: The Juvenile Justice System* (New York: Clark Boardman, 1983), 5.27–5.29.

38. The results of the General Hospital examination are contained in a letter dated December 22, 1961, from the hospital's chief psychiatrist and clinical director of psychiatry. The St. Elizabeth's results are contained in a letter dated April 6, 1962, from the hospital's superintendent. Both letters are reprinted in Arens, *Make Mad the Guilty,* 57–59. During the psychiatric examinations of Kent, his counsel continued to seek procedural relief for his client prior to trial. On November 16, Kent's attorney filed a motion to dismiss the criminal indictments for housebreaking, robbery, and rape. During a hearing on this motion, the chief judge of the district court expressed concern about the case's relationship to the *Durham* project and questioned both the motives and activities of the project's staff. After criticizing the appearance of an independent expert witness on Kent's behalf as a "stimulated activity," the chief judge denied the motion to dismiss the indictments and directed Kent's counsel to file a report on the activities of the Washington School of Psychiatry in the case.

39. *Kent v. Reid,* 316 F.2d 331, 334, 336 (D.C. Cir. 1963).

40. Brief for Petitioner, *Kent v. United States,* 383 U.S. 541, 73–78 (appendix A).

See also Brief for the United States, *Kent v. United States,* 383 U.S. 541 (1966), 6a–7a (appendix A).

41. Indeed, Sandground did not think the waiver question was the issue for which the case would become known (letter to the author from Mark B. Sandground [Kent's trial attorney], March 10, 1986).

42. *Kent v. United States,* 343 F.2d 247 (D.C. Cir. 1965).

43. Ibid., 250–51.

44. Ibid., 259.

45. Ibid., 260–61.

46. Ibid., 256.

47. Ibid.

48. Ibid., 252–56.

49. Ibid., 253.

50. Ibid., 256.

51. See, e.g., *Frigillana v. United States,* 307 F.2d 665 (1962).

52. Brief for Petitioner, *Kent v. United States,* 383 U.S. 541 (1966), 49–56.

53. Ibid., 19.

54. Arens, *Make Mad the Guilty,* 59.

55. Brief for Petitioner, *Kent v. United States,* 383 U.S. 541 (1966), 54–56.

56. Ibid., 7.

57. Ibid., 5–7.

58. Ibid., 11.

59. Ibid., 16.

60. Ibid., 30–39.

61. *Escobedo v. Illinois,* 378 U.S. 478 (1964).

62. *Linkletter v. Walker,* 381 U.S. 618 (1965). For a general discussion of the retroactivity problem, see Ralph A. Rossum, "New Rights and Old Wrongs: The Supreme Court and the Problem of Retroactivity," *Emory Law Journal* 23 (1974): 381–420, and Francis X. Beytagh, "Ten Years of Non-retroactivity: A Critique and a Proposal," *Virginia Law Review* 61 (1975): 1557–1625.

63. Brief for Petitioner, *Kent v. United States,* 383 U.S. 541 (1966), 26.

64. Ibid., 28.

65. Ibid., 30, 26.

66. Ibid., 38.

67. Ibid., 26.

68. These cases are discussed at notes 22–25.

69. Brief for amicus curiae, *Kent v. United States,* 383 U.S. 541 (1966), 1–2.

70. Ibid., 12–13.

71. Ibid., 2, 14.

72. Ibid., 2.

73. Brief for the United States, *Kent v. United States,* 383 U.S. 541 (1966), 43.

74. Ibid., 15.

75. Ibid., 17, 30.

76. Ibid., 26.

77. Ibid.

78. Ibid., 32 (emphasis in original).

79. Ibid., 19–20.

80. Ibid., 20, 24.

81. Ibid., 35.

82. Ibid., 16.

83. Ibid., 32–35.

84. Ibid., 38.

85. *Kent v. United States,* 383 U.S. 541, 568 (1966), Stewart, J., dissenting.

86. 383 U.S. 550, 552 (Fortas, J., majority opinion).

87. Ibid., 552 n. 13.

88. Ibid., 554–55.

89. Joel Handler, "The Juvenile Court and the Adversary System: Problems of Function and Form," *Wisconsin Law Review* (1965): 7–51; Note, "Juvenile Delinquents: The Police, State Courts, and Individualized Justice," *Harvard Law Review* 79 (1966): 775–810.

90. 383 U.S., 555–56.

91. Ibid., 556–57.

92. Ibid., 561.

93. Ibid., 543.

94. Ibid., 551.

95. See Citizens' Committee for Children of New York, *The Experiment That Failed: The New York Juvenile Offender Law—A Study Report* (New York: CCNY, 1984).

96. 383 U.S., 543.

97. Ibid., 562.

4. *GAULT:* THE ROAD TO WASHINGTON

1. Jack L. Walker Jr., "The Diffusion of Innovations Among the States," *American Political Science Review* 63 (1969): 883; Virginia Gray, "Innovation in the States: A Diffusion Study," *American Political Science Review* 67 (1973): 1192.

2. Robert L. Savage, "Policy Innovativeness as a Trait of American States," *Journal of Politics* 40 (1978): 216, 218.

3. Jay J. Wagoner, *Arizona Territory, 1863–1912: A Political History* (Tucson: University of Arizona Press, 1970), 441.

4. Quoted in John J. Molloy, "Juvenile Court—A Labyrinth of Confusion for the Lawyer," *Arizona Law Review* 4 (1962): 1, 5.

5. See *Arizona Constitution* Art. 6, s. 6. When the Arizona Constitution was amended in 1960, this provision became Art. 6, s. 15.

6. *Arizona Revised Statutes,* ss. 8–201 to 8–239 (1956).

7. Note, "Criminal Law—Evidence—Juvenile's Confession Obtained in Violation of Statute Inadmissible," *Arizona Law Review* 5 (1964): 286–91.

8. Molloy, "Juvenile Court," 15.

9. *Burrows v. State,* 297 P. 1029, 1034 (Ariz. Sup. Ct. 1931).

10. *State v. Guerrero,* 120 P.2d 798, 802 (Ariz. Sup. Ct. 1942).

11. *State v. Shaw,* 378 P.2d. 487 (Ariz. Sup. Ct. 1963).

12. *Ginn v. Superior Court,* 404 P.2d 721 (Ariz. Sup. Ct. 1965).

13. *Harper v. Tipple,* 184 P. 1005, 1007 (Ariz. Sup. Ct. 1919). See also *In re Mandevil,* 193 P. 17 (Ariz. Sup. Ct. 1920).

14. *Ex parte Winn,* 63 P.2d 198, 202 (Ariz. Sup. Ct. 1936).

15. 296 P.2d 298 (Ariz. Sup. Ct. 1956).

16. Ibid., 299–301.

17. John A. Yogis, *Canadian Law Dictionary* (Toronto: Barron's Educational Series, 1983), 98.

18. Application for Habeas Corpus (Arizona), August 3, 1964, 8–9.

19. Ibid., 7.

20. Appellant's Opening Brief, *Application of Gault,* 407 P.2d 760 (Ariz. Sup. Ct. 1965), 2–3.

21. Ibid. Citing Sen. Rept. 130 on Juvenile Delinquency, March 4, 1957, 178.

22. Ibid., 3.

23. Ibid., 9–11.

24. Ibid., 22.

25. Ibid., 13.

26. Jack Greenberg, *Crusaders in the Courts* (New York: Basic Books, 1994), 68, 73, 102–6.

27. Appellant's Opening Brief, 9–10.

28. Ibid., 28–40.

29. Ibid., 41.

30. Ibid., 12.

31. *Application of Gault,* 407 P.2d 760 (Ariz. Sup. Ct. 1965). For an early analysis of this decision, see Monrad G. Paulsen, "*Kent v. United States:* The Constitutional Context of Juvenile Cases," *Supreme Court Review* (1966): 184–86.

32. 407 P.2d, 766.

33. Ibid., 765–66.

34. Ibid.

35. Ibid., 764–68.

36. Ibid., 767.

37. Ibid., 768.

38. Ibid., 767.

39. *Brown v. Board of Education,* 347 U.S. 483 (1954).

40. Richard Kluger, *Simple Justice* (New York: Vintage Books, 1975), 424.

41. *Plessy v. Ferguson*, 163 U.S. 537 (1896).

42. Ralph A. Rossum and G. Alan Tarr, *American Constitutional Law: Cases and Interpretation*, 2d ed. (New York: St. Martin's Press, 1987), 502.

43. Amelia Lewis to Melvin Wulf, November 17, 1965. Correspondence among the principals in the case is preserved in the ACLU archives at Princeton University, indexed under ACLU, 1966, vol. 19.

44. William A. Donohue, *The Politics of the American Civil Liberties Union* (New Brunswick, NJ: Transaction Books, 1985), 16. Baldwin's text was *Juvenile Courts and Probation* (New York: Century Company, 1916).

45. See Charles Reasons, "*Gault:* Procedural Change and Substantive Effect," *Crime and Delinquency* 16 (1970): 165 n. 11.

46. American Civil Liberties Union, *Annual Reports* (New York: Arno Press and *New York Times*, 1970), vol. 6 (1956), 55–56.

47. Ibid., (1959), 6:97.

48. Alan Reitman (Florida Civil Liberties Union) to Leonard Scheff, November 29, 1965.

49. Wulf to Lewis, January 31, 1966.

50. Samuel D. Warren and Louis D. Brandeis, "The Right to Privacy," *Harvard Law Review* 4 (1890): 193–220.

51. *Griswold v. Connecticut*, 381 U.S. 479 (1965).

52. These amendments included the First (freedom of speech and religion), Third (prohibition on the quartering of soldiers in private homes during peacetime), Fourth (prohibition against unwarranted searches and seizures), Fifth (right against self-incrimination), and Ninth (unenumerated rights).

53. Lewis to Wulf, March 8, 1966.

54. Lewis to Norman Dorsen and Wulf, September 27, 1966. See also Dorsen to Lewis, September 30, 1966, and Wulf to Lewis, October 11, 1966.

55. Samuel Walker, *In Defense of American Liberties: A History of the ACLU* (New York: Oxford University Press, 1990), 252, 313.

56. Wulf to Gertrude Mainzer, March 16, 1966.

57. Mainzer to Wulf, April 5, 1966.

58. *Interest of Long*, 184 So. 2d 861, 862 (Miss. Sup. Ct. 1966).

59. Wulf to Mainzer, April 5, 1966.

60. Jurisdictional Statement for Appellants, *In re Gault*, 387 U.S. 1 (1967), 1.

61. Wulf to Lewis, November 30, 1965.

62. Rossum and Tarr, *American Constitutional Law*, 23.

63. David M. O'Brien, *Storm Center: The Supreme Court in American Politics*, 2d ed. (New York: W. W. Norton, 1990), 197.

64. Jurisdictional Statement, 3.

65. Amelia Lewis to the author, April 1, 1986.

66. Jurisdictional Statement, 10.

67. 383 U.S., 555–56.

68. Jurisdictional Statement, 12.

69. 384 U.S. 997 (1966).

70. *Miller v. Rhay,* 383 U.S. 965 (1966). Certiorari granted, April 4, 1966.

71. *Dillenburg v. Maxwell,* 413 P.2d 940 (Wash. Sup. Ct. 1966).

72. *Miller v. Rhay,* 384 U.S. 892 (1966).

73. Franklin Zimring, *The Changing Legal World of Adolescence* (New York: Free Press, 1982), 77–80.

5. *GAULT* IN THE SUPREME COURT

1. Samuel Walker, *In Defense of American Liberties: A History of the ACLU* (New York: Oxford University Press, 1990), 246.

2. Ibid., 251.

3. Ibid., 254.

4. James Murray, Draft Brief for Appellants, *In re Gault,* 387 U.S. 1 (1967), 7 (emphasis in original).

5. This organization later became the National Council on Crime and Delinquency.

6. Draft Brief, 13, 15.

7. Dorsen to the author, November 1, 1985.

8. Rezneck to the author, October 17, 1985.

9. Brief for Appellants, *In re Gault,* 387 U.S. 1 (1967), 9.

10. Ibid., 13.

11. Ibid., 17 (emphasis in original).

12. Ibid., 22.

13. Ibid.

14. Dorsen to the author, November 1, 1985.

15. Ibid. The justices supportive of selective incorporation, according to Dorsen, were Warren, Clark, Brennan, and White. Justices Black and Douglas supported total incorporation, and Justices Harlan and Stewart supported fundamental fairness. Dorsen was uncertain about Fortas's views. Selective incorporation had also been advocated by scholarly commentators after *Kent.* See Monrad G. Paulsen, "*Kent v. United States:* The Constitutional Context of Juvenile Cases," *Supreme Court Review* (1966): 186.

16. Brief for Appellants, 29.

17. Ibid., 30.

18. Ibid., 33.

19. Ibid.

20. Ibid., 44.

21. Ibid., 45, 47–48. The brief cited *Greene v. McElroy,* 360 U.S. 474 (1959); *Wilner v. Committee on Character & Fitness,* 373 U.S. 96 (1963); *Williams v. Zuckert,* 371 U.S. 531 (1963).

22. Brief for Appellants, 47.

23. Ibid., 51.

24. Ibid., 50.

25. Ibid., 56.

26. Ibid., 57.

27. See *New York Family Court Act,* ss. 711, 742–45 (1962). See also Nanette Dembitz, "Ferment and Experiment in New York: Juvenile Cases in the New Family Court," *Cornell Law Quarterly* 48 (1963): 505, and Michael Fabricant, *Juveniles in the Family Court* (Lexington, MA: D. C. Heath, 1983), 25.

28. Brief for Appellants, 34.

29. Ibid.

30. Ibid., 35. See *Powell v. Alabama,* 287 U.S. 45 (1932), right to counsel in state capital offense proceedings; *Gideon v. Wainwright,* 372 U.S. 335 (1963), right to court-appointed counsel in state felony proceedings.

31. Brief for Appellants, 38. Dorsen and Rezneck cited data from the Biographical Data Survey of Juvenile Court Judges conducted in 1964 by the Center of Behavioral Sciences at George Washington University. These data indicated that 20 percent of juvenile court judges were not lawyers and that over half devoted less than one-quarter of their time to juvenile and family law matters.

32. Brief for Appellants, 58.

33. Ibid., 61.

34. Ibid., 63.

35. See Charles Schinitsky, "The Role of the Lawyer in Children's Court," *Record of the Bar Association of New York City* 17 (1962): 10–26.

36. Dembitz to Wulf, June 30, 1966.

37. Dorsen to deB. Katzenbach, July 7, 1966; Dorsen to Marshall, July 7, 1966.

38. David M. O'Brien, *Storm Center: The Supreme Court in American Politics,* 2d ed. (New York: W. W. Norton, 1990), 250.

39. Polsky to Getty, June 30, 1966.

40. Brief of the National Legal Aid and Defender Association as amicus curiae, *In re Gault,* 387 U.S. 1 (1967), 4.

41. Ibid., 5.

42. Ibid., 8.

43. Ibid., 7.

44. Ibid., 9. The extension of the right to counsel to all cases in which liberty is at stake was the outcome of *Argersinger v. Hamlin,* 407 U.S. 25 (1972), and *Scott v. Illinois,* 440 U.S. 367 (1979).

45. Brief, NLADA, 10–11.

46. Ibid.

47. Memorandum from F. E. Andrew to John J. Cleary, September 9, 1966, 3 (on file with author).

48. Ibid., 4.

49. Brief, NLADA, 11.

50. Brief of the Legal Aid Society of New York as amicus curiae, *In re Gault,* 387 U.S. 1 (1967), 2–3.

51. Ibid., 5.

52. Ibid., 11.

53. Ibid., 19–20.

54. Ibid., 14, 16–17.

55. Ibid., 7, 24–25.

56. Ibid., 25–27.

57. Ibid., 28.

58. Brief of the American Parents' Committee as amicus curiae, *In re Gault,* 387 U.S. 1 (1967), 2.

59. Ibid., 3.

60. Ibid., 17.

61. Ibid., 17–18.

62. Ibid., 25–26.

63. Judge Don J. Young to the author, January 28, 1986. Young's former colleagues at the NCJCJ, however, officially supported the ACLU's position.

64. Brief for the State of Arizona, *In re Gault,* 387 U.S. 1 (1967), 8.

65. Ibid.

66. Ibid., 12.

67. Ibid., 14.

68. Ibid., 17.

69. Ibid., 18.

70. Ibid., 9

71. Ibid., 30–31.

72. Ibid., 22.

73. Ibid.

74. Ibid., 28.

75. Ibid., 24.

76. Ibid., 23. See *Pee v. United States,* 274 F.2d 556 (D.C. Cir. 1959).

77. Julian W. Mack, "The Juvenile Court," *Harvard Law Review* 23 (1909): 104.

78. Brief of the Ohio Association of Juvenile Court Judges as amicus curiae, *In re Gault,* 387 U.S. 1 (1967), 3.

79. Ibid., 12.

80. Ibid.

81. Ibid., 17.

82. Ibid., 4.

83. Ibid., 3–4.

84. Ibid.,., 20.

85. Ibid., 19.

86. Laura Kalman, *Abe Fortas: A Biography* (New Haven: Yale University Press, 1990), 250.

87. Ibid., 252–53.

88. *In re Gault,* 387 U.S. 1, 13 (1967).

89. Ibid., 16.

90. Ibid., 18.

91. Ibid., 18–19.

92. Ibid., 26.

93. Ibid., 21.

94. Ibid., 20.

95. Ibid., 28.

96. Ibid.

97. Ibid., 29–30.

98. Ibid., 21.

99. Ibid., 22. Fortas referred specifically to separate treatment of adults and juveniles, immunity from the civil disabilities associated with criminal conviction, and confidentiality.

100. Ibid., 26 (citing President's Commission on Law Enforcement and Administration of Justice, *The Challenge of Crime in a Free Society* [Washington, DC: Government Printing Office, 1967], 85).

101. President's Commission, *Challenge of Crime in a Free Society,* 80.

102. For a discussion of Fortas's use of the President's Commission report, see Donald Horowitz, *The Courts and Social Policy* (Washington, DC: Brookings Institution, 1977), 177–83.

103. 387 U.S., 58.

104. Ibid., 36, 41.

105. Bernard Schwartz, *Super Chief: Earl Warren and His Supreme Court—A Judicial Biography* (New York: New York University Press, 1983), 673.

106. Ibid., 47.

107. *Miranda v. Arizona,* 384 U.S. 430, 448, 445, 455, 467, 460 (1966).

108. 387 U.S., 48.

109. See *Cole v. Arkansas,* 333 U.S. 196, 201 (1948); *Gideon v. Wainwright,* 372 U.S. 335, 344 (1963); *Malloy v. Hogan,* 378 U.S. 1, 8 (1964); *Pointer v. Texas,* 380 U.S. 400, 405, 406–8 (1965). It should not be surprising that Fortas would adopt the Court's reasoning from *Gideon* so easily, since he had argued the case in the Supreme Court on behalf of Gideon.

110. See *Estes v. Texas,* 381 U.S. 532, 587 (1965), Harlan, J., concurring.

111. 387 U.S., 78, Stewart, J., dissenting.

112. Ibid., 78.

113. Ibid., 79.

114. Ibid.

115. 387 U.S., 67, Harlan, J., concurring in part, dissenting in part.

116. Ibid., 67.

117. Ibid., 74.

118. Ibid., 68–69.

119. Ibid., 71. Harlan rejected the argument that there was little or no connection between procedure and rehabilitation in juvenile courts.

120. Ibid., 72. "In this way, the Court may guarantee the fundamental fairness of the proceeding, and yet permit the State to continue development of an effective response to the problems of juvenile crime."

121. Ibid.

122. 387 U.S., 64–65, White, J., concurring.

123. Ibid., 60–61, Black, J., concurring.

124. Bruce Allen Murphy, *Fortas: The Rise and Ruin of a Supreme Court Justice* (New York: William Morrow and Company, 1988), 216, 222, 229–33, 535–41.

125. According to Kalman, "Fortas made *Gault* a good case by emphasizing the facts" (*Abe Fortas,* 252).

6. CONSTITUTIONAL CHALLENGES BEYOND *GAULT*

1. Dorsen and Rezneck commented on these unanswered questions shortly after the Court's decision in *Gault.* See Norman Dorsen and Daniel Rezneck, "*In re Gault* and the Future of Juvenile Law," *Family Law Quarterly* 1 (1967), 13–46.

2. *Application of Gault,* 407 P.2d 760, 768 (Ariz. Sup. Ct. 1965).

3. *In re Gault,* 387 U.S. 1, 11 (1967).

4. Dorsen and Rezneck, "*In re Gault* and the Future of Juvenile Law," 22–27. This consistency was particularly true of the criminal standard of proof "beyond a reasonable doubt." According to Dorsen and Rezneck, once the Supreme Court rejected the "civil label of convenience" formerly applicable to juvenile proceedings, other procedures imported into juvenile proceedings from civil cases, such as the preponderance of the evidence standard of proof, automatically became suspect.

5. See, e.g., James Hillson Cohen, "The Standard of Proof in Juvenile Proceedings: *Gault* Beyond a Reasonable Doubt," *Michigan Law Review* 68 (1970): 567.

6. *In re Urbasek,* 232 N.E. 2d 716 (Ill. Sup. Ct. 1967). For other state court decisions, see Cohen, "Standard of Proof," 587.

7. 232 N.E. 2d, 719.

8. Ibid.

9. *United States v. Costanzo,* 395 F.2d 441 (4th Cir. 1968).

10. Ibid., 444, 445.

11. *In re Whittington,* 391 U.S. 341 (1968). The Court granted certiorari in this case on October 9, 1967 (389 U.S. 819 [1967]). It was argued on April 2, 1968, and decided on May 20, 1968. In addition to Rezneck, Whittington involved some of the other participants in *Gault,* including Merrit Green and Leon Polsky.

12. 391 U.S., 344. Justices White and Black dissented from the Court's

disposition of the case. They would have dismissed the appeal entirely on the grounds that the Ohio court's delinquency adjudication did not constitute a final judgment within the Court's appellate jurisdiction over state court proceedings, (344-45). Their reasoning was that there had yet to be a disposition order in Whittington's case.

13. *DeBacker v. Brainard*, 396 U.S. 28 (1969).

14. Ibid., 31.

15. *In re Winship*, 397 U.S. 358 (1970).

16. *People v. Fitzgerald*, 155 N.E. 584, 587–88 (N.Y. Ct. App. 1927); *In re Madik*, 251 N.Y. S. 765 (N.Y. App. Div. 1931).

17. See, e.g., *In re Ronny*, 242 N.Y. S. 2d 844, 848 (1963); *In re Doe*, 255 N.Y. S. 2d 33, 37 (1964); *In re Williams*, N.Y. S. 2d 91, 99 (1966); *In re W.*, 224 N.E. 2d 102, 106 (1966); and *In re Rust*, 278 N.Y. S. 2d 333, 338 (1967).

18. 255 N.Y. S. 2d, 35.

19. 242 N.Y. S. 2d, 860. The judge in this case presided over Samuel Winship's delinquency hearing four years later.

20. Ibid.

21. 267 N.Y. S. 2d, 99, 107.

22. Ibid., 108.

23. Ibid., 109.

24. *In re W.*, 224 N.E. 2d 102, 106 (N.Y. Ct. App. 1966). But see the dissent by Bergan, J., 224 N.E. 2d, 107. Bergan argued that "since the adjudication of juvenile delinquency is not a conviction for a crime and is made in a civil proceeding . . . the purpose of which is to protect and treat a child and not to punish him, the preliminary questioning of the child by police and other authorities should not be measured precisely by the standards which would apply to a criminal case."

25. Letter to the author from Rena Uviller, January 8, 1986.

26. Record of the Family Court of the State of New York, City of New York, County of Bronx, March 30, 1967, 55–56.

27. Ibid., 57.

28. Ibid., 58.

29. Ibid., 59.

30. Ibid., 59–60.

31. Rena Uviller to the author, January 8, 1986.

32. *W. v. Family Court*, 247 N.E. 2d 253 (N.Y. Ct. App. 1969).

33. *People v. Lewis*, 183 N.E. 353 (N.Y. Ct. App. 1932).

34. 247 N.E. 2d, 254 (Bergan, J.).

35. Ibid., 257.

36. Ibid., 256.

37. Ibid., 258 (Fuld, C. J., dissenting).

38. See Comment, "The *Gault* Decision and the New York Family Court Act," *Syracuse Law Review* 19 (1968): 753.

39. Jurisdictional Statement of Appellants, *In re Winship,* 397 U.S. 358 (1970), 2.

40. Ibid., 8.

41. Ibid., 25.

42. Ibid., 25–26.

43. Brief for Appellants, *In re Winship,* 397 U.S. 358 (1970), 9.

44. Ibid., 14–15, 17–18.

45. Ibid., 11, 23.

46. Ibid., 24.

47. Brief of the Neighborhood Legal Services Program and the Legal Aid Agency for the District of Columbia as amici curiae, *In re Winship,* 397 U.S. 358 (1970), 13, 5, 46, 51.

48. Ibid., 33.

49. Ibid., 44–45.

50. Ibid., 39.

51. Ibid., 35, 10–13.

52. Ibid., 54. There is a parallel between this argument and the one underlying the juvenile court diversion movement.

53. For analysis of how adjudication procedures in juvenile courts might serve rehabilitative ends, see Note, "Rights and Rehabilitation in the Juvenile Court," *Columbia Law Review* 67 (1967): 281–341.

54. Stanley Buchsbaum to the author, January 5, 1986.

55. Appellee's Motion to Dismiss Appeal, *In re Winship,* 397 U.S. 358 (1970), 4.

56. Ibid., 3. Buchsbaum also questioned whether adult defendants possess a constitutional right not to be convicted except by proof beyond a reasonable doubt. He argued that the Court needed to resolve this question before reaching the issue of the reasonable doubt standard's applicability to juvenile proceedings. This, of course, the Court did.

57. See Brief for Appellee, *In re Winship,* 397 U.S. 358 (1970), 34, 36.

58. Ibid., 27.

59. Ibid., 15.

60. Ibid., 18.

61. Ibid., 8. Buchsbaum was also worried about the potential impact of a successful appeal on other civil commitment proceedings.

62. Ibid., 16.

63. Ibid., 18.

64. Ibid., 17.

65. Brief of the Attorney General of New York as amicus curiae, *In re Winship,* 397 U.S. 358 (1970), 7, 13.

66. Ibid., 13.

67. Ibid., 5.

68. Ibid., 10 (emphasis in original).

69. *In re Gault,* 387 U.S. 1, 36 (1967).

70. *In re Winship,* 397 U.S. 358, 359.

71. Ibid., n. 1.

72. Ibid., 361–64. See Ronald J. Allen, "The Restoration of *In re Winship:* A Comment on Burdens of Persuasion in Criminal Cases after *Patterson v. New York,*" *Michigan Law Review* 76 (1977): 41.

73. *In re Winship,* 397 U.S. 363–64.

74. Ibid., 363.

75. Ibid., 361.

76. Ibid., 361–62 (citing *Duncan v. Louisiana,* 391 U.S. 145, 155 [1968]).

77. The information in this paragraph relies on Anthony A. Morano, "A Reexamination of the Development of the Reasonable Doubt Rule," *Boston University Law Review* 55 (1975): 507–28.

78. New York, however, was one of the earliest states to adopt the standard (ibid., 519, n. 89).

79. 397 U.S., 361–62.

80. Ibid., 365.

81. Ibid., 366–67. Brennan included among these "beneficial aspects" confidentiality, speed, and flexibility.

82. Ibid., 367.

83. Ibid.

84. Ibid.

85. The compromises involved in writing the *Winship* opinion are recounted in Bernard Schwartz, *The Ascent of Pragmatism: The Burger Court in Action* (Reading, MA: Addison-Wesley Publishing Company, 1990), 341–46.

86. 397 U.S., 374–75 (Harlan, J., concurring).

87. Ibid., 371.

88. Ibid., 373–74. Two consequences noted by Harlan were loss of liberty and stigmatization.

89. Ibid., 374. Harlan also agreed with the majority that requiring a higher standard of proof would not interfere with the juvenile court's rehabilitative goals, would not increase the stigma attached to being found delinquent, and would not overburden juvenile courts with unnecessary procedure delays or rigidity.

90. 397 U.S., 377 (Black, J., dissenting).

91. Ibid., 386.

92. Ibid.

93. Ibid.

94. Ibid., 378.

95. 397 U.S., 375–76 (Burger, C. J., dissenting).

96. Ibid.

97. Ibid., 376.

98. Ibid.

99. According to Schwartz, Justice Douglas, who had the task of assigning the

Winship opinion, believed that the reasonable doubt standard was the one aspect of criminal due process that could be introduced into juvenile proceedings with little disruption (see *Ascent of Pragmatism*, 342).

100. See Marc Miller, "Changing Legal Paradigms in Juvenile Justice" in *The Juvenile Rehabilitation Reader*, ed. Peter Greenwood (Santa Monica, CA: Rand Corporation, 1985).

101. *McKeiver v. Pennsylvania*, 403 U.S. 528 (1971).

102. Ibid., 533 (emphasis in original). Blackmun also mentioned that the Court had noted "widespread disaffection" with the accomplishments of juvenile courts and that its decisions had been tailored to ensure that they would "not spell the doom of the juvenile court system or even deprive it of its informality, flexibility, or speed."

103. Ibid., 541.

104. Ibid., 543.

105. *Duncan v. Louisiana*, 397 U.S. 145, 149–50 n.14, 158 (1965).

106. *Williams v. Florida*, 399 U.S. 78 (1970).

107. 403 U.S., 550.

108. Dorsen and Rezneck, "*In re Gault* and the Future of Juvenile Law," 10.

109. *Breed v. Jones*, 421 U.S. 519 (1975).

110. Ibid., 528–29.

111. Ibid., 535.

112. Ibid., 540.

113. Ibid., 541, 540. The Court worried that the possibility of transfer after adjudication presented juveniles with a difficult dilemma: failure to cooperate with the juvenile court might produce an adverse adjudication and an unfavorable dispositional recommendation; cooperation, on the other hand, might prejudice their case in a criminal court.

114. Ibid., 540.

115. *In re Gault*, 387 U.S. 1, 22 (1967).

116. *Fare v. Michael C.*, 442 U.S. 707 (1979).

117. *Miranda v. Arizona*, 384 U.S. 436 (1966).

118. 442 U.S., 721.

119. Ibid., 723.

120. *Goss v. Lopez*, 419 U.S. 565 (1975).

121. *Schall v. Martin*, 467 U.S. 253 (1984).

122. Ibid., 274.

123. Ibid.

124. Ibid., 265.

125. The argument that children are always in some form of custody had been made by the Arizona Supreme Court in 1936 and was an integral part of the brief submitted by the Ohio Association of Juvenile Court Judges in *Gault*.

126. Ibid. (quoting from *Santosky v. Kramer*, 455 U.S. 745, 766 [1982]).

127. Ibid., 263.

128. The Court was planning to consider the applicability of the exclusionary rule to juvenile proceedings in *New Jersey v. T.L.O.*, 469 U.S. 325 (1985). It decided against doing so when it became apparent that the case raised the more basic issue of whether the Fourth Amendment's prohibition against unreasonable search and seizure applies to school authorities (see 469 U.S., 332).

129. It is significant that in both this decision and *Michael C.*, the Court reversed state court decisions expanding juvenile due process.

7. CONSTITUTIONAL DOMESTICATION AND THE NEW JUVENILE COURT

1. According to David Rothman, the juvenile court thus has the distinction of being the first criminal justice reform of the Progressive Era to be challenged successfully in the 1960s. See Rothman, *Conscience and Convenience: The Asylum and Its Alternatives in Progressive America* (Boston: Little, Brown, 1980), 205.

2. See, e.g., Monrad Paulsen, "*Kent v. United States:* The Constitutional Context of Juvenile Cases," *Supreme Court Review* (1966): 167; Robert Gardner, "The *Kent* Case and the Juvenile Court: A Challenge to Lawyers," *American Bar Association Journal* 52 (1966): 923–25; Monrad G. Paulsen, "The Constitutional Domestication of the Juvenile Court," *Supreme Court Review* (1967): 233; James Hillson Cohen, "The Standard of Proof in Juvenile Proceedings: *Gault* Beyond a Reasonable Doubt," *Michigan Law Review* 68 (1970): 567–602.

3. Some analysts of the decisions conclude that the Court did not alter the fundamental premises of juvenile jurisprudence. See J. Lawrence Schultz and Fred Cohen, "Isolationism in Juvenile Court Jurisprudence" in *Pursuing Justice for the Child,* ed. Margaret Rosenheim (Chicago: University of Chicago Press, 1976), 20–42.

4. *In re Gault,* 387 U.S. 1, 21 (1967); *In re Winship,* 397 U.S. 358, 367 (1970).

5. Orman W. Ketcham, "Guidelines from *Gault:* Revolutionary Requirements and Reappraisal," *Virginia Law Review* 53 (1967): 1718. At least one commentator, however, disagreed with this assessment. Spencer Coxe argued that *Gault* marked the demise of traditional juvenile jurisprudence, which he viewed as a positive development (see Coxe, "Lawyers in Juvenile Court," *Crime and Delinquency* 13 [1967]: 493).

6. Norman Dorsen and Daniel Rezneck, "*In re Gault* and the Future of Juvenile Law," *Family Law Quarterly* 1 (1967): 5.

7. Norman Lefstein, Vaughan Stapleton, and Lee Teitelbaum, "In Search of Juvenile Justice: *Gault* and Its Application," *Law and Society Review* 3 (1969): 491–562; Elyce Ferster, Thomas Courtless, and Edith Snethen, "The Juvenile Justice System: In Search of the Role of Counsel," *Fordham Law Review* 39 (1971): 375–412; B. C. Canon and K. L. Kolson, "Rural Compliance with *Gault:* Kentucky, a Case Study," *Journal of Family Law* 10 (1971): 300–326.

8. Lefstein, Stapleton, and Teitelbaum, "In Search of Juvenile Justice," 510, 531.

9. Ferster, Courtless, and Snethen, "The Juvenile Justice System," 379; Canon and Kolson, "Rural Compliance with *Gault*," 318.

10. M. A. Bortner, *Inside a Juvenile Court: The Tarnished Ideal of Individualized Justice* (New York: New York University Press, 1982), 139; the figure cited by Bortner is 60 percent. See also Barry C. Feld, "Criminalizing Juvenile Justice: Rules of Procedure for the Juvenile Court," *Minnesota Law Review* 69 (1984): 189–90; Feld, "The Juvenile Court Meets the Principle of the Offense: Legislative Changes in Juvenile Waiver Statutes," *Journal of Criminal Law and Criminology* 78 (1987): 531; Feld, "*In re Gault* Revisited: A Cross-State Comparison of the Right to Counsel in Juvenile Court," *Crime and Delinquency* 34 (1988): 393–424.

11. 387 U.S., 36; Sanford J. Fox, "Juvenile Justice Reform: An Historical Perspective," *Stanford Law Review* 22 (1970): 1239; Anthony M. Platt, *The Child Savers: The Invention of Delinquency* (Chicago: University of Chicago Press, 1969), 172.

12. Ferster, Courtless, and Snethen, "Juvenile Justice System," 406.

13. Platt, *Child Savers,* 167; Donald Horowitz, *The Courts and Social Policy* (Washington, DC: Brookings Institution, 1977), 191.

14. Richard Kay and Daniel Segal, "The Role of the Attorney in Juvenile Court Proceedings: A Non-polar Approach," *Georgetown Law Journal* 61 (1973): 1411.

15. Elyce Ferster and Thomas Courtless, "Pre-dispositional Data, Role of Counsel and Decisions in a Juvenile Court," *Law and Society Review* 7 (1972): 209.

16. See Vaughan Stapleton and Lee Teitelbaum, *In Defense of Youth: A Study of the Role of Counsel in American Juvenile Courts* (New York: Russell Sage Foundation, 1972); Platt, *Child Savers,* 178; Lefstein, Stapleton, and Teitelbaum, "In Search of Juvenile Justice," 543.

17. Gerald Rosenberg, *The Hollow Hope: Can Courts Bring About Social Change?* (Chicago: University of Chicago, 1991), 316.

18. See Ralph A. Rossum, Benedict J. Koller, and Christopher P. Manfredi, *Juvenile Justice Reform: A Model for the States* (Claremont, CA: Rose Institute of State and Local Government and American Legislative Exchange Council, 1987), 112–14.

19. Ariz. Rev. Stat. Ann. s. 8-231.01 (1978); Cal. Welf. & Inst. Code s. 677 (West 1984); Colo. Rev. Stat. s. 19-1-107 (3) (1984); Ga. Code Ann. s. 24A-1801 (b) (1981); Hawaii Rev. Stat. s. 571-41 (a) (Supp. 1984); Idaho Code s. 16-1621 (Supp. 1987); Iowa Code Ann. s. 232.41 (West 1985); Kan. Stat. Ann. s. 38-834 (f) (1981); La. Rev. Stat. Ann. s. 13:1586 (West 1983); Me. Rev. Stat. Ann. tit. 15, s. 3405 (1980); Mich. Comp. Laws s. 712A.17 (1) (Supp. 1986); Minn. Stat. Ann. s. 260.161 (1) (West 1982); Miss. Code Ann. s. 43-21-203 (7) (1981); Mo. Rev. Stat. s. 211.171 (4) (1983); Mont. Code Ann. s. 41-5-521 (3) (1985); N.M. Stat. Ann. s. 32-1-31 (A) (Supp. 1985); N.C. Gen. Stat. s. 7A-675 (a) (1981); N.D. Cent. Code s. 27-20-24 (4) (Supp. 1985); Ohio Rev. Code Ann. s. 2151.35 (Page 1978); 42 Pa. Cons. Stat. s. 6336 (c) (1982); S.D. Codified Laws Ann. s. 26-8-32.4 (1984); Tex. Fam. Code Ann. 54.09 (Vernon 1975);

Utah Code Ann. s. 78-3a-35 (Supp. 1985); Wash. Rev. Code Ann. s. 13.40.140 (5) (Supp. 1987); W. Va. Code s. 49-5-11 (c) (1980); Wyo. Stat. s. 14-6-224 (a) (1978).

20. See Alaska Stat. s. 47.10.070 (1985); Colo. Rev. Stat. s. 19-1-106 (4) (1984); Kan. Stat. Ann. s. 38-8-8 (a) (1981); Mass. Gen. Laws Ann. ch. 119, s. 55a (West 1986); Mich. Comp. Laws s. 712A.17 (2) (Supp. 1986); Mont. Code Ann. s. 41-5-521 (1) (1985); N.M. Stat. Ann. s. 32-1-31 (A) (Supp. 1985); Okla. Stat. Ann. tit. 10, s. 1110 (West 1985); S.D. Codified Laws Ann. s. 26-8-31 (1984); Tex. Fam. Code Ann. s. 54.03 (c) (1975); W. Va. Code s. 49-5-6 (1980); Wis. Stat. s. 48.31 (2) (Supp. 1985); Wyo. Stat. s. 14-6-223 (c) (1978).

21. See Colo. Rev. Stat. s. 19-2-103 (7) (1984); Conn. Gen. Stat. s. 46b-131 (1979); Del. Code Ann. tit. 10, s. 936 (1) (Supp. 1984); Ga. Code Ann. s. 24A-1402 (d) (1981); Kan. Stat. Ann. s. 38-815e (1981); Mass. Gen. Laws Ann. ch. 119, s. 67 (West 1986); Mich. Comp. Laws s. 712A.17 (3) (Supp. 1986); Neb. Rev. Stat. s. 43-205.03 (1978); Tenn. Code Ann. s. 37-1-117 (e) (1984); S.D. Codified Laws Ann. s. 26-8-21 (1984); Vt. Stat. Ann. tit. 33, s. 641 (c) (1981); Va. Code s. 16.1-247 (D) (1) (Supp. 1985); Wash. Rev. Code Ann. s. 13.40.040 (4) (Supp. 1987); W. Va. Code s. 49-5-8 (d) (1980). Connecticut, Georgia, Massachusetts, Michigan, South Dakota, Washington, and West Virginia provided for bail as a matter of right in all cases; Vermont and Virginia provided for it as a matter of right in felony cases. Colorado, Delaware, Kansas, Nebraska, and Tennessee allowed for bail at the discretion of the court. Only Hawaii, Indiana, New Jersey, North Carolina, Ohio, Oregon, and Utah specifically prohibited bail.

22. Feld, "Criminalizing Juvenile Justice," 274.

23. On abolishing juvenile courts, see Francis McCarthy, "Should Juvenile Delinquency Be Abolished?" *Crime and Delinquency* 23 (1977): 196–203, and S. Wizner and M. F. Keller, "The Penal Model of Juvenile Justice: Is Juvenile Court Delinquency Jurisdiction Obsolete?" *New York University Law Review* 52 (1977): 1120–35. But see H. Ted Rubin, "Retain The Juvenile Court? Legislative Developments, Reform Directions, and the Call for Abolition," *Crime and Delinquency* 25 (1979): 281–98. Another more moderate but still significant reform proposal is advanced by Gary B. Melton, "Taking *Gault* Seriously: Toward a New Juvenile Court," *Nebraska Law Review* 68 (1989): 146–81.

24. Both quotations are from McCarthy, "Should Juvenile Delinquency Be Abolished?," 196.

25. Barbara D. Flicker, *Standards for Juvenile Justice: A Summary and Analysis* (Cambridge, MA: Ballinger, 1977).

26. Ibid., 3, 4, 133.

27. Ibid., 43, 49, 178.

28. Ibid., 191, 12, 22–23.

29. Ibid., 23.

30. Ibid., 196.

31. Ibid., 193.

32. Ibid., 192.

33. Ibid., 196, 204, 207, 148.

34. Ibid., 138–39. The commission argued that counsel represents the most effective means of ensuring that rules are followed and discretion reduced in juvenile courts (148).

35. Ibid., 167–74.

36. Ibid., 182.

37. Ibid., 164–65.

38. Twentieth Century Fund, *Confronting Youth Crime: Sentencing Policy Toward Young Offenders* (New York: Holmes and Meier, 1978), 11.

39. Ibid., 12.

40. Ibid., 5.

41. Ibid., 6, 72–73.

42. Ibid., 6–7.

43. Ibid., 80.

44. Ibid., 7.

45. Ibid., 15–16.

46. Ibid., 10.

47. Ibid., 16.

48. Ibid., 25 (dissent of Marvin Wolfgang).

49. Ibid., 7.

50. Public Law No. 93-415, amended by Public Law No. 95-417.

51. National Advisory Committee for Juvenile Justice and Delinquency Prevention, *Standards for the Administration of Juvenile Justice* (Washington, DC: Department of Justice, 1980), ix.

52. Ibid., xiii–xiv.

53. Ibid., 243, 244.

54. Ibid., 245 (Standard 3.11); 247 (Standard 3.111).

55. Ibid., 260 (Standard 3.115).

56. Ibid., 249 (Standard 3.112).

57. Ibid., 254 (Standard 3.113).

58. Ibid., 262 (Standard 3.116).

59. Ibid. (Commentary on Standard 3.116).

60. Ibid., 243.

61. Ibid., 325 (Standard 3.171).

62. Ibid., 326 (Commentary on Standard 3.171). See also 330 (Commentary on Standard 3.173, discussing recommendation against trial by jury). The NAC concluded that public trials would serve the same purpose as trial by jury.

63. Ibid., 278 (Standard 3.134).

64. Ibid. (Commentary on Standard 3.134).

65. Ibid., 352 (Standard 3.188).

66. Ibid., 337 (Standard 3.181). As with *Confronting Youth Crime*, this

recommendation was also an attempt to establish determinate sentencing without presumptive sentences.

67. Ibid., 340 (Standard 3.182).

68. Ibid. (Commentary on Standard 3.182).

69. Ibid.

70. Ibid. (Standard 3.182).

71. Ibid., xiii. Citing *Kent v. United States*, 383 U.S 541, 556 (1966).

72. National Advisory Committee, *Serious Juvenile Crime: A Redirected Federal Effort* (Washington, DC: Department of Justice, 1984), iii.

73. Ibid., 3–8.

74. Ibid., 12.

75. Ibid., 11.

76. Ibid., 13–14.

77. National Council of Juvenile and Family Court Judges, "The Juvenile Court and Serious Offenders: 38 Recommendations," *Juvenile and Family Court Judges Journal* 35 (Special Issue 1984).

78. Ibid. (Preamble).

79. Ibid., 12 (Recommendations 10, 11, 12).

80. Ibid., 9 (Recommendations 2, 3).

81. Ibid., 18 (Recommendations 27, 28).

82. Feld, "Criminalizing Juvenile Justice," 163. See also Andrew Walkover, "The Infancy Defense in the New Juvenile Court," *UCLA Law Review* 31 (1984): 517–23.

83. See, e.g., Del. Code Ann. tit. 10, s. 902 (1974); Fla. Stat. Ann. s. 39.001 (Supp. 1983); Me. Rev. Stat. Ann. tit. 15, s. 3002 (Supp. 1982–1983); Minn. Stat. Ann. s. 260.011 (West 1982); Neb. Rev. Stat. s. 43-246 (Supp. 1982); Wash. Rev. Code Ann. s. 13.40.010 (Supp. 1983–1984). See also Walkover, "Infancy Defense," 523.

84. Horowitz, *Courts and Social Policy*, 205–9.

85. See, e.g., Ga. Code Ann. s. 15-11-33(d) (1982); Ill. Ann. Stat. ch. 37, s. 705-1(1) (1972); N.M. Stat. Ann. s. 32-1-31(G) (1978); N.D. Cent. Code s. 27-20-29(4) (1974); Pa. Stat. Ann. tit. 42, s. 6341(d) (1982); Tenn. Code Ann. s. 37-1-129(d) (1977).

86. States providing for both examination of the report and cross-examination of the writer included Alabama, California, Georgia, Maryland, Minnesota, Mississippi, Montana, North Carolina, Pennsylvania, Rhode Island, South Dakota, Tennessee, Utah, Vermont, Washington, Wisconsin, and Wyoming. States providing only for examination of the report included Arkansas, Illinois, Iowa, Kansas, Massachusetts, New Hampshire, New Mexico, New York, Ohio, Oregon, Texas, and Virginia. States providing only for cross-examination of the report's writer included Colorado, Hawaii, Maine, Nevada, and South Carolina.

87. Samuel M. Davis, *The Rights of Juveniles: The Juvenile Justice System*, 2d ed. (New York: Clark Boardman, 1987), 6.5.

88. See John L. Roche, "Juvenile Court Dispositional Alternatives: Imposing a Duty on the Defense," *Santa Clara Law Review* 27 (1987): 281–89.

89. Barry C. Feld, "Reference of Juvenile Offenders for Adult Prosecution: The Legislative Alternative to Asking Unanswerable Questions," *Minnesota Law Review* 62 (1978): 608.

90. Davis, *Rights of Juveniles,* 6.22. See, e.g., Ga. Code Ann. s. 15-11-41(b) (1982), N.D. Cent. Code s. 27-20-36(2) (1974), and Conn. Gen. Stat. Ann. s. 46b-141(a)-(b) (1986). Each of these states placed a two-year limit on commitment. See also Martin L. Forst, Bruce A. Fisher, and Robert B. Coates, "Indeterminate and Determinate Sentencing of Juvenile Delinquents: A National Survey of Approaches to Commitment and Release Decision-making," *Juvenile and Family Court Journal* 36 (Summer 1985): 1–12; their survey of dispositional practices classified the commitment or release decisionmaking structures of five states—Arizona, California, Georgia, Minnesota, and Washington—as determinate.

91. According to Davis, *Rights of Juveniles,* 6.12, Arkansas, Connecticut, Indiana, Maryland, Minnesota, and North Carolina provided for restitution as an outright disposition; New York, North Carolina, and South Carolina permitted it as a condition of probation. See also Calif. Welf. & Inst. Code ss. 728, 729, 729.6, 730.6 (West 1986).

92. Note, "The Transfer of Juvenile Offenders to Adult Courts in Massachusetts: Reevaluating the Rehabilitative Ideal," *Suffolk University Law Review* 20 (1986): 990. See also Barry C. Feld, "Delinquent Careers and Criminal Policy: Just Deserts and the Waiver Decision," *Criminology* 21 (1983): 195–96.

93. See Barry C. Feld, "Legislative Policies Toward the Serious Juvenile Offender," *Crime and Delinquency* 27 (1981): 497–521.

94. See Feld, "Reference of Juvenile Offenders for Adult Prosecution," "Delinquent Careers and Criminal Policy," and "Juvenile Court Meets the Principle of the Offense," 487–94.

95. Feld, "Delinquent Careers and Criminal Policy," 202.

96. Ibid., 197; Feld, "Legislative Policies Toward the Serious Juvenile Offender," 518.

97. Feld, "Juvenile Court Meets the Principle of the Offense," 511–13. The states were Arkansas, Colorado, Connecticut, Delaware, Florida, Georgia, Idaho, Illinois, Indiana, Kansas, Louisiana, Maryland, Mississippi, Nebraska, Nevada, New York, Ohio, Oklahoma, Pennsylvania, Rhode Island, Utah, Vermont, and Wyoming.

98. The exceptions were Ark. Stat. Ann. s. 41-617 (1975), Neb. Rev. Stat. s. 43-247 (1974), and Wy. Stat. s. 14-6-203(c) (1971).

99. Feld, "Juvenile Court Meets the Principle of the Offense," 514.

100. Citizens' Committee for Children of New York, *The Experiment That Failed: The New York Juvenile Offender Law—A Study Report* (New York: CCNY,

1984). See also M. A. Bortner, "Traditional Rhetoric, Organizational Realities: Remand of Juveniles to Adult Court," *Crime and Delinquency* 32 (1986): 56.

101. Note, "Transfer of Juvenile Offenders to Adult Courts in Massachusetts," 1006–7.

102. Feld, "Delinquent Careers and Criminal Policy," 206.

103. Joan Petersilia, "Juvenile Record Use in Adult Court Proceedings: A Survey of Prosecutors," *Journal of Criminal Law and Criminology* 72 (1981): 1746–71.

104. Forst, Fisher, and Coates, "Indeterminate and Determinate Sentencing of Juvenile Delinquents," 8–10.

105. Ibid., 10.

106. Ill. Rev. Stat. ch. 37, ss.705–712 (1983 & Supp. 1984). There is no possibility of parole under this statute, although the juvenile's period of confinement may be reduced by earning credits for good conduct.

107. Note, "Mandatory Sentencing for Habitual Juvenile Offenders: *People v. J.A.*," *Depaul Law Review* 34 (1985): 1094.

108. Ibid., 1090. See *People v. J.A.* (1984) 469 N.E. 2d 449 (Ill. App. Ct.).

109. Wash. Rev. Code Ann. s. 13.40.010 (2) (Supp. 1984).

110. Washington State Juvenile Disposition Standards Commission, *Washington State Juvenile Dispositions Standards Philosophy and Guide* (1984), 9.

111. Wash. Rev. Code Ann. s. 13.40.020 (Supp. 1984).

112. Anne Larason Schneider and Donna D. Schram, "The Washington State Juvenile Justice System Reform: A Review of Findings," *Criminal Justice Policy Review* 1 (1986): 211–35.

113. Andrew von Hirsch, *Doing Justice: The Choice of Punishments* (New York: Hill and Wang, 1976). Other future-oriented goals criticized by the just deserts approach are deterrence and incapacitation. Von Hirsch responded to critics and elaborated his own theory in *Past or Future Crimes* (New Brunswick, NJ: Rutgers University Press, 1985).

114. Wash. Rev. Code Ann. s.13.40.110 (Supp. 1977).

115. *State v. Lawley*, 591 P.2d 772 (Wash. Sup. Ct. 1979).

116. Alexander Bickel, *The Supreme Court and the Idea of Progress* (New York: Harper and Row, 1970), 175.

8. LITIGATION AND JUVENILE COURT REFORM

1. Donald Horowitz, *The Courts and Social Policy* (Washington, DC: Brookings Institution, 1976), 264.

2. Gerald N. Rosenberg, *The Hollow Hope: Can Courts Bring About Social Change?* (Chicago: University of Chicago Press, 1991), 341.

3. Judge David Bazelon announced the existence of a statutory right to treatment in the District of Columbia and hinted at the existence of a similar

constitutional right in 1966. See *Rouse v. Cameron*, 373 F.2d 541 (D.C. Cir. 1966). The right to treatment attracted strong support among leading mental-health-law practitioners, who used leading law journals to advocate their position. See Symposium, "Observations on the Right to Treatment," *Georgetown Law Journal* 57 (1969): 673–817, and Symposium, "The Mentally Ill and the Right to Treatment," *University of Chicago Law Review* 36 (1969): 742-801. These developments are discussed in Phillip J. Cooper, *Hard Judicial Choices: Federal District Court Judges and State and Local Officials* (New York: Oxford University Press, 1988), 141–42, 151–52.

4. Anne Larason Schneider and Donna D. Schramm, "The Washington State Juvenile Justice System Reform: A Review of Findings," *Criminal Justice Policy Review* 1 (1986): 217, 231.

5. Horowitz, *Courts and Social Policy*, 38–45.

6. See Stephen L. Wasby, "Civil Rights Litigation by Organizations: Constraints and Choices," *Judicature* 68 (1985): 345–50.

7. Bruce C. Hafen, "Exploring Test Cases in Child Advocacy," *Harvard Law Review* 100 (1986): 437.

8. For a discussion of these issues, see Gary B. Melton, "Litigation in the Interest of Children: Does Anybody Win?" *Law and Human Behavior* 10 (1986): 337–53.

9. Rena K. Uviller to the author, January 8, 1986.

10. Daniel Rezneck to the author, October 17, 1985; Norman Dorsen to the author, November 1, 1985; Uviller to the author, January 8, 1986.

11. Hafen, "Exploring Test Cases in Child Advocacy," 439–40; Rachel F. Moran, "Reflections on the Enigma of Indeterminacy in Child Advocacy Cases," *California Law Review* 74 (1986): 628.

12. Dorsen to the author, November 1, 1985.

13. Arthur Selwyn Miller and Jerome A. Barron, "The Supreme Court, the Adversary System, and the Flow of Information to the Justices: A Preliminary Inquiry," *Virginia Law Review* 61 (1975): 1187–89.

14. Ibid., 1227.

15. Michael S. Wald, "Thinking About Public Policy Toward Abuse and Neglect of Children: A Review of *Before the Best Interests of the Child*," *Michigan Law Review* 78 (1980): 678–79.

16. *Gault* raised two constitutional claims—the rights to a written transcript and to appellate review—that the Court simply did not decide upon.

17. *Breed v. Jones*, 421 U.S. 519 (1975). The issue here was double jeopardy from juvenile and criminal proceedings stemming from the same offense.

18. Fred P. Graham, *The Due Process Revolution: The Warren Court's Impact on Criminal Law* (New York: Hayden Book Company, 1970), 221–22.

19. Ibid., 302–3.

20. Eleanor Wolf, *Trial and Error: The Detroit School Segregation Case* (Detroit:

Wayne State University Press, 1981), 259–60. See also Rogers Elliott, *Litigating Intelligence: IQ Tests, Special Education, and Social Science in the Courtroom* (Dover, MA: Auburn House, 1987).

21. On the information-gathering weaknesses of appellate courts, see Thomas Marvell, *Appellate Courts and Lawyers: Information Gathering in the Adversary System* (Westport, CT: Greenwood Press, 1978), 184. See also Jethro Lieberman, *The Role of Courts in American Society: Final Report of the Council on the Role of Courts* (St. Paul, MN: West Publishing Company, 1984), 148. On the axiomatic treatment of hypotheses, see Ralph A. Rossum, "The Problem of Prison Crowding: On the Limits of Prison Capacity and Judicial Capacity," *Benchmark* 1 (1984): 23.

22. See Peggy C. Davis, " 'There Is a Book Out . . . ': An Analysis of Judicial Absorption of Legislative Facts," *Harvard Law Review* 100 (1987): 1539–1604.

23. Wolf, *Trial and Error,* 275.

24. See chapter 2, Table 2.1.

25. Miller and Barron, "Supreme Court, Adversary System, and Flow of Information to the Justices," 1213.

26. Jack W. Peltason, *Federal Courts in the Judicial Process* (New York: Random House, 1955), 52; Chester A. Newland, "Legal Periodicals and the United States Supreme Court," *Midwest Journal of Political Science* 3 (1959): 60–61; Clement Vose, *Caucasians Only: The Supreme Court, the NAACP, and the Restrictive Covenant Cases* (Berkeley: University of California Press, 1959), 161.

27. Rossum, "Problem of Prison Crowding," 30.

28. Brief for Appellee, *In re Winship,* 397 U.S. 358 (1970), 13–14.

29. Wolf, *Trial and Error,* 268.

30. 383 U.S., 543. To be accurate, Fortas also admitted that "some" of these issues were not "within judicial competence." Still, they were an implicit theme throughout the decision, as was evident in Fortas's concern that juvenile courts provide children with the "worst of both worlds" (383 U.S., 556). Moreover, by excluding some issues of juvenile justice policy from judicial competence, Fortas subtly implied that other issues might be within that competence, thus providing an open invitation to future judicial review of custodial and treatment policies.

31. Norman Lefstein, Vaughan Stapleton, and Lee Teitelbaum, "In Search of Juvenile Justice: *Gault* and Its Application," *Law and Society Review* 3 (1969): 491–562. The study was not cited in any of the concurring or dissenting opinions, either.

32. Moran, "Reflections on the Enigma of Indeterminacy in Child Advocacy Cases," 627.

33. Hafen, "Exploring Test Cases in Child Advocacy," 441.

34. John Hart Ely, *Democracy and Distrust: A Theory of Judicial Review* (Cambridge: Harvard University Press), 21, 88.

35. The judicially created exclusionary rule is a case in point. The purpose of

the rule is to deter law enforcement authorities from engaging in illegal searches and seizures. It operates most directly, however, on prosecutors and thus assumes a certain type and level of communication between prosecutors and law enforcement officials. This communication varies widely among jurisdictions, a fact that significantly affects the rule's operation. See Stephen R. Schlesinger, "Criminal Procedure in the Courtroom," in *Crime and Public Policy,* ed. James Q. Wilson (San Francisco: ICS Press, 1983), 192–200.

36. Wolf, *Trial and Error,* 278.

37. Horowitz, *Courts and Social Policy,* 52–53.

38. Ibid., 137.

39. 410 U.S. 113 (1973).

40. Eva Rubin, *Abortion, Politics, and the Courts: Roe v. Wade and Its Aftermath* (Westport, CT: Greenwood Press, 1982), 161.

41. Miller and Barron, "Supreme Court, Adversary System, and Flow of Information to the Justices," 1222.

Bibliography

Allen, Francis A. "Criminal Justice, Legal Values and the Rehabilitative Ideal," *Journal of Criminal Law, Criminology and Police Science* 50 (1959): 226–32.

Allen, Francis A. *The Decline of the Rehabilitative Ideal: Penal Policy and Social Purpose.* New Haven: Yale University Press, 1981.

Allen, Ronald J. "The Restoration of *In re Winship*: A Comment on Burdens of Persuasion in Criminal Cases after *Patterson v. New York*," *Michigan Law Review* 76 (1977): 30–63.

American Civil Liberties Union. *Annual Reports.* New York: Arno Press and *New York Times,* 1970.

Antieau, Chester James. "Constitutional Rights in Juvenile Courts," *Cornell Law Quarterly* 46 (1961): 387–415.

Arens, Richard. *Make Mad the Guilty.* Springfield, IL: Charles C. Thomas, 1969.

Baker, Liva. *Miranda: Crime, Law and Politics.* New York: Atheneum, 1983.

Bazelon, David. *Questioning Authority: Justice and Criminal Law.* New York: Knopf, 1988.

Beemsterboer, Mathew J. "The Juvenile Court—Benevolence in the Star Chamber," *Journal of Criminal Law, Criminology and Police Science* 50 (1960): 464–75.

Berger, Mark. *Taking the Fifth: The Supreme Court and the Privilege Against Self-incrimination.* Lexington, MA: Lexington Books, 1980.

Beytagh, Francis X. "Ten Years of Non-retroactivity: A Critique and a Proposal," *Virginia Law Review* 61 (1975): 1557–1625.

Bickel, Alexander. *The Supreme Court and the Idea of Progress.* New York: Harper and Row, 1970.

Binder, Arnold. "The Juvenile Justice System: Where Pretence and Reality Clash," *American Behavioral Scientist* 22 (1979): 621–52.

Binder, Arnold, Gilbert Geiss, and Dickson Bruce. *Juvenile Delinquency: Historical, Cultural, Legal Perspectives.* New York: Macmillan, 1988.

Bogen, David. " 'Justice' Versus 'Individualized Treatment' in Juvenile Court," *Journal of Criminal Law, Criminology and Police Science* 35 (1944): 249–52.

Bortner, M. A. *Inside a Juvenile Court: The Tarnished Ideal of Individualized Justice.* New York: New York University Press, 1982.

Bortner, M. A. "Traditional Rhetoric, Organizational Realities: Remand of Juveniles to Adult Court," *Crime and Delinquency* 32 (1986): 53–73.

Breckenridge, Sophonisba P., and Edith Abbott. *The Delinquent Child and the Home.* New York: Russell Sage Foundation, 1912.

Canon, B. C., and K. L. Kolson. "Rural Compliance with *Gault:* Kentucky, A Case Study," *Journal of Family Law* 10 (1971): 300–326.

Cavanagh, Ralph, and Austin Sarat. "Thinking About Courts: Toward and Beyond a Jurisprudence of Judicial Competence," *Law and Society Review* 14 (1980): 371–420.

Chayes, Abram. "The Role of the Judge in Public Law Litigation," *Harvard Law Review* 89 (1976): 1281–1316.

Citizens' Committee for Children of New York. *The Experiment That Failed: The New York Juvenile Offender Law—A Study Report.* New York: CCNY, 1984.

Cohen, James Hillson. "The Standard of Proof in Juvenile Proceedings: *Gault* Beyond a Reasonable Doubt," *Michigan Law Review* 68 (1970): 567–602.

Comment. "The *Gault* Decision and the New York Family Court Act," *Syracuse Law Review* 19 (1968): 753–68.

Cooper, Phillip J. *Hard Judicial Choices: Federal District Court Judges and State and Local Officials.* New York: Oxford University Press, 1988.

Corsi, Jerome R. *Judicial Politics: An Introduction.* Englewood Cliffs, NJ: Prentice-Hall, 1984.

Cover, Robert M. "The Origins of Judicial Activism in the Protection of Minorities," *Yale Law Journal* 91 (1982): 1287–1316.

Coxe, Spencer. "Lawyers in Juvenile Court," *Crime and Delinquency* 13 (1967): 488–93.

Dahl, Robert. "Decision-making in a Democracy: The Supreme Court as a National Policy Maker," *Journal of Public Law* 6 (1957): 279–95.

Davis, Allen F. *American Heroine: The Life and Legend of Jane Addams.* New York: Oxford University Press, 1973.

Davis, Kenneth Culp. *Discretionary Justice: A Preliminary Inquiry.* Baton Rouge: Louisiana State University Press, 1969.

Davis, Peggy C. " 'There Is a Book Out . . . ': An Analysis of Judicial Absorption of Legislative Facts," *Harvard Law Review* 100 (1987): 1539–1604.

Davis, Samuel M. *The Rights of Juveniles: The Juvenile Justice System.* 2d ed. New York: Clark Boardman, 1987.

Dembitz, Nanette. "Ferment and Experiment in New York: Juvenile Cases in the New Family Court," *Cornell Law Quarterly* 48 (1963): 499–523.

Diana, Lewis. "The Rights of Juvenile Delinquents: An Appraisal of Juvenile Court Procedures," *Journal of Criminal Law, Criminology and Police Science* 47 (1957): 561–69.

Diver, Colin S. "The Judge as Political Powerbroker: Superintending Structural Change in Public Institutions," *Virginia Law Review* 65 (1979): 43–106.

Donohue, William A. *The Politics of the American Civil Liberties Union.* New Brunswick, NJ: Transaction Books, 1985.

Dorsen, Norman, and Daniel Rezneck. "*In re Gault* and the Future of Juvenile Law," *Family Law Quarterly* 1 (1967): 1–46.

Elliott, Rogers. *Litigating Intelligence: IQ Tests, Special Education, and Social Science in the Courtroom.* Dover, MA: Auburn House, 1987.

Ellrod, Fred E., and Don H. Melaney. "Juvenile Justice: Treatment or Travesty?" *University of Pittsburgh Law Review* 11 (1950): 277–87.

Ely, John Hart. *Democracy and Distrust: A Theory of Judicial Review.* Cambridge: Harvard University Press, 1980.

Epstein, Lee, and Joseph Kobylka. *The Supreme Court and Legal Change: Abortion and the Death Penalty.* Chapel Hill: University of North Carolina Press, 1992.

Epstein, Lee, Thomas G. Walker, and William J. Dixon. "The Supreme Court and Criminal Justice Disputes: A Neo-institutional Perspective," *American Journal of Political Science* 33 (1989): 825–41.

Fabricant, Michael. *Juveniles in the Family Court.* Lexington, MA: D. C. Heath, 1983.

Federal Bureau of Investigation. *Uniform Crime Reports.* Washington, DC: Government Printing Office, 1950–1965.

Feld, Barry C. "Criminalizing Juvenile Justice: Rules of Procedure for the Juvenile Court," *Minnesota Law Review* 69 (1984): 141–276.

Feld, Barry C. "Delinquent Careers and Criminal Policy: Just Deserts and the Waiver Decision," *Criminology* 21 (1983): 195–212.

Feld, Barry C. "*In re Gault* Revisited: A Cross-State Comparison of the Right to Counsel in Juvenile Court," *Crime and Delinquency* 34 (1988): 393–424.

Feld, Barry C. "The Juvenile Court Meets the Principle of the Offense: Legislative Changes in Juvenile Waiver Statutes," *Journal of Criminal Law and Criminology* 78 (1987): 471–533.

Feld, Barry C. "Legislative Policies Toward the Serious Juvenile Offender," *Crime and Delinquency* 27 (1981): 497–521.

Feld, Barry C. "Reference of Juvenile Offenders for Adult Prosecution: The Legislative Alternative to Asking Unanswerable Questions," *Minnesota Law Review* 62 (1978): 515–618.

Ferster, Elyce, and Thomas Courtless. "Pre-dispositional Data, Role of Counsel and Decisions in a Juvenile Court," *Law and Society Review* 7 (1972): 195–222.

Ferster, Elyce, Thomas Courtless, and Edith Snethen. "The Juvenile Justice System: In Search of the Role of Counsel," *Fordham Law Review* 39 (1971): 375–412.

Flexner, Bernard, and Roger N. Baldwin. *Juvenile Courts and Probation.* New York: Century Company, 1916.

Flicker, Barbara D. *Standards for Juvenile Justice: A Summary and Analysis.* Cambridge, MA: Ballinger, 1977.

Forst, Martin L., Bruce A. Fisher, and Robert B. Coates. "Indeterminate and Determinate Sentencing of Juvenile Delinquents: A National Survey of Approaches to Commitment and Release Decision-making," *Juvenile and Family Court Journal* 36 (Summer 1985): 1–12.

Fox, Sanford J. "Juvenile Justice Reform: An Historical Perspective," *Stanford Law Review* 22 (1970): 1187–1239.

Galanter, Marc. "Why the 'Haves' Come Out Ahead: Speculations on the Limits of Legal Change," *Law and Society Review* 9 (1974): 95–160.

Gardner, John, ed. *Public Law and Public Policy.* New York: Praeger, 1977.

Gardner, Robert. "The *Kent* Case and the Juvenile Court: A Challenge to Lawyers," *American Bar Association Journal* 52 (1966): 923–25.

George, Tracey E., and Lee Epstein. "On the Nature of Supreme Court Decision Making," *American Political Science Review* 86 (1992): 323–37.

Gibson, James L. "Judges' Role Orientations, Attitudes, and Decisions: An Interactive Model," *American Political Science Review* 72 (1978): 911–24.

Gilbert, James. *A Cycle of Outrage: America's Reaction to the Juvenile Delinquent in the 1950s.* New York: Oxford University Press, 1986.

Glaab, Charles N., and A. Theodore Brown. *A History of Urban America.* New York: Macmillan, 1967.

Goodin, Robert E. *Political Theory and Public Policy.* Chicago: University of Chicago Press, 1982.

Graglia, Lino. "When Honesty Is 'Simply . . . Impractical' for the Supreme Court: How the Constitution Came to Require Busing for School Racial Balance," *Michigan Law Review* 85 (1987): 1153–82.

Graham, Fred P. *The Due Process Revolution: The Warren Court's Impact on Criminal Law.* New York: Hayden Book Company, 1970.

Gray, Virginia. "Innovation in the States: A Diffusion Study," *American Political Science Review* 67 (1973): 1174–93.

Greenberg, Jack. *Crusaders in the Courts.* New York: Basic Books, 1994.

Greenwood, Peter, ed. *The Juvenile Rehabilitation Reader.* Santa Monica, CA: Rand Corporation, 1985.

Gwynn, William B., and George C. Edwards III, eds. *Perspectives on Public Policy-making.* New Orleans: Tulane University Press, 1975.

Hafen, Bruce C. "Exploring Test Cases in Child Advocacy," *Harvard Law Review* 100 (1986): 435–49.

Handler, Joel. "The Juvenile Court and the Adversary System: Problems of Function and Form," *Wisconsin Law Review* (1965): 7–51.

Handler, Joel F. *Social Movements and the Legal System: A Theory of Law Reform and Social Change.* New York: Academic Press, 1978.

Hart, Hastings M. *Juvenile Court Laws in the United States Summarized.* New York: Russell Sage Foundation, 1910.

Hartmann, Francis X., ed. *From Children to Citizens.* Volume 2. *The Role of the Juvenile Court.* New York: Springer-Verlag, 1987.

Hawes, Joseph. *Children in Urban Society: Juvenile Delinquency in Nineteenth-Century America.* New York: Oxford University Press, 1971.

Hirsch, Andrew von. *Doing Justice: The Choice of Punishments.* New York: Hill and Wang, 1976.

Hirsch, Andrew von. *Past or Future Crimes.* New Brunswick, NJ: Rutgers University Press, 1985.

Holmes, Oliver Wendell. *The Common Law.* Boston: Little, Brown, 1940.

Horowitz, Donald. *The Courts and Social Policy.* Washington, DC: Brookings Institution, 1977.

Horowitz, Donald L. "Decreeing Organizational Change: Judicial Supervision of Public Institutions," *Duke Law Journal* (1983): 1265–1307.

Horowitz, Donald. "The Judiciary: Umpire or Empire?" *Law and Human Behavior* 6 (1982): 129–43.

Hughes, Charles Evans. "Forward," *Yale Law Journal* 50 (1941): 737–38.

Kalman, Laura. *Abe Fortas: A Biography.* New Haven: Yale University Press, 1990.

Kalman, Laura. *Legal Realism at Yale, 1927–1960.* Chapel Hill: University of North Carolina, 1986.

Kay, Richard, and Daniel Segal. "The Role of the Attorney in Juvenile Court Proceedings: A Non-polar Approach," *Georgetown Law Journal* 61 (1973): 1401–24.

Ketcham, Orman W. "Guidelines from *Gault:* Revolutionary Requirements and Reappraisal," *Virginia Law Review* 53 (1967): 1700–1718.

Kluger, Richard. *Simple Justice.* New York: Vintage Books, 1975.

Lawrence, Susan E. *The Poor in Court: The Legal Services Program and Supreme Court Decision Making.* Princeton, NJ: Princeton University Press, 1990.

Lefstein, Norman, Vaughan Stapleton, and Lee Teitelbaum. "In Search of Juvenile Justice: *Gault* and Its Application," *Law and Society Review* 3 (1969): 491–562.

Lemert, Edwin. *Social Action and Legal Change: Revolution Within the Juvenile Court.* Chicago: Aldine, 1970.

Levine, Daniel. *Jane Addams and the Liberal Tradition.* Westport, CT: Greenwood, 1971.

Lewis, Anthony. *Gideon's Trumpet.* New York: Vintage Books, 1966.

Lieberman, Jethro. *The Role of Courts in American Society: Final Report of the Council on the Role of Courts.* St. Paul, MN: West Publishing Company, 1984.

Lindsey, Edward. "The Juvenile Court Movement from a Lawyer's Standpoint," *Annals of the American Academy of Political and Social Science* 52 (1914): 140–48.

Lofgren, Charles. *The Plessy Case: A Legal-Historical Interpretation.* New York: Oxford University Press, 1987.

Lou, Herbert H. *Juvenile Courts in the United States.* Chapel Hill: University of North Carolina Press, 1927.

Louthan, William C. *The Politics of Justice.* Port Washington, NY: Kennikat Press, 1979.

Mack, Julian. "The Juvenile Court," *Harvard Law Review* 23 (1909): 104–22.

Manfredi, Christopher P. "Human Dignity and the Psychology of Interrogation in *Miranda v. Arizona*," *Canadian Journal of Law and Society* 1 (1986): 109–24.

Manzer, Ronald. "Public Policy-making as Practical Reasoning," *Canadian Journal of Political Science* 17 (1984): 577–94.

Marvell, Thomas. *Appellate Courts and Lawyers: Information Gathering in the Adversary System*. Westport, CT: Greenwood Press, 1978.

Matza, David. *Delinquency and Drift*. New York: John Wiley and Sons, 1964.

McCarthy, Francis. "Should Juvenile Delinquency Be Abolished?" *Crime and Delinquency* 23 (1977): 196–203.

McKelvey, Blake. *The Urbanization of America, 1860–1915*. New Brunswick, NJ: Rutgers University Press, 1963.

McKesson, William B. "Right to Counsel in Juvenile Proceedings," *Minnesota Law Review* 45 (1961): 843–52.

Melnick, R. Shep. *Regulation and the Courts: The Case of the Clean Air Act*. Washington, DC: Brookings Institution, 1983.

Melton, Gary B. "Litigation in the Interest of Children: Does Anybody Win?" *Law and Human Behavior* 10 (1986): 337–53.

Melton, Gary B. "Taking *Gault* Seriously: Toward a New Juvenile Court," *Nebraska Law Review* 68 (1989): 146–81.

Mennell, Robert M. *Thorns and Thistles: Juvenile Delinquents in the United States, 1825–1940*. Hanover, NH: University Press of New England, 1973.

Mezey, Susan Gluck. *Children in Court: Public Policymaking and Federal Court Decisions*. Albany: State University of New York Press, 1996.

Miller, Arthur Selwyn, and Jerome A. Barron, "The Supreme Court, the Adversary System, and the Flow of Information to the Justices: A Preliminary Inquiry," *Virginia Law Review* 61 (1975): 1187–1245.

Mnookin, Robert. *In the Interests of Children: Advocacy, Law Reform, and Public Policy*. New York: W. H. Freeman, 1985.

Molloy, John J. "Juvenile Court—A Labyrinth of Confusion for the Lawyer," *Arizona Law Review* 4 (1962): 1–25.

Moran, Rachel F. "Reflections on the Enigma of Indeterminacy in Child Advocacy Cases," *California Law Review* 74 (1986): 603–48.

Morano, Anthony A. "A Reexamination of the Development of the Reasonable Doubt Rule," *Boston University Law Review* 55 (1975): 507–28.

Murphy, Bruce Allen. *Fortas: The Rise and Ruin of a Supreme Court Justice*. New York: William Morrow and Company, 1988.

National Advisory Committee for Juvenile Justice and Delinquency Prevention. *Serious Juvenile Crime: A Redirected Federal Effort*. Washington, DC: Department of Justice, 1984.

National Advisory Committee for Juvenile Justice and Delinquency Prevention. *Standards for the Administration of Juvenile Justice*. Washington, DC: Department of Justice, 1980.

National Council of Juvenile and Family Court Judges. "The Juvenile Court and Serious Offenders: 38 Recommendations," *Juvenile and Family Court Judges Journal* 35 (Special Issue 1984): 1–21.

Newland, Chester A. "Legal Periodicals and the United States Supreme Court," *Midwest Journal of Political Science* 3 (1959): 58–74.

Note. "Criminal Law—Evidence—Juvenile's Confession Obtained in Violation of Statute Inadmissible," *Arizona Law Review* 5 (1964): 286–91.

Note. "Juvenile Delinquents: The Police, State Courts, and Individualized Justice," *Harvard Law Review* 79 (1966): 775–810.

Note. "Mandatory Sentencing for Habitual Juvenile Offenders: *People v. J.A.*," *Depaul Law Review* 34 (1985): 1089–1107.

Note. "Rights and Rehabilitation in the Juvenile Court," *Columbia Law Review* 67 (1967): 281–341.

Note. "The Transfer of Juvenile Offenders to Adult Courts in Massachusetts: Reevaluating the Rehabilitative Ideal," *Suffolk University Law Review* 20 (1986): 989–1028.

O'Brien, David M. *Constitutional Law and Politics*. Volume 2. *Civil Rights and Civil Liberties*. New York: W. W. Norton, 1991.

O'Brien, David M. *Storm Center: The Supreme Court in American Politics*. 2d ed. New York: W. W. Norton, 1990.

O'Connor, Karen. *Women's Organizations' Use of the Courts*. Lexington, MA: D. C. Heath, 1980.

O'Connor, Karen, and Lee Epstein, "Rebalancing the Scales of Justice: Assessment of Public Interest Law," *Harvard Journal of Law and Public Policy* 7 (1984): 483–505.

O'Connor, Karen, and Lee Epstein. "The Rise of Conservative Interest Group Litigation," *Journal of Politics* 45 (1983): 479–89.

Olson, Susan. "Interest Group Litigation in Federal District Courts: Beyond the Political Disadvantage Theory," *Journal of Politics* 52 (1990): 854–82.

Packer, Herbert L. *The Limits of the Criminal Sanction*. Palo Alto, CA: Stanford University Press, 1968.

Paulsen, Monrad G. "The Constitutional Domestication of the Juvenile Court," *Supreme Court Review* (1967): 233–66.

Paulsen, Monrad. "Fairness to the Juvenile Offender," *Minnesota Law Review* 41 (1957): 547–76.

Paulsen, Monrad G. "*Kent v. United States:* The Constitutional Context of Juvenile Cases," *Supreme Court Review* (1966): 167–92.

Peltason, Jack W. *Federal Courts in the Judicial Process*. New York: Random House, 1955.

Perrin, Solon L. "The Future of the Children's Court," *American Bar Association Journal* 8 (1922): 767–69.

Petersilia, Joan. "Juvenile Record Use in Adult Court Proceedings: A Survey of Prosecutors," *Journal of Criminal Law and Criminology* 72 (1981): 1746–71.

Pisciotta, Alexander W. "Treatment on Trial: The Rhetoric and Reality of the New York House of Refuge, 1857–1935," *American Journal of Legal History* 29 (1985): 151–81.

Platt, Anthony M. *The Child Savers: The Invention of Delinquency.* Chicago: University of Chicago Press, 1969.

President's Commission on Law Enforcement and Administration of Justice. *The Challenge of Crime in a Free Society.* Washington, DC: Government Printing Office, 1967.

President's Commission on Law Enforcement and Administration of Justice. *Task Force Report: Juvenile Delinquency and Youth Crime.* Washington, DC: Government Printing Office, 1967.

Pritchett, C. Herman. *The Roosevelt Court: A Study in Judicial Politics and Values, 1937–1947.* New York: Macmillan, 1948.

Rabin, Robert L. "Perspectives on Public Interest Law," *Stanford Law Review* 28 (1976): 207–61.

Rappeport, Jack J. "Some Legal Aspects of Juvenile Court Proceedings," *Virginia Law Review* 46 (1960): 908–25.

Reasons, Charles. "*Gault:* Procedural Change and Substantive Effect," *Crime and Delinquency* 16 (1970): 163–71.

Rhoden, Nancy K. "Trimesters and Technology: Revamping *Roe v. Wade,*" *Yale Law Journal* 95 (1986): 639–97.

Ripley, Randall B., and Grace A. Franklin. *Congress, the Bureaucracy, and Public Policy.* Homewood, IL: Dorsey Press, 1980.

Roche, John L. "Juvenile Court Dispositional Alternatives: Imposing a Duty on the Defense," *Santa Clara Law Review* 27 (1987): 279–97.

Rosenberg, Gerald N. *The Hollow Hope: Can Courts Bring About Social Change?* Chicago: University of Chicago Press, 1991.

Rosenheim, Margaret, ed. *Pursuing Justice for the Child.* Chicago: University of Chicago Press, 1976.

Rossum, Ralph A. "New Rights and Old Wrongs: The Supreme Court and the Problem of Retroactivity," *Emory Law Journal* 23 (1974): 381–420.

Rossum, Ralph A. "*Plessy, Brown,* and the Reverse Discrimination Cases: Consistency and Continuity in Judicial Approach," *American Behavioral Scientist* 28 (1985): 785–806.

Rossum, Ralph A. *The Politics of the Criminal Justice System: An Organizational Analysis.* New York: Marcel Dekker, 1978.

Rossum, Ralph A. "The Problem of Prison Crowding: On the Limits of Prison Capacity and Judicial Capacity," *Benchmark* 1 (1984): 22–30.

Rossum, Ralph A., and G. Alan Tarr. *American Constitutional Law: Cases and Interpretation.* 2d ed. New York: St. Martin's Press, 1987.

Rossum, Ralph A., Benedict J. Koller, and Christopher P. Manfredi. *Juvenile Justice Reform: A Model for the States.* Claremont, CA: Rose Institute of State and Local Government and American Legislative Exchange Council, 1987.

Rothman, David. *Conscience and Convenience: The Asylum and Its Alternatives in Progressive America.* Boston: Little, Brown, 1980.

Rothman, David. *The Discovery of the Asylum: Social Order and Disorder in the New Republic.* Boston: Little, Brown, 1971.

Rubin, Eva. *Abortion, Politics, and the Courts: Roe v. Wade and Its Aftermath.* Westport, CT: Greenwood Press, 1982.

Rubin, H. Ted. "Retain the Juvenile Court? Legislative Developments, Reform Directions, and the Call for Abolition," *Crime and Delinquency* 25 (1979): 281–98.

Rubin, Sol. "Protecting the Child in the Juvenile Court," *Journal of Criminal Law, Criminology and Police Science* 43 (1952): 425–40.

Ryerson, Ellen. *The Best-Laid Plans: America's Juvenile Court Experiment.* New York: Hill and Wang, 1978.

Savage, Robert L. "Policy Innovativeness as a Trait of American States," *Journal of Politics* 40 (1978): 212–24.

Schinitsky, Charles. "The Role of the Lawyer in Children's Court," *Record of the Bar Asscociation of New York City* 17 (1962): 10–26.

Schneider, Anne Larason, and Donna D. Schram. "The Washington State Juvenile Justice System Reform: A Review of Findings," *Criminal Justice Policy Review* 1 (1986): 211–35.

Schubert, Glendon. *The Judicial Mind.* Chicago: Northwestern University Press, 1965.

Schubert, Glendon. *The Judicial Mind Revisited: Psychometric Analysis of Supreme Court Ideology.* New York: Oxford University Press, 1974.

Schultz, J. Lawrence. "The Cycle of Juvenile Court History," *Crime and Delinquency* 19 (1973): 457–76.

Schur, Edwin M. *Radical Nonintervention: Rethinking the Delinquency Problem.* Englewood Cliffs, NJ: Prentice-Hall, 1973.

Schwartz, Bernard. *The Ascent of Pragmatism: The Burger Court in Action.* Reading, MA: Addison-Wesley Publishing Company, 1990.

Schwartz, Bernard. *Super Chief: Earl Warren and His Supreme Court—A Judicial Biography.* New York: New York University Press, 1983.

Segal, Jeffrey A. "Supreme Court Justices as Human Decision Makers: An Individual-Level Analysis of the Search and Seizure Cases," *Journal of Politics* 48 (1986): 938–55.

Shapiro, Martin. *Courts: A Comparative Analysis.* Chicago: University of Chicago Press, 1981.

Sheehan, Reginald S., William Mishler, and Donald R. Songer. "Ideology, Status, and the Differential Success of Direct Parties Before the Supreme Court," *American Political Science Review* 86 (1992): 464–71.

Siegel, Richard L., and Leonard B. Weinberg. *Comparing Public Policies: United States, Soviet Union and Europe.* Homewood, IL: Dorsey Press, 1977.

Smith, T. Alexander. *The Comparative Policy Process.* Santa Barbara, CA: Clio Books, 1975.

Stapleton, Vaughan, and Lee Teitelbaum. *In Defense of Youth: A Study of the Role of Counsel in American Juvenile Courts.* New York: Russell Sage Foundation, 1972.

Steffens, Lincoln. *Upbuilders.* New York: Doubleday, Page and Company, 1909. Reprint, Seattle: University of Washington Press, 1968.

Symposium. "The Mentally Ill and the Right to Treatment," *University of Chicago Law Review* 36 (1969): 742–801.

Symposium. "Observations on the Right to Treatment," *Georgetown Law Journal* 57 (1969): 673–817.

Tappan, Paul. *Juvenile Delinquency.* New York: McGraw Hill, 1949.

Tribe, Laurence H. *American Constitutional Law.* Mineola, NY: Foundation Press, 1978.

Tsebelis, George. *Nested Games: Rational Choice in Comparative Politics.* Berkeley: University of California Press, 1990.

Tushnet, Mark V. *The NAACP's Legal Strategy Against Segregated Education, 1925–1950.* Chapel Hill: University of North Carolina Press, 1987.

Twentieth Century Fund. *Confronting Youth Crime: Sentencing Policy Toward Young Offenders.* New York: Holmes and Meier, 1978.

Twichell, Robert H. "Current Legislation: New York State's Family Court Act," *Syracuse Law Review* 14 (1963): 481–96.

Ulmer, S. Sidney. "Dissent Behavior and the Social Background of Supreme Court Justices," *Journal of Politics* 32 (1970): 580–98.

Ulmer, S. Sidney. "Social Background as an Indicator to the Votes of Supreme Court Justices in Criminal Cases, 1947–1956 Terms," *American Journal of Political Science* 17 (1973): 622–30.

U.S. Bureau of the Census. Statistical Research Division. *Historical Statistics of the United States.* Series A 119–134. *Population, by Age, Sex, Race, and Nativity: 1790 to 1970.* Washington, DC: GPO, 1971.

U.S. Congress. House. *Children's Courts in the United States: Their Origin, Development and Results.* H. Doc. 701, 58th Cong., 2d sess., 1904.

U.S. Congress. Senate. *A Report Covering the Work of the Juvenile Court During the Period from July 1, 1906, to June 30, 1926.* S. Doc. 236, 69th Cong., 2d sess., 1927.

Vose, Clement E. *Caucasians Only: The Supreme Court, the NAACP, and the Restrictive Covenant Cases.* Berkeley: University of California Press, 1959.

Vose, Clement E. *Constitutional Change: Amendment Politics and Supreme Court Litigation Since 1900.* Lexington, MA: Lexington Books, 1972.

Vose, Clement. "Litigation as a Form of Pressure Group Activity," *Annals of the American Academy of Political and Social Science* 319 (1958): 20–31.

Wagoner, Jay J. *Arizona Territory, 1863–1912: A Political History.* Tucson: University of Arizona Press, 1970.

Wald, Michael S. "Thinking About Public Policy Toward Abuse and Neglect of Children: A Review of *Before the Best Interests of the Child,*" *Michigan Law Review* 78 (1980): 645–93.

Walker, Jack L. "The Diffusion of Innovations Among the States," *American Political Science Review* 63 (1969): 880–99.

Walker, Jack L. Jr. *Mobilizing Interest Groups in America: Patrons, Professions and Social Movements.* Ann Arbor: University of Michigan Press, 1991.

Walker, Samuel. *In Defense of American Liberties: A History of the ACLU.* New York: Oxford University Press, 1990.

Walkover, Andrew. "The Infancy Defense in the New Juvenile Court," *UCLA Law Review* 31 (1984): 503–62.

Warren, Earl. "Equal Justice for Juveniles," *Juvenile Court Judges Journal* 15 (1964): 14–16.

Warren, Samuel D., and Louis D. Brandeis. "The Right to Privacy," *Harvard Law Review* 4 (1890): 193–220.

Wasby, Stephen L. "Civil Rights Litigation by Organizations: Constraints and Choices," *Judicature* 68 (1985): 337–52.

Wasby, Stephen L. *The Impact of the United States Supreme Court.* Homewood, IL: Dorsey Press, 1970.

Washington State Juvenile Disposition Standards Commission. *Washington State Juvenile Dispositions Standards Philosophy and Guide* (1984).

White, Welsh S. "Police Trickery in Inducing Confessions," *University of Pennsylvania Law Review* 127 (1979): 581–629.

Wilson, James Q., ed. *Crime and Public Policy.* San Francisco: ICS Press, 1983.

Winnet, Nochem. "Fifty Years of the Juvenile Court: An Evaluation," *American Bar Association Journal* 36 (1950): 363–66.

Wizner, S., and M. F. Keller. "The Penal Model of Juvenile Justice: Is Juvenile Court Delinquency Jurisdiction Obsolete?" *New York University Law Review* 52 (1977): 1120–35.

Wolf, Eleanor. *Trial and Error: The Detroit School Segregation Case.* Detroit: Wayne State University Press, 1981.

Wolfgang, Marvin E., Robert M. Figlio, and Thorsten Sellin. *Delinquency in a Birth Cohort.* Chicago: University of Chicago Press, 1972.

Wood, Robert C., ed. *Remedial Law: When Courts Become Administrators.* Amherst: University of Massachusetts Press, 1990.

Yarborough, Tinsley E. "The Political World of Federal Judges as Managers," *Public Administration Review* 45 (1985): 660–66.

Yogis, John A. *Canadian Law Dictionary.* Toronto: Barron's Educational Series, 1983.

Zimring, Franklin. *The Changing Legal World of Adolescence.* New York: Free Press, 1982.

Index